**Kursk—July 8, 1943**
Rudel's cannon-armed Stuka
flies into the midst of World War II's
greatest armored battle.
Painting by Gunther Scherrer

# ATTACK!

We fly in low over the water from the south; it is dark and murky; I cannot distinguish anything more than 2000 to 2500 feet ahead. Now I see straight in the line of my flight a black moving mass: the road, tanks, vehicles, Russians. I at once yell: "Attack!" Already at almost point blank range the defence looses off a concentrated fire from in front of me, twin and quadruple flak, machine guns, revealing everything with a livid brightness in this foggy light. I am flying at 90 feet and have bumped right into the middle of this hornet's nest. Shall I get out of it? I twist and turn in the craziest defensive maneuvers to avoid being hit; I shoot without taking aim . . . my head is as hot as the metal screaming past me. A few seconds later a tell-tale hammering. "Engine on fire!" Flames lick the cockpit. Our kite will be our crematorium. Can we bail out in time?

## STUKA PILOT

# THE BANTAM WAR BOOK SERIES

This is a series of books about a world on fire.

These carefully chosen volumes cover the full dramatic sweep of World War II. Many are eyewitness accounts by the men who fought in this global conflict in which the future of the civilized world hung in balance. Fighter pilots, tank commanders and infantry commanders, among others, recount exploits of individual courage in the midst of the large-scale terrors of war. They present portraits of brave men and true stories of gallantry and cowardice in action, moving sagas of survival and tragedies of untimely death. Some of the stories are told from the enemy viewpoint to give the reader an immediate sense of the incredible life and death struggle of both sides of the battle.

Through these books we begin to discover what it was like to be there, a participant in an epic war for freedom.

---

Each of the books in the Bantam War Book series contains a dramatic color painting and illustrations specially commissioned for each title to give the reader a deeper understanding of the roles played by the men and machines of World War II.

# STUKA PILOT

## by Hans Ulrich Rudel

FOREWORD BY
GROUP CAPTAIN DOUGLAS BADER,
D.S.O., D.F.C.

INTRODUCTION BY JOHANNES AND
MARTHA RUDEL

TRANSLATED BY LYNTON HUDSON

▰

STUKA PILOT
*A Bantam Book*

*PRINTING HISTORY*
First American edition published by Ballantine Books in
*December 1958*
*Bantam edition | February 1979*

*Drawings by Greg Beecham.*
*Map by Benjamin F. Klaessig.*

*Bantam Books are published by Bantam Books, Inc. Its trade-
mark, consisting of the words "Bantam Books" and the por-
trayal of a bantam, is Registered in U.S. Patent and Trademark
Office and in other countries. Marca Registrada. Bantam
Books, Inc., 666 Fifth Avenue, New York, New York 10019.*

# CONTENTS

# FOREWORD

As so often occurs during a war, particularly in the Air Forces, you often hear the names of pilots on the opposite side. It is seldom that you meet them subsequently. At the end of this war some of us had the opportunity of meeting several well-known pilots of the German Air Force, who had hitherto been just names to us. Now, seven years later, some of the names escape me, but I well remember Galland, Rudel and a German night fighter pilot called Mayer. They visited the Central Fighter Establishment at Tangmere in June 1945 for a couple of days and some of their opposite numbers in the Royal Air Force were able to exchange views on air tactics and aircraft, always an absorbing topic amongst pilots. A coincidence which amused all of us, if I may be excused this anecdote, occurred when Mayer was talking to our well-known fighter pilot Brance Burbidge and discovered that Brance had shot him down over his own aerodrome one night as he was circling to land.

Having been a prisoner in Germany for much of the war I had heard of Hans Ulrich Rudel. His exploits on the Eastern Front with his dive bomber were from time to time given much publicity in the German press. It was therefore with great interest that I met him when he came over in June 1945. Not long before he arrived Rudel had lost one leg below the knee, as he describes in this book. At the time of this visit that well-known R.A.F. character, Dick Atcherley, was the Commandant

viii                  STUKA PILOT

at Tangmere. Others there were Frank Carey, Bob Tuck (who had been a prisoner-of-war in Germany with me), "Raz" Berry, Hawk Wells and Roland Beamont (now Chief Test Pilot for English Electric). We all felt that somehow we should try and get an artificial leg for Rudel. It was very sad that we were unable to do this because although a plaster cast and the requisite measurements were taken it was discovered that his amputation was too recent for an artificial leg to be made and fitted and we were reluctantly compelled to give up the idea.

We all read an autobiography written by someone we have met, if only for a short time, with more interest than that of a stranger. This book of Rudel's is a first-hand account of his life in the German Air Force throughout the war, mainly in the East. I do not agree with a number of the conclusions he draws or with some of his thoughts. I was, after all, on the other side.

The book is not broad in its scope because it is confined to the activities of one man—and a brave one—waging a war in very single-minded fashion. It does however shed an interesting light on Rudel's opposite numbers on the Eastern Front, the Russian Air Force pilots. This is perhaps the most revealing part of the whole book.

I am happy to write this short foreword to Rudel's book, since although I only met him for a couple of days he is, by any standards, a gallant chap and I wish him luck.

DOUGLAS BADER.

# INTRODUCTION

It is not customary for a father and mother to write an introduction to their son's book, but we believe it would be wrong to refuse the invitation even though at the present time it may appear imprudent to write a preface to a "war book."

It has been said with competent authority: ". . . that Hans-Ulrich Rudel (as from the 1st January, 1945, Wing Commander of the Luftwaffe—at the age of 28½) has distinguished himself far beyond the measure of all officers and men, and his operational flights at focal points and in frontal sectors have been decisive for the general situation (wherefore he has been the first and only soldier to be awarded the highest decoration— the Golden Oakleaves with Swords and Diamonds to the Knight's Cross of the Iron Cross) . . ."

". . . Rudel is pre-eminently equipped to write his war experiences. The stupendous events of the war are still too close for it to be possible to present a comprehensive picture of them. It is therefore all the more important that those who did their duty at their post *until the bitter end* should record their experiences *truthfully*. It is only on the basis of a balanced objectivity and first hand individual experience that the Second World War will one day appear in full perspective. With 2,530 operational flights to his credit, Rudel—and this is admitted also by fair-minded enemies—is the foremost war pilot in the world . . ."

Throughout the long war he was hardly ever on leave;

even after he was wounded he immediately hurried back
to the front. At the beginning of April 1945 he lost his
right leg (below the knee) in action. He refused to wait
until he was fully convalescent, but despite an open
wound forced himself to go on flying with an artificial
limb. It was his creed that an officer has a vocation in
which he does not belong to himself, but to his fatherland and to the subordinates committed to his charge,
and that he must therefore—in war even more than in
peace time—show an example to his men without
regard for his own person or his life. On the other hand
he did not mince his words to his superiors, but spoke
his mind openly and honestly. By his forthrightness he
gave his successes their real foundation, for only where
mutual confidence prevails can superior and subordinate
achieve the highest and the best.

The old soldierly virtues of loyalty and obedience
determined his whole life. "Only he is lost who gives
himself up for lost" is a maxim which our son made
devotedly his own. And in obedience to it he now lives
in the Argentine.

We—his parents and his two sisters, and countless
others besides—have often feared and prayed for him,
but we could always repeat—as he did—with Eduard
Mörike: "May all things, both the beginning and the
end, be given into His hands!"

May his book bring words of cheer to his many
friends and admirers, a message of inspiration to all
readers from afar.

JOHANNES RUDEL,
*Retired Minister of Christ.*

Sausenhofen bei Gunzenhausen/Mfr.
   *September,* 1950.

*       *       *

For the comfort of every mother of a boy I should
like to mention that our Hans-Ulrich was a delicate and

nervous child (he weighed five and three quarter pounds when he was born). Until his twelfth year I had to hold his hand during a thunderstorm. His older sister used to say: "Uli will never be any good in life, he is afraid of going into the cellar by himself." It was just this ridicule that put Uli on his mettle and he began to toughen himself in every way and to devote himself to sport. But through this he got behindhand with his school work and his bad reports, which had to be initialled by his father, were kept back until the last day of the holidays. His form master whom I once asked: "How is he getting on at school?" gave me this answer: "He is a charming boy, but a shocking scholar."—Many tales could be repeated of his boyish pranks, but I am happy that he was granted a carefree youth.

His mother: MARTHA RUDEL.

Hans Ulrich Rudel

# 1

## FROM UMBRELLA TO DIVE BOMBER

*"Only he is lost who gives himself up for lost!"*

1924. My home is the rectory of the little village of Seiferdau in Silesia; I am eight. One Sunday my father and mother go into the neighbouring town of Schweidnitz for an "Aviation Day." I am furious that I am not allowed to go with them, and when they return my parents have to tell me over and over again what they have seen there. And so I hear about a man who jumped from a great height with a parachute and came safely down to earth. This delights me, and I badger my sisters for an exact description of the man and the parachute. Mother sews me a little model, I attach a stone to it and am proud when stone and parachute slowly drift to the ground. I think to myself that what a stone can do I must be able to do too, and when I am left alone for a couple of hours the following Sunday I lose no time in exploiting my new discovery.

Upstairs to the first floor! I climb on to the window-sill with an umbrella, open it up, take a quick look down, and before I have time to be afraid I jump. I land on a soft flower-bed and am surprised to find that I have twisted every muscle and actually broken a leg. In the tricky way in which umbrellas are apt to behave, the thing has turned inside out and hardly braked my fall. But nevertheless I abide by my resolve: I will be an airman.

After a brief flirtation with modern languages at the local school I take up classics, and learn Greek and Latin. At Sagen, Niesky, Görlitz and Lauban—my father is moved to these different parishes in the lovely province of Silesia—my schooling is completed. My holidays are devoted almost exclusively to sport, including motor-cycling; athletics in summer, and skiing in winter lay the foundations of a robust constitution for later life. I enjoy everything; so I do not specialize in any particular field. Our little village does not offer very much scope—my knowledge of sporting tackle is derived solely from magazines—so I practise pole-jumping by using a long tree-prop to vault over my mother's clothesline. Thus later with a proper bamboo pole I can clear a respectable height. . . As a ten year old I go off into the Eulengebirge, twenty three miles away, with the six foot long skis given to me as a Christmas present, and teach myself skiing. . . I stand a couple of planks resting on a sawing-horse of my father's, this gives me an upward slope. I give the contraption the once-over to make sure it is firmly fixed. No funking now—I open the throttle of my motorbike and sail up the boards . . . and over. I land on the other side, swerve wildly and back again for another run at the planks and the trusty sawing-horse! It never enters my head that in addition to all this I ought to be a good scholar, much to my parents' distress. I play almost every conceivable prank on my teachers. But the question of my future becomes a more serious problem as matriculation looms nearer. One of my sisters is studying medicine, and consequently the possibility of finding the large sum of money needed to have me trained as a civil air-pilot does not even come under consideration—a pity. So I decide to become a sports instructor.

Quite unexpectedly the Luftwaffe is created, and with it a demand for applicants for a reserve of officers. Black sheep that I am, I see little hope of passing the difficult entrance examination. Several fellows I know, rather older than myself, who have previously tried to get in have been unlucky. Apparently only sixty out of six hundred candidates will be selected, and I cannot imagine any likelihood of my being among this ten per cent. Fate, however, disposes otherwise; and in August 1936 I have in my pocket the notification of my admission to the Military School at Wildpark-Werder for next December. Two months Labour Service work on the regulation of the Neisse at Muskau follow matriculation in the autumn. In the first term at Wildpark-Werder we recruits are put through the mill. Our infantry training is completed in six months. Aircraft we see only from the ground, with an especial longing when we happen to be flat on our faces. The rule of no smoking and no drinking, the virtual restriction of all leisure time to physical exercise and games, the pretence of indifference to the distractions of the near-by capital, are tiresome. I take a rather dim view of my milk-drinking existence, and that is putting it mildly. I earn no black marks in my military and athletic training and so my supervisional officer, Lt. Feldmann, is not dissatisfied. In some respects, however, I am not altogether successful in living down the reputation of being a "queer fish."

The second term finds us in the neighbouring town of Werder, a holiday resort in the Havel lake district. At last we are taught to fly. Competent instructors are at pains to initiate us into the mysteries of aviation. We practise circuits and landings with Flt. Sgt. Dieselhorst. After about the sixtieth time I am able to undertake a solo flight, and this achievement makes me an average pupil of my class. In conjunction with our flying lessons the technical and military curriculum is continued, as well as an advanced course for a commission. Our flying training finishes at the end of this second term and we receive our flight authority. The third term, back at Wildpark, is no longer so diversified. Little stress is laid on flying; instead air tactics, ground tactics, defence methods and other special subjects figure more largely in our work. Meanwhile I am seconded for a short spell and sent to Giebelstadt near Würzburg, the lovely old city on the Main, where I am attached to a combat unit as officer cadet. Gradually the date of our passing-out examination draws near, and speculation is rife as to what unit and what branch of the service we shall eventually be posted to. Almost to a man we would like to be fighter pilots, but this is clearly impossible. There is a rumour going about that our whole class is to be assigned to Bomber Command. Promotion to the rank of officer senior cadet and posting to a definite formation follows for those who pass the difficult examination.

Shortly before leaving the Military School we are sent on a visit to an anti-aircraft gunnery school on the Baltic coast. Quite unexpectedly Goering arrives and addresses us. At the end of his speech he asks for dive bomber volunteers. He tells us he still requires a number of young officers for the newly-formed Stuka formations. It does not take me long to make up my mind. "You would like to become a fighter," I argue, "but you will have to be a bomber; so you might as well volunteer for the Stukas and be done with it." In any case I do not fancy myself flying the heavy bomber aircraft. A little quick thinking and my name is entered on the list of Stuka candidates. A few days later we all get our postings. Almost the whole of the class is assigned—to Fighter Command! I am bitterly disappointed, but there is nothing to be done about it. I am a Stuka pilot. And so I watch my comrades happily depart.

In June 1938 I arrive at Graz, in the picturesque province of Steiermark, to report to a Stuka formation as officer senior cadet. It is three months since German troops marched into Austria, and the population is enthusiastic. The squadron which is stationed outside the town in the village of Thalerhof has recently received the type 87 Junkers; the single-seater Henschel will no longer be used as a dive-bomber. Learning to dive at all angles up to ninety degrees, formation flying, aerial gunnery and bombing are the fundamentals of the new arm. We are soon familiar with it. It cannot be said that I am a rapid learner; furthermore the rest of the squadron have already passed all their tests when I join it. It takes a long time to ring the bell, too long to please my squadron leader. I catch on so slowly that he ceases to believe that it will ever ring at all.

Ju. 87 Stuka

The fact that I spend my leisure hours in the mountains, or at sport, rather than in the officers' mess, and that on the rare occasions when I put in an appearance there my only beverage is milk does not make my position any easier.

Meanwhile I have received my commission as pilot officer, and at Christmas 1938 the squadron is instructed to submit the name of an officer for special training in operational reconnaissance. Other squadrons all return a blank form; none of them is willing to release a man. It is, however, a splendid opportunity for the "1st" to be able at last to send the milk-drinker into the wilderness. Naturally I object; I want to stay with the Stukas. But my efforts to put a spoke in the wheels of the military machine are fruitless.

So in January 1939 I find myself on a course at the Reconnaissance Flying School at Hildesheim, and in the depths of despair. We are given instruction in the theory and practice of aerial photography, and it is whispered that at the end of the course we are to be posted to formations whose task it will be to fly special missions for operational air command. In reconnaissance aircraft the observer is also the skipper, and so we all become observers. Instead of piloting our aircraft we have now to sit still and trust ourselves to a pilot whom we naturally set down as a duffer, prophesying that he is certain to crash one day—with us. We learn aerial photography, taking vertical and oblique photographs, etc., here in the region of Hildesheim. The rest of the time is devoted to monotonous theory. At the end of the course we are assigned to our formations. I am transferred to Distance Reconnaissance Squadron 2F 121 at Prenzlau.

Two months later we move to the Schneidemühl area. The war against Poland breaks out! I shall never forget my first flight across the frontier of another country. I sit tensely in my aircraft, waiting for what is now going to happen. We are awed by our first experience of flak and treat it with considerable respect. The rare appearance of a Polish fighter is always for a long time afterwards a topic of conversation. What has been hitherto the dry stuff of the classroom now becomes an exciting reality. We take photographs of the railway yards at Thorn, Kulm, etc., to ascertain troop movements and concentrations. Later our missions take us further East to the railway line Brest Litovsk—Kovel—Luck. The High Command wishes to know how the Poles are regrouping in the East and what the Russians are doing.

We use Breslau as our base for missions in the Southern zone.

The war days in Poland are soon over and I return to Prenzlau with the EK II. Here my flight commander guesses at once that my heart is not in reconnaissance flying. But he thinks that in the present state of high pressure activity there is little sense in my making an application for a retransfer to Stuka command; I do make one or two attempts without success.

We spend the winter at Fritzlar near Kassel in Hesse. From here our squadron carries out missions to the West and the North West, taking off from advanced bases further W. or N.W. as the case may be. We fly them at very high altitudes and therefore every crew has to undergo a special examination for high level reconnaissance. In Berlin the verdict is that I have failed to pass the test of altitude fitness. As the Stukas operate at a lower level, my squadron now endorses my application for transfer to Dive Bomber Command, and so I am hopeful of getting back to my "first love." When, however, two crews are successively reported missing I am sent up again for re-examination. This time I am pronounced 'exceptionally able to stand high altitudes'; apparently they were wrong the previous time. But although the Ministry issues no definite orders for my disposal I am transferred to Stammersdorf (Vienna), to an Aviation Training Regiment which later moves to Crailsheim.

I am acting adjutant while the campaign in France begins. All my attempts to circumvent the proper channels by ringing up the personnel department of the Luftwaffe do not help me—the radio and the newspapers are my only contact with the war. Never have I been so downhearted as during this time. I feel as though I was being severely punished. Sport alone, to which I devote all my energies and every free minute, brings me some relief in my distress. During this period I have few opportunities to fly, and when I do it is only in little sporting aircraft. My main job is the military training of our recruits. On a weekend flight in the foulest weather in a Heinkel 70 with the C.O. as passenger I nearly crash in the Suabian Alps. But I am lucky and get back to Crailsheim safely.

My countless letters and telephone calls are at last successful. Presumably I am a nuisance which must be got rid of. Back I go to my old Graz Stuka formation, at the moment stationed at Caen on the English Channel. Operations here are practically over and a friend in the squadron who served with me at Graz gives me the benefit of his experiences in Poland and France in practice flights. I am certainly not lacking in keenness, for I have been longing for this moment for two years. But one cannot catch up with everything in a couple of days and even now I am not a quick learner. I have not the practice. Here in the pleasure-seeking atmosphere of France my clean living, my addiction to sport and my everlasting habit of drinking milk are more conspicuous than ever. And so when the squadron is transferred to S.E. Europe I am sent to a Reserve Flight at Graz for further instruction. Will I ever learn my job?

The Balkan campaign begins—once again I am kept out of it. Graz is being temporarily used as a base for Stuka formations. It is hard to have to look on. The war surges forward across Jugoslavia into Greece, but I sit at home and practise formation flying, bombing and gunnery. I put up with it for three weeks, and then one morning I suddenly say to myself: "Now at last you have rung the bell and you can make an aircraft do anything you like." And that is the truth. My instructors are amazed. Dill and Joachim can pull any stunts they choose when leading our so-called circus, but my machine will always keep station right behind them as if attached by an invisible tow rope whether they go into a loop or dive or fly upside down. At bombing practice I hardly ever drop a bomb thirty feet wide of the target. In gunnery from the air I score over ninety out of a possible hundred. In a word, I have made the grade. Next time a call comes for replacements from the squadrons at the front I shall be one of them.

Soon after the Easter holidays, which I spend with colleagues skiing in the vicinity of Prebichl, the longed-for moment arrives. An order comes through for aircraft to be flown to the Stuka squadron stationed in the South of Greece. With it comes the order for my transfer to this unit. Over Agram-Skoplje to Argos. There I learn that I am to proceed further South. The 1 Stuka 2 is at Molai on the southernmost tip of the Peloponnesus. To a classical scholar the flight is especially impressive and revives many schoolroom memories. On arrival I lose no time in reporting to the station commander of my new unit. I am keenly excited, for at last the hour has come and I am about to take part in serious combat operation. The first person to greet me is the squadron adjutant; his face and mine cloud simultaneously. We are old acquaintances . . . he is my instructor from Caen.

"What are you doing here?" he asks. His tone takes all the wind out of my sails.

"I am reporting for duty."

"There'll be no operational flying for you till you've learnt how to manage a Stuka." I can hardly contain my anger, but I keep my self-control even when he adds with a supercilious smile: "Have you learnt that much yet?"

An icy silence—until I break the intolerable pause: "I am completely master of my aircraft."

Almost contemptuously—or is it only my momentary impression?—he says with an emphasis that sends a shiver down my spine:

"I will put your case before the C.O. and we'll hope for the best. It's for him to decide. That's all; you can go and get yourself fixed up."

As I come out of the tent into the blazing sunshine I blink my eyes—not only because of the glare. I am battling with a steadily growing feeling of desperation. Then common sense tells me there is no reason to give up hope: the adjutant may be prejudiced against me, but his opinion of me is one thing, the C.O.'s decision another. And even supposing the adjutant to have so much influence over the C.O.—could that be possible? No, the C.O. is unlikely to be swayed because he does not even know me and will surely form an independent judgment. An order to report immediately to the C.O. puts an end to my brooding. I am confident that he will make up his mind for himself. I report. He returns my salute rather lackadaisically and submits me to a prolonged and silent scrutiny. Then he drawls: "We already know each other," and, probably noticing an expression of contradiction on my face, waves aside my unuttered protest with a motion of his hand. "Of course we do, for my adjutant knows all about you. I know you so well that until further orders you are not to fly with my squadron. If at some future date we are under strength . . ."

I do not hear another word of what he says. For the first time something comes over me, a feeling in the pit of my stomach: a feeling I never have again until years later when I am crawling home in an aircraft riddled by enemy bullets and serious loss of blood has sapped all my physical strength. This "something" is a dark intuition that despite everything the human factor is the criterion of war and the will of the individual the secret of victory.

How long the C.O. goes on talking I have not the least idea and as little of what he is saying. Rebellion seethes inside me and I feel the warning hammering in my head: "Don't . . . don't . . . don't . . ." Then the adjutant's voice recalls me to reality:

"You are dismissed."

I look at him now for the first time. I had not until that moment been aware that he was present. He returns me a stony stare. Now I have completely recovered control of my temper.

A few days later Operation Crete begins. The engines roar on the airfield; I sit in my tent. Crete is the trial of strength between the Stukas and the Navy. Crete is an island. According to all accepted military axioms only superior naval forces can wrest the island from the British. And England is a sea power; we are not. Certainly not where the Straits of Gibraltar prevent us from bringing up our naval units. The hitherto accepted military axioms, the English superiority at sea, are being wiped out by Stuka bombs. I sit in my tent.

". . . that until further orders you are not to fly with my squadron!" A thousand times a day this sentence riles me, mocking, contemptuous, derisive. Outside I listen to the returning crews excitedly chatting of their experiences and of the effective landings of our airborne troops. Sometimes I try to persuade one of them to let me fly in his place. It is useless. Even friendly bribes avail me nothing. Occasionally I fancy I can read something like sympathy in the faces of my colleagues, and then my throat goes dry with bitter fury. Whenever the aircraft take off on a sortie I feel like stuffing my fists into my ears so as not to hear the music of the engines. But I cannot. I have to listen. I cannot help myself! The Stukas go out on sortie after sortie. They are making history out there in the battle for Crete; I sit in my tent and weep with rage.

"We already know each other!" That is just what we do not. Not in the very least. I am positive that even now I should be a useful member of the squadron. I am completely master of my aircraft. I have the will to carry out an operation. A prejudice stands between me and the chance of winning my spurs. A prejudice on the part of my superiors who refuse to give me the opportunity to convince them of the wrongness of their "judgment."

I mean to prove in spite of them that an injustice has been done me. I will not let their prejudice stop me getting at the enemy. This is no way to treat a subordinate; I realize that now. Time and again the flames of insubordination blaze inside me. Discipline! Discipline! Discipline! Control yourself, it is only by self-restraint that you can achieve anything. You must have an understanding for everything, even for the mistakes, the crass blunders of your superior officers. There is no

CENTRAL EUROPE A...

Circa 1939-44

EUROPEAN RUSSIA

Area of Pilot Rudel's sorties

other way to make yourself more fit than they to hold a command. And to have an understanding for the mistakes of your subordinates. Sit calmly in your tent and keep your temper. Your time will come when you will really count for something. Never lose confidence in yourself!

## 2

# WAR AGAINST THE SOVIETS

Slowly Operation Crete draws to its conclusion. I am told to fly a damaged aircraft to a repair shop at Kottbus and wait there for further orders. Back again to Germany over Sofia—Belgrade.

I am left at Kottbus without news of the squadron and without any idea as to what they intend to do with me. During the last few days there have been constant rumours of a new campaign, based on the fact that numerous ground crews and flying formations as well have been moved East. Most of those with whom I discuss these rumours believe that the Russians are going to allow us to push forward across Russia to the Near East so that we can get near the oilfields, other raw materials and war potential of the allies from this side. But all this is the merest speculation.

At 4 A.M. on the 22nd June I hear on the radio that war with Russia has just been declared. As soon as it is daylight I go into the hangar where the aircraft belonging to the "Immelmann" squadron are under repair and ask if any one of them is serviceable. Shortly before noon I have attained my object, and now nothing holds me back. My squadron is believed to be stationed somewhere on the East Prussian-Polish frontier. I land first at Insterburg to make enquiries. Here I get the information from a Luftwaffe H.Q. The place I am bound for is called Razci and lies to the S.E. I land there half an hour later among a crowd of aircraft which have just returned from a sortie and are about to take off again after being overhauled. The place is crawling with aircraft. It takes me quite a while to find my last squadron which had rather cold shouldered me when we were in Greece, and which I had not seen since. They have not much time for me at squadron H.Q. They have their hands full with operations.

The C.O. tells me via the adjutant to report to the first flight. There I report to the flight commander, a Flying Officer, who has also been in the doldrums and welcomes me if for no other reason than because the squadron has branded me a black sheep. As he is now sceptical of everything told him by his colleagues in the squadron I have the initial advantage that he is not ill disposed towards me. I have to hand over the aircraft I brought with me from Kottbus, but am allowed to join the next sortie flying an ancient aeroplane. From now on I am dominated by only one idea: "I am going to show all of you that I have learnt my job and that your prejudice is unjust." I fly as No. 2 behind the flight commander, who has detailed me to look after the technical requirements of the flight when not on operations. With the assistance of the Senior Fitter it is my business to see that as many aircraft as possible are serviceable for each sortie and to maintain liaison with the engineer officer of the squadron.

During operations I stick like a burr to the tail of my No. 1's aircraft so that he becomes nervous of my ramming him from behind until he sees that I have mine thoroughly under control. By the evening of the first day I have been out over the enemy lines four times in the area between Grodno and Wolkowysk. The Russians have brought up huge masses of tanks together with their supply columns. We mostly observe the types KW I, KW II and T 34. We bomb tanks, flak artillery and ammunition dumps supplying the tanks and infantry. Ditto the following day, taking off at 3 A.M. and coming in from our last landing often at 10 P.M. A good night's rest goes by the board. Every spare minute we stretch out underneath an aeroplane and instantly fall asleep. Then if a call comes from anywhere we hop to it without even knowing where it is from. We move as though in our dreams.

On my very first sortie I notice the countless fortifications along the frontier. The fieldworks run deep into Russia for many hundreds of miles. They are partly positions still under construction. We fly over half-completed airfields; here a concrete runway is just being built; there a few aircraft are already standing on an aerodrome. For instance, on the road to Witebsk along which our troops are advancing there is one of these half-finished airfields packed with Martin bombers. They must be short either of petrol or of crews. Flying in this way over one airfield after another, over one strongpoint after another, one reflects: "It is a good thing we struck" . . . It looks as if the Soviets meant to build all these preparations up as a base for invasion against us. Whom else in the West could Russia have wanted to attack? If the Russians had completed their preparations there would not have been much hope of halting them anywhere.

We are fighting in front of the spearhead of our armies; that is our task.

We stay for short periods at Ulla, Lepel and Janowici. Our targets are always the same: tanks, motor vehicles, bridges, fieldworks and A.A. sites. On and off our objectives are the enemy's railway communications or an armoured train when the Soviets bring one up to support their artillery. All resistance in front of our spearheads has to be broken so as to increase the speed and impetus of our advance. The defence varies in strength. The ground defence is in the main considerable, ranging from infantry small arms fire to flak, not to mention M.G. fire from the air. The only fighter aircraft the Russians have at this time is the Rata J 15, very much inferior to our Me 109. Wherever the Ratas put in an appearance they are shot down like flies. They are no serious match for our Messerschmitts, but they are easy to manoeuvre and of course a great deal faster than we Stukas. Consequently we cannot afford entirely to ignore them. The Soviet operational air force, its fighter and bomber units, is remorselessly destroyed both in the air and on the ground. Their fighting power is small; their types, like the Martin bomber and the DB III, mostly obsolete. Very few aircraft of the new type, P II, are to be seen. It is not until later that American deliveries of the twin-engined Boston are noticeable even on this front. We are frequently subjected to raids by small aircraft at night with the object of, disturbing our sleep and interrupting our supplies. Their evident successes are generally few. We get a taste of it at Lepel. Some of my colleagues sleeping under canvas in a wood are casualties. Whenever the "wire crates," as we call the little wire-braced biplanes, observe a light they drop their small shrapnel bombs. They do this everywhere, even in the front line. Often they shut off their engines so as to make it difficult to locate them and go into a glide; then all we can hear is the wind humming through their wires. The tiny bomb drops out of this silence and immediately their engines begin to purr again. It is less a normal method of warfare than an attempt to fray our nerves.

The flight has a new skipper, Flt. Lt. Steen. He joined us originally from the same formation in which I received my first instruction in flying a Stuka. He gets accustomed to my sticking close behind him like a shadow on a sortie and keeping only a few yards distance even when diving. His marksmanship is excellent —if he misses the bridge it is a certainty I hit it. The flight aircraft following us can then drop their bombs on the A.A. guns and other targets. He is delighted when the squadron at once give him their opinion of his pet lambs, among which I am included. He makes no bones about it when one day they ask him: "Is Rudel O.K. yet?" When he replies: "He is the best man I have in the flight" there are no more questions. He recognizes my keenness, but on the other hand he gives me only a short lease of life because I am "crazy." The term is used half in jest; it is the appreciation of one airman by another. He knows that I generally dive to too low a level in order to make sure of hitting the target and not to waste ammunition.

"That is bound to land you in trouble in the long run," is his opinion. By and large he may be right, if it were not that at this time I am having a run of luck. But one gains experience with every fresh sortie. I owe a lot to Steen and count myself fortunate to be flying with him.

In these first few weeks, however, it looks very much as if he is likely to be proved right in his predictions. In low level attacks on a road along which the Russians are advancing, damage by enemy flak compels one of our aircraft to make a forced landing. Our comrade's aircraft comes down in a little clearing surrounded on three sides by scrub and Russians. The crew take cover behind their machine. I can see the Russian M.G. bursts spattering up the sand. Unless my colleagues are picked up they are lost. But the Reds are right among them. What the heck! I must bring it off. I lower my landing flaps and already I am gliding down to land. I can spot the Ivans' light grey uniforms among the bushes. Whang! A burst of M.G. fire hits my engine! There seems no sense in landing with a crippled aircraft; if I do we shall not be able to take off again. My comrades are done for. Their waving hands are the last I see of them. The engine conks like mad, but picks up and is running just sufficiently for me to pull out on the other side over a copse. The oil has plastered the window of my cockpit and I expect a piston seizure at any moment. If that happens my engine will stop for good. The Reds are below me; they throw themselves on the ground in front of my kite while some of them shoot at it. The flight has climbed to nearly a thousand feet and is out of range of the tornado of small arms fire. My engine just holds out till I reach our front line; there I land. Then I hare back to base in an army lorry.

Here Officer Cadet Bauer has just arrived. I know him from my time with the reserve flight at Graz. He later distinguishes himself and is to be one of the few of us who survive this campaign. But this day on which he joins us is an unlucky one. I damage the right wing plane of my aircraft because when taxying in I am blinded by the thick swirl of dust and collide with another aircraft. That means I must change my wing plane, but there is not one on the airfield. They tell me that a damaged aircraft is still standing on our last runway at Ulla, but it still has a sound right wing plane. Steen is furious with me. "You may fly when your aircraft is serviceable again and not before." To be grounded is the severest punishment. Anyhow we have flown the last sortie for today, and I fly back at once to Ulla. Two mechanics from another flight have been left behind there; they help me. During the night we take off the wing planes with the assistance of a couple of comrades from the infantry. We are through by three in the morning. All one needs is a break. I report my return with a whole aircraft in time for the first sortie at half past four. My skipper grins and shakes his head.

A few days later I am transferred to the 3rd squadron as engineer officer and have therefore to bid the first flight good-bye. Steen cannot pull any strings to stop my transfer and so I am now engineer officer of the 3rd squadron. I have barely arrived when the squadron commander leaves the unit and a new one takes his place. Who is he? Flt./Lt. Steen! All one needs is a break.

"Your transfer was only half as bad as you thought, you see that now. Yes, it is a mistake to be too eager to play providence!" says Steen as he greets me. When he joins us in the squadron mess tent for the first time at Janowici there is the dickens of a racket going on. An ancient L.A.C. had been trying to fill his lighter from a large petrol tin. He does it by tilting the tin with the result that the petrol spills over the lighter whereupon he keeps flicking it to see if it is already working. There is a terrific bang; the tin explodes in his face and the L.A.C. pulls a face as if the explosion were a breach of military regulations. A sad waste of good petrol; for many old women are only too glad to swap eggs for a little petrol. This is of course forbidden, because petrol is meant for other uses than the concoction of spirituous liquor by old women. Even one drop of the stuff they manufacture burns our skin. Everything is a question of habit. The chancel of the village church has been converted into a cinema, the nave into a stables. "Different people, different customs," says Flt./Lt. Steen with a chuckle.

The great motor road from Smolensk to Moscow is the objective of many of our sorties; it is crowded with immense quantities of Russian material. Lorries and tanks are parked there beside one another at the closest intervals, often in three parallel columns. "If this mass of material had poured over us . . ." I cannot help thinking as I attack this sitting target. Now in a few days' time it will all be a vast sea of wreckage. The advance of the army goes forward irresistibly. Soon we are taking off from Duchowtchina, not far from the railway station of Jarzewo the possession of which is later hotly contested.

On one of the following days a Rata dives from above into our formation and rams Bauer; the Rata crashes and Bauer flies home with a severely damaged aircraft. That evening the Moscow radio sings a hymn of praise for the Soviet pilot officer who "rammed and brought down a Stuka swine." The radio must be right, and we since childhood have always enjoyed listening to fairy stories.

About two miles away from us the army is preparing a new major operation. So quite unexpectedly we receive orders to move to another area. Our new station is called Rehilbitzy and lies some ninety miles West of Lake Ilmen. From dawn till dusk we support the army to the East and to the North.

# 3

## BAD WEATHER FLYING

At Rehilbitzy the summer months are very hot; the minute we come off duty we lie down on our campbeds in the coolness of our tents. Our skipper is living with us under canvas. We have not much to say to each other, but we have a feeling of mutual understanding. We must be essentially alike in character. In the evenings after ops, he strolls off into the forest or across the steppe, and if I do not accompany him I am pretty sure to be either putting the weight or throwing the discus or taking a long distance run round the airfield. These are the ways in which each of us finds recreation after a hard day's flying and is fresh for the next day. Afterwards we sit about in our tent. He is not much of a drinker, and does not hold it against me that I do not drink at all. After reading a book for a while he will look up at someone in the circle and remark:

"Well, Weinicke, you must be pretty well fagged out?" And before one can deny it: "All right, then, let's turn in." So we always go to bed early, and that suits me. "Live and let live" is his motto. Steen's previous experiences have been much the same as mine; he has profited by them and is determined to be a better C.O. than those he served under. On operations he exerts a peculiar influence over us. He dislikes heavy flak just as much as the rest of us, but no defence can be so strong as to make him drop his bombs from a greater altitude. He is a grand fellow, an exceptionally good officer and a first rate airman, a combination of virtues which makes him a very rare bird. Steen has the oldest rear-gunner in our formation, W. O. Lehmann. I have the youngest, Corporal Alfred Scharnovski. Alfred is the thirteenth child of a simple East Prussian family; he seldom speaks and perhaps for that reason nothing ruffles him. With him I never have to worry about enemy fighters, for not even Ivan can be as dour as Alfred.

Here at Rehilbitzy we sometimes get storms of terrific violence. Over vast areas Russia has a continental climate, and the blessing of cooler weather has to be paid for by thunderstorms that are thunderstorms. It suddenly gets pitch dark in the middle of the day and the clouds hang almost on the ground; the rain comes down in sheets. Even on the ground visibility is reduced to a few yards. As a rule when in the air we give the storm centres a wide berth. It seems, however, inevitable that one day or another I shall get a close view of all this.

We are giving offensive and defensive support to the army in the Luga sector of the front. Occasionally we are also sent out on operational missions far into the interior. The objective of one of these missions is the railway station at Tschudowo, a very important junction on the Leningrad-Moscow line. We know the enemy's flak and fighter strength from earlier missions there. The A.A. defence is heavy, but unless fresh fighter formations have recently arrived in this area we do not anticipate any particular surprises.

Just before we take off a formation of Russian battle aircraft which we call "Iron Gustavs" attacks our air-

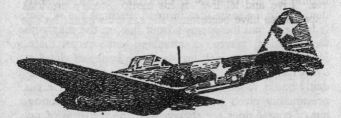

**IL 2 "Iron Gustav"**

field. We tumble into the split trenches behind our aircraft. Plt./Off. Stahl is the last to jump in, and lands
right in the small of my back. That is more uncomfortable than the Iron Gustavs' raid. Our flak opens up on
them, Gustav jettisons his bombs and makes off at low
level. Then we take off, setting a N.W. vector at an attitude of 9,000 feet. Not a cloud in the sky. I am flying
as No. 2 behind the skipper. During flight I bring my
wing plane level with his and look straight into his
cockpit. His face is calm confidence personified.

After a while the deep blue of Lake Ilmen sparkles
ahead of us. How many times have we come this way,
to Nowgorod at the northern end of the lake or near
Starja Rusa to the South! Both are key points, and with
a rush memories of the tight corners we have been in
come to mind. As we approach our objective a sheer
black wall of storm blots out the horizon. Is it just before or beyond our target? I see Flt./Lt. Steen studying
his map and now we are flying through a development
of dense cloud, the advance guard of the storm front.

I cannot make out the target. It must therefore lie
below the storm. We should now be very near it by the
clock. In this monotonous landscape the tattered clouds
increase the difficulty of finding one's bearing by eye.
For seconds we are in darkness, then it is light again. I
close up to an interval of perhaps 3 to 6 feet so as not
to lose sight of the wing plane of my skipper's aircraft in
the clouds. If I do I run the risk of a collision. Why
does not Steen turn back? Surely we shall not try to
attack in this storm. It would not be possible. The
flights behind us have already taken positions, evidently with the same idea in mind. Perhaps the skipper
is trying to find the enemy's front line on the map with
the intention, maybe, of attacking some target there.
He loses a little height, but there are banks of cloud at
every level. Steen looks up from his map and suddenly banks round at an angle of 180 degrees. He has
presumably given heed to the bad weather situation,
but of course does not reckon with the nearness of my
wing-plane. My reaction is instantaneous; I bank sharp-

ly, and still more sharply, and so avoid a collision. I have turned over so far that I am almost flying upside down. My aircraft is carrying 700 Kg. bombs and now this weight pulls my aircraft at a terrific speed onto her nose, and I disappear in the inky sea of clouds.

It is pitch dark all around me. I hear the whistling and the howling of the wind. Rain pours into the cockpit. From time to time a flash of lightning illumines everything bright as day. Fierce gusts of wind shake and rattle the aircraft, and send violent shudders through the structure. No earth is visible; there is no horizon by which I can right my aircraft. The needle of the vertical speed indicator has ceased to oscillate. The ball and arrow which indicate the aircraft's position in relation to its lateral and longitudinal axes and which should be nicely one above the other, are both in one corner of the dial. The vertical speed indicator points to zero. The air speed indicator accelerates with every second. I must do something to bring the instruments back into a normal position and that as quickly as possible, for the altimeter shows that we are racing madly downwards.

The A.S.I. soon registers 375 m.p.h. It is clear that I am in an almost perpendicular dive. I read on the illuminated figures of the altimeter 6900, 6600, 6000, 5400, 5100, 4800, 4500 feet. At this rate it is only a matter of seconds before there will be a crash, and that will be the end. I am in a sweat; water just pours off me. Is it rain or is it sweat? 3900, 3300, 2400, 1800, 1500 on the altimeter. Gradually I succeed in getting the other instruments functioning properly except for an alarming pressure on the joy stick.

So I continue to hurdle earthwards. The vertical speed indicator is still set at maximum. All this time I am completely benighted. Ghostly lightning flashes stab the darkness, making it even more difficult to fly by instruments. I pull on the stick with both hands to bring the aircraft back into a horizontal position. Altitude 1500, 1200 feet! The blood is throbbing in my temples, I gasp for breath. Something inside me urges me to give up this struggle with the unleashed forces of the elements. Why go on? All my efforts are of no avail. Now it also strikes me that the altimeter has stopped at 600 feet; it still oscillates feebly like an exhausted barometer. That means the crash will come at any moment with the altimeter still registering 600 feet. No, carry on, dourly, with might and main. A groaning thump. There now, I am dead. . . I think. Dead? If I were I should not be able to think. Besides, I can still hear the noise of the engine. It is still as dark all around as it was before. And now the unruffled voice of Scharnovski says serenely:

"It looks as if we had bumped into something or other, sir."

Scharnovski's imperturbable calm leaves me speech-less. But one thing I now know: I am still airborne. And this knowledge helps me to go on concentrating. It is true that even at full throttle I travel no faster, but the instruments show that I am beginning to climb, and that is already enough. The compass points due West; not exactly unlucky. It is to be hoped the thing is still working. I keep my eyes rigidly fixed on my instru-ments, hypnotising them with all the power of my will. Our salvation depends on them! I have to pull my stick for all I am worth, otherwise the "ball" pops back into the corner. I handle the aircraft gingerly as if she were a living thing. I coax her out loud and suddenly cannot help thinking of Old Shatterhand and his horse Rih.

Scharnovski interrupts my thoughts.

"We have two holes in the wings—there are a couple of birch trees sticking out of them—we have also lost a large bit of one aileron and landing flap."

I look out and perceive that I have climbed out of the lowest bank of cloud and am now flying above it. We are back in daylight! I see that Scharnovski is right. Two great holes in the wings on either side reaching to the main spar with small birch saplings sticking through them. The aileron and the landing flap are in the condition described. Now I begin to understand: the air is caught in the wings which explains the loss of speed; the difficulties in steering are also accounted for. How long will the valiant Ju 87 be able to carry on? I reckon I must be about thirty miles behind the Russian front. Now, and not till now, do I remember my load of bombs. I jettison them, and this makes flying easier. We usually meet with enemy fighters on every sortie. Today one of them would not have to shoot me down; a dirty look would be quite sufficient to do the trick. I cannot discover even one. At last I am across the front line and slowly approach our airfield.

I warn Scharnovski to bale out immediately. I give the order in case I find the aircraft no longer controllable. I reconstruct in my mind the recent miracle which has given me an extended lease of life: the storm blew up; after I had got the other instruments back to normal by constantly pulling the stick I must have been close to the ground at the very moment the aircraft recovered a horizontal position. At this speed I must have swept along an avenue of birch trees or between two single birches, and that was where I picked up the broken saplings. It was a stroke of uncanny luck that they tore holes exactly in the centre of the wings and did not catch the propeller, otherwise it would have become unbalanced and flown off in a matter of seconds. Still to maintain stability after such a jar and actually to bring me safely home is a thing no aircraft could possibly do except a Ju 87.

The return flight takes much too long for my liking, but at last I see Stoltzy ahead of me. The tension relaxes sensibly and I stretch my shoulders again. There are some of our fighters at Stoltzy, and now it will not be long before we are back at our station.

"Scharnovski, you are to bale out over the airfield."

I have no idea what my machine looks like from the ground nor how the holes in the wings will affect its aerodynamic characteristics when landing. There must be no unnecessary damage now.

"I won't. You'll make it all right, sir," he replies in an almost level voice. What can one answer to that?

The airfield is below us. I see it with new eyes; it has a more homelike appearance than usual. There my Ju can have a good rest; there are my comrades, the familiar faces. Somewhere down there hangs my tunic and in one of the pockets the last letter received from home. What was it my mother wrote? A chap ought to read his mother's letters through more carefully!

The squadron has apparently been paraded for dispersal. Are they perhaps being briefed for another sortie? In that case we must hurry. Now they are all staring up at our aircraft and moving away. I get ready to land and in order to have a safety factor I come in at a pretty fair speed. After taxying for a considerable distance I am safely back. Some of the chaps have run alongside us for the last hundred yards. I climb out of the aircraft; so does Scharnovski with perfect nonchalance. Now our colleagues cluster round us and pat us on the back. I hurriedly push my way through this welcoming committee and report to the skipper:

"Pilot Officer Rudel returning from ops. Special incident—contact with the ground in the target area—aircraft unserviceable."

He shakes us by the hand; a smile on his face. Then with a shake of the head he walks away towards the squadron tent. Of course we have to repeat the whole story to the others. They tell us they had just been paraded to hear the skipper deliver a short obituary speech. "Pilot Officer Rudel and his crew attempted the impossible. They tried to attack the set target by diving through the storm, and death has claimed them." He was just filling his lungs to start a new sentence when the battered Ju 87 appeared on the edge of the airfield. Then he turned even paler and quickly dismissed the parade. Even now in the tent he flatly refuses to believe that I did not purposely dive into the storm instead of being plunged into pitch black darkness because I was flying so close to his aircraft when he suddenly banked round.

"I assure you, sir, it wasn't intentional."

"Rubbish! You are exactly that kind of idiot. You were absolutely determined to attack the railway station."

"You overestimate me, sir."

"The future will prove I was right. Incidentally, we are going out again presently."

An hour later I am flying next to him with another aircraft again in the Luga sector. In the evening I work off my inner tension and my physical lassitude in a game. After that I do something immensely important: I sleep like a top.

The following morning our objective is Nowgorod, where the big bridge that spans the Wolchow collapses under our bombs. The Soviets are trying to get as many men and as much material as possible across the Wolchow and the Lowat, which flows into Lake Ilmen from the South, before it is too late. Therefore we have to keep on attacking the bridges. Their destruction delays the enemy, but not for long; we very soon realize that. Pontoons are quickly constructed in between them and in this way the Soviets perseveringly patch up the damage we have caused.

This constant operational flying without intermission brings on many symptoms of fatigue, sometimes with distressing results. The skipper is very quick at noticing them, too. Operational instructions from the wing, transmitted over the telephone at midnight or even later, must now be listened to and taken down by two of us. On more than one occasion misunderstandings have arisen in the morning for which every one is convinced that the others blame him. The reason is really general exhaustion.

The C.O. and I are detailed to listen jointly to the wing's nocturnal briefings. One night the telephone rings in the squadron tent. It is the wing commander on the line.

"Steen, we meet our fighter escort tomorrow morning at 5 A.M. over Batjeskoje."

The exact point is very important. We hunt for it on the map by the light of a pocket torch, but we find no

Batjeskoje. We have no clue as to where to look for it. Our desperation is as vast as Russia. Finally he says:

"I am sorry, sir. I can't find the place on the map."

Now the wing commander's angry voice yaps in his Berlin accent:

"What! Call yourself a squadron leader and don't know where Batjeskoje is!"

"Can you please give me the map reading, sir," says Steen.

A lengthy silence, endlessly prolonged. I look at him, he looks at me. Then suddenly:

"Damned if I know the place either, but I'm putting Pekrun on the line. He knows where it is."

His adjutant then quietly explains the exact location of the tiny village in the fen lands. A peculiar fellow, our wing commander; when he is angry or when he particularly wishes to be friendly, in either case, he talks like a typical Berliner. Where discipline and system are concerned our wing owes a lot to him.

# 4

# THE BATTLE FOR THE FORTRESS OF LENINGRAD

The centre of the fighting is gravitating more and more Northwards. So, in September 1941, we are sent to Tyrkowo, South of Luga, in the Northern sector of the Eastern front. We go out daily over the Leningrad area where the army has opened an offensive from the West and from the South. Lying as it does between the Finnish Gulf and Lake Ladoga, the geographical position of Leningrad is a big advantage to the defenders since the possible ways of attacking it are strictly limited. For some time progress here has been slow. One almost has the impression that we are merely marking time.

On the 16th September Flight Lieutenant Steen summons us to a conference. He explains the military situation and tells us that the particular difficulty holding up the further advance of our armies is the presence of the Russian fleet moving up and down the coast at a certain distance from the shore and intervening in the battles with their formidable naval guns. The Russian fleet is based on Kronstadt, an island in the Gulf of Finland, the largest war harbour in the U.S.S.R. Approximately 12½ miles from Kronstadt lies the harbour of Leningrad and South of it the ports of Oranienbaum and Peterhof. Very strong enemy forces are massed round these two towns on a strip of coast some six miles long. We are told to mark all the positions precisely on our maps so as to ensure our being able to recognize our own front line. We are beginning to guess that these troop concentrations will be our objective when Flt./Lt. Steen gives another turn to the briefing. He comes back to the Russian fleet and explains that our chief concern is the two battleships *Marat* and *Oktobrescaja Revolutia*. Both are ships of about 23,000 tons. In addition, there are four or five cruisers, among them the *Maxim Gorki* and the *Kirov,* as well as a number of destroyers. The ships constantly change their positions according to which parts of the mainland require the support of their devastating and accurate gunfire.

As a rule, however, the battleships navigate only in the deep channel between Kronstadt and Leningrad. Our wing has just received orders to attack the Russian fleet in the Gulf of Finland. There is no question of using normal bomber-aircraft, any more than normal bombs, for this operation, especially as intense flak must be reckoned with. He tells us that we are awaiting the arrival of two thousand pounder bombs fitted with a special detonator for our purpose. With normal detonators the bomb would burst ineffectively on the armoured main deck and though the explosion would be sure to rip off some parts of the upper structure it would not result in the sinking of the ship. We cannot expect to succeed and finish off these two leviathans except by the use of a delayed action bomb which must first pierce the upper decks before exploding deep down in the hull of the vessel.

A few days later, in the foulest weather, we are suddenly ordered to attack the battleship *Marat;* she has just been located in action by a reconnaissance patrol. The weather is reported as bad until due South of Krasnowardeisk, 20 miles South of Leningrad. Cloud density over the Gulf of Finland 5-7/10; cloud base 2400 feet. That will mean flying through a layer of cloud which where we are is 6000 feet thick. The whole wing takes off on a Northerly course. Today we are about thirty aircraft strong; according to our establishment we should have eighty, but numbers are not invariably the decisive factor. Unfortunately the two thousand pounders have not yet arrived. As our single engined Stukas are not capable of flying blind our No. 1 has to do the next best thing and keep direction with the help of the few instruments: ball, bank indicator and vertical speed indicator. The rest of us keep station by flying close enough to one another to be able to catch an occasional glimpse of our neighbour's wing. Flying in the dense, dark clouds it is imperative never to let the interval between the tips of our wings exceed 9-12 feet. If it is greater we risk losing our neighbour for good and running full tilt into another aircraft. This is an awe-inspiring thought! In such weather conditions therefore the safety of the whole wing is in the highest degree dependent on the instrument flying of our No. 1.

Below 6000 feet we are in a dense cloud cover; the individual flights have slightly broken formation. Now they close up again. There is still no ground visibility. Reckoning by the clock we must pretty soon be over the Gulf of Finland. Now, too, the cloud cover is thinning out a little. There is a glint of blue sky below us; *ergo* water. We should be approaching our target, but where exactly are we? It is impossible to tell because the rifts in the clouds are only infinitesimal. The cloud density can no longer be anything like 5-7/10; only here and there the thick soup dissolves to reveal an isolated gap. Suddenly through one such gap I see something and instantly contact Flt. Lt. Steen over the radio.

"König 2 to König 1 . . . come in, please."

He immediately answers:

"König 1 to König 2 . . . over to you."

"Are you there? I can see a large ship below us . . . the battleship *Marat*, I guess."

We are still talking as Steen loses height and disappears into the gap in the clouds. In mid-sentence I also go into a dive. Pilot Officer Klaus behind me in the other staff aeroplane follows suit. Now I can make out the ship. It is the *Marat* sure enough. I suppress my excitement with an iron will. To make up my mind, to grasp the situation in a flash: for this I have only seconds. It is *we* who must hit the ship, for it is scarcely likely that all the flights will get through the gap. Both gap and ship are moving. We shall not be a good target for the flak until in our dive we reach the cloud base at 2400 feet. As long as we are above the unbroken cloud base the flak can only fire by listening apparatus, they cannot open up properly. Very well then: dive, drop bombs and back into the clouds! The bombs from Steen's aircraft are already on their way down . . . near misses. I press the bomb switch . . . dead on. My bomb hits the after deck. A pity it is only a thousand pounder! All the same I see flames break out. I cannot afford to hang about to watch it, for the flak barks furiously. There, the others are still diving through the gap. The Soviet flak has by this time realized where the "filthy Stukas" are coming from and concentrate their fire on this point. We exploit the favourable cloud cover and climb back into it. Nevertheless, at a later date, we are not to escape from this area so relatively unscathed.

Once we are home again the guessing game immediately begins: what can have been the extent of the damage to the ship after the direct hit? Naval experts claim that with a bomb of this small calibre a total success must be discounted. A few optimists, on the other hand, think it possible. As if to confirm their opinion, in the course of the next few days our reconnaissance patrols, despite the most enterprising search, are quite unable to find the *Marat*.

In an ensuing operation a cruiser sinks in a matter of minutes under my bomb.

After the first sortie our luck with the weather is out. Always a brilliant blue sky and murderous flak. I never again experience anything to compare with it in any place or theatre of war. Our reconnaissance estimates that a hundred A.A. guns are concentrated in an area of six-square miles in the target zone. The flak bursts form a whole cumulus of cloud. If the explosions are more than ten or twelve feet away one cannot hear the flak from the flying aircraft. But we hear no single bursts; rather an incessant tempest of noise like the clap of doomsday. The concentrated zones of flak in the air space begin as soon as we cross the coastal strip which is still in Soviet hands. Then come Oranienbaum and Peterhof; being harbours, very strongly defended. The open water is alive with pontoons, barges, boats and tiny craft, all stiff with flak. The Russians use every possible site for their A.A. guns. For instance, the mouth of Leningrad harbour is supposed to have been closed to our U-boats by means of huge steel nets suspended from a chain of concrete blocks floating on the surface of the water. Even from these blocks A.A. guns bark at us.

After about another six miles we sight the island of Kronstadt with its great naval harbour and the town of the same name. Both harbour and town are heavily defended, and besides the whole Russian Baltic fleet is anchored in the immediate vicinity, in and outside the harbour. And it can put up a murderous barrage of flak. We in the leading staff aircraft always fly at an altitude between 9,000 and 10,000 feet; that is very low, but after all we want to hit something. When diving onto the ships we use our diving brakes in order to check our diving speed. This gives us more time to sight our target and to correct our aim. The more carefully we aim, the better the results of our attack, and everything depends on them. By reducing our diving speed we make it easier for the flak to bring us down, especially as if we do not overshoot we cannot climb so fast after the dive. But, unlike the flights behind us, we do not generally try to climb back out of the dive. We use different tactics and pull out at low level close above the water. We have then to take the widest evasive action over the enemy-occupied coastal strip. Once we have left it behind we can breathe freely again.

We return to our airfield at Tyrkowo from these sorties in a state of trance and fill our lungs with the air we have won the right to continue to breathe. These days are strenuous, very strenuous. On our evening walks Steen and I are now mostly very silent, each of us guessing the other's thoughts. It is our task to destroy the Russian fleet; so we are reluctant to discuss its difficulties. Argument would be merely a waste of breath. Those are our orders and we obey them. So in an hour we come back to the tent, inwardly relaxed and ready to go out again into this hell in the morning.

On one of these walks with Flt./Lt. Steen I break the customary silence and ask him rather hesitantly:

"How do you manage to be so cool and so collected?"

He stops for a moment, looks at me out of the corner of his eye, and says:

"My dear chap, don't imagine for a moment that I have always been so cool. I owe my indifference to hard years of bitter experience. You know something of what one is up against in the service if one doesn't see eye to eye with one's superiors . . . and if they are not big enough to leave such differences behind in the mess and refuse to forget them on duty, it can be plain hell. But the most finely tempered steel comes out of the hottest fire. And if you go your own gait alone, without necessarily losing touch with your fellows, you grow strong."

There is a long pause, and I realize why it is that he understands me so well. Although I am aware that my next remark is not very military, I say to him:

"I, too, when I was a subaltern sometimes promised myself that if I were ever given a command I wouldn't at any rate behave like some of my superiors."

Steen is silent for quite a while before he adds:

"There are other things besides which form a man. Only a few of our colleagues know that and so are able to understand my serious views on life. I was once engaged to a girl I loved very deeply. She died on the day we were to have been married. When a thing like that happens to you, you don't easily forget it."

I relapse into silence and go into the tent. For a long time afterwards the man Steen is the subject of my thoughts. Now I understand him better than I did. I realize how much virile strength and strength-giving understanding can be passed from one man to another in a quiet talk at the front. It is not the soldier's way to be communicative. He expresses himself very differently from a civilian. His talk is every bit as uncivilian and tongue-tied as it is popularly represented. And because war jerks a man out of all pretence and hypocrisy, the things a soldier says, even if they only take the form of an oath or a primitive sentimentality, are integrally sincere and genuine, and therefore finer than all the glib rhetoric of the civilian world.

War awakes primitive strength in its servants, and primitive strength is only to be found in subjectivity, never in objectivity.

On the 21st September our two thousand pounders arrive. The next morning reconnaissance reports that the *Marat* is lying in Kronstadt harbour. They are evidently repairing the damage sustained in our attack of the 16th. I just see red. Now the day has come for me to prove my ability. I get the necessary information about the wind, etc., from the reconnaissance men. Then I am deaf to all around me; I am longing to be off. If I reach the target, I am determined to hit it. I must hit it!—We take off with our minds full of the attack; beneath us, the two thousand pounders which are to do the job today.

Brilliant blue sky, without a rack of cloud. The same even over the sea. We are already attacked by Russian fighters above the narrow coastal strip; but they cannot deflect us from our objective, there is no question of that. We are flying at 9000 feet; the flak is deadly. About ten miles ahead we see Kronstadt; it seems an infinite distance away. With this intensity of flak one stands a good chance of being hit at any moment. The waiting makes the time long. Dourly, Steen and I keep on our course. We tell ourselves that Ivan is not firing at single aircraft; he is merely putting up a flak barrage at a certain altitude. The others are all over the shop, not only in the squadrons and the flights, but even in the pairs. They think that by varying height

and zigzagging they can make the A.A. gunners' task
more difficult. There go the two blue-nosed staff aircraft sweeping through all the formations, even the
separate flights. Now one of them loses her bomb. A
wild helter-skelter in the sky over Kronstadt; the danger
of ramming is great. We are still a few miles from our
objective; at an angle ahead of me I can already make
out the *Marat* berthed in the harbour. The guns boom,
the shells scream up at us, bursting in flashes of livid
colours; the flak forms small fleecy clouds that frolic
around us. If it was not in such deadly earnest one
might use the phrase: an aerial carnival. I look down
on the *Marat*. Behind her lies the cruiser *Kirov*. Or is
it the *Maxim Gorki?* These ships have not yet joined
in the general bombardment. But it was the same the
last time. They do not open up on us until we are diving
to the attack. Never has our flight through the defence
seemed so slow or so uncomfortable. Will Steen use
his diving brakes today or in the face of this opposition will he go in for once "without"? There he goes.
He has already used his brakes. I follow suit, throwing
a final glance into his cockpit. His grim face wears an
expression of concentration. Now we are in a dive,
close beside each other. Our diving angle must be between seventy and eighty degrees. I have already
picked up the *Marat* in my sights. We race down towards her; slowly she grows to a gigantic size. All
their A.A. guns are now directed at us. Now nothing
matters but our target, our objective; if we achieve our
task it will save our brothers in arms on the ground
much bloodshed. But what is happening? Steen's aircraft suddenly leaves mine far behind. He is travelling
much faster. Has he after all again retracted his diving
brakes in order to get down more quickly? So I do
the same. I race after his aircraft going all out. I am
right on his tail, travelling much too fast and unable to
check my speed. Straight ahead of me I see the horri-
fied face of W.O. Lehmann, Steen's rear-gunner. He expects every second that I shall cut off his tail unit with

my propeller and ram him. I increase my diving angle with all the strength I have got—it must surely be 90 degrees—sit tight as if I were sitting on a powder-keg. Shall I graze Steen's aircraft which is right on me or shall I get safely past and down? I streak past him within a hair's breadth. Is this an omen of success? The ship is centered plumb in the middle of my sights. My Ju 87 keeps perfectly steady as I dive; she does not swerve an inch. I have the feeling that to miss is now impossible. Then I see the *Marat* large as life in front of me. Sailors are running across the deck, carrying ammunition. Now I press the bomb release switch on my stick and pull with all my strength. Can I still manage to pull out? I doubt it, for I am diving without brakes and the height at which I have released my bomb is not more than 900 feet. The skipper has said when briefing us that the two thousand pounder must not be dropped from lower than 3000 feet as the fragmentation effect of this bomb reaches 3000 feet and to drop it at a lower altitude is to endanger one's aircraft. But now I have forgotten that!—I am intent on hitting the *Marat*. I tug at my stick, without feeling, merely exerting all my strength. My acceleration is too great. I see nothing, my sight is blurred in a momentary blackout, a new experience for me. But if it can be managed at all I must pull out. My head has not yet cleared when I hear Scharnovski's voice:

"She is blowing up, sir!"

Now I look out. We are skimming the water at a level of ten or twelve feet and I bank round a little. Yonder lies the *Marat* below a cloud of smoke rising up to 1200 feet; apparently the magazine has exploded.

"Congratulations, sir."

Scharnovski is the first. Now there is a babel of congratulations from all the other aircraft over the radio. From all sides I catch the words: "Good show!" Hold on, surely I recognize the Wing Commander's voice? I am conscious of a pleasant glow of exhilaration such as one feels after a successful athletic feat. Then I fancy that I am looking into the eyes of thousands of grateful infantrymen. Back at low level in the direction of the coast.

"Two Russian fighters, sir," reports Scharnovski.

"Where are they?"

"Chasing us, sir.—They are circling round the fleet in their own flak.—Cripes! They will both be shot down together by their own flak."

This expletive and, above all, the excitement in Scharnovski's voice are something quite new to me. This has never happened before. We fly on a level with the concrete blocks on which A.A. guns have also been posted. We could almost knock the Russian crews off them with our wings. They are still firing at our comrades who are now attacking the other ships. Then for a moment there is nothing visible through the pall of smoke rising from the *Marat*. The din down below on the surface of the water must be terrific, for it is not until now that a few flak crews spot my aircraft as it roars close past them. Then they swivel their guns and fire after me; all have had their attention diverted by the main formation flying off high above them. So the luck is with me, an isolated aircraft. The whole neighbourhood is full of A.A. guns; the air is peppered with shrapnel. But it is a comfort to know that this weight of iron is not meant exclusively for me! I am now crossing the coast line. The narrow strip is very unpleasant. It would be impossible to gain height because I could not climb fast enough to reach a safe altitude. So I stay down. Past machine guns and flak. Panic-stricken Russians hurl themselves flat on the ground. Then again Scharnovski shouts:

"A Rata coming up behind us!"

I look round and see a Russian fighter about 300 yards astern.

"Let him have it, Scharnovski!"

Scharnovski does not utter a sound. Ivan is blazing away at a range of only a few inches. I take wild evasive action.

"Are you mad, Scharnovski? Fire! I'll have you put under arrest." I yell at him!

Scharnovski does not fire. Now he says deliberately:

"I am holding fire, sir, because I can see a German Me coming up behind and if I open up on the Rata I may damage the Messerschmitt." That closes the sub-

I 16 Rata

ject, as far as Scharnovski is concerned; but I am sweating with the suspense. The tracers are going wider on either side of me. I weave like mad.

"You can turn round now, sir. The Me has shot down the Rata." I bank round slightly and look back. It is as Scharnovski says; there she lies down below. Now a Me passes groggily.

"Scharnovski, it will be a pleasure to confirm our fighter's claim to have shot that one down." He does not reply. He is rather hurt that I was not content to trust his judgment before. I know him; he will sit there and sulk until we land. How many operational flights have we made together when he has not opened his lips the whole time we have been in the air.

After landing, all the crews are paraded in front of the squadron tent. We are told by Flt./Lt. Steen that the

Wing Commander has already rung up to congratulate the 3rd squadron on its achievement. He had personally witnessed the very impressive explosion. Steen is instructed to report the name of the officer who was the first to dive and drop the successful two thousand pounder in order that he may be recommended for the Knight's Cross of the Iron Cross.

With a side-glance in my direction he says:

"Forgive me for telling the Kommodore that I am so proud of the whole squadron that I would prefer it if our success is attributed to the squadron as a whole."

In the tent he wrings my hand. "You no longer need a battleship for special mention in despatches," he says with a boyish laugh.

The Wing Commander rings up. "It is sinking day for the 3rd. You are to take off immediately for another attack on the *Kirov* berthed behind the *Marat*. Good hunting!" The photographs taken by our latest aircraft show that the *Marat* has split in two. This can be seen on the picture taken after the tremendous cloud of smoke from the explosion had begun to dissipate. The telephone rings again:

"I say, Steen, did you see my bomb? I didn't and neither did Pekrun."

"It fell into the sea, sir, a few minutes before the attack."

We youngsters in the tent are hard put to it to keep a straight face. A short crackling on the receiver and that is all. We are not the ones to blame our Wing Commander, who is old enough to be our father, if presumably out of nervousness he pressed the bomb release switch prematurely. He deserves all praise for flying with us himself on such a difficult mission. There is a big difference between the ages of fifty and twenty five. In dive bomber flying this is particularly true.

Out we go again on a further sortie to attack the *Kirov*. Steen had a slight accident taxying back after landing from the first sortie: one wheel ran into a large crater, his aircraft pancaked and damaged the propeller. The 7th flight provides us with a substitute aircraft, the flights are already on dispersal and we taxi off from our squadron base airfield. Flt./Lt. Steen again hits an obstacle and this aircraft is also unserviceable. There is no replacement available from the flights; they are of course already on dispersal. No one else on the staff is flying except myself. He therefore gets out of his aircraft and climbs onto my wingplane.

"I know you are going to be mad at me for taking your aircraft, but as I am in command I must fly with the squadron. I will take Scharnovski with me for this one sortie."

Vexed and disgruntled I walk over to where our aircraft are overhauled and devote myself for a time to my job as engineer officer. The squadron returns at the end of an hour and a half. No. 1, the green-nosed staff aircraft—mine—is missing. I assume the skipper has made a forced landing somewhere within our lines.

As soon as my colleagues have all come in I ask what has happened to the skipper. No one will give me a straight answer until one of them says:

"Steen dived onto the *Kirov*. He was caught by a direct hit at 5000 or 6000 feet. The flak smashed his rudder and his aircraft was out of control. I saw him try to steer straight at the cruiser by using the ailerons, but he missed her and nose-dived into the sea. The explosion of his two thousand pounder seriously damaged the *Kirov*."

The loss of our skipper and my faithful Cpl. Scharnovski is a heavy blow to the whole squadron and makes a tragic climax to our otherwise successful day. That fine lad Scharnovski gone! Steen gone! Both in their way were paragons and they can never be fully replaced. They are lucky to have died at a time when they could still hold the conviction that the end of all this misery would bring freedom to Germany and to Europe.

The senior staff captain temporarily takes over command of the squadron. I chose A.C. 1st class Henschel to be my rear-gunner. He has been sent to us by the reserve flight at Graz where he flew with me on several operational exercises. Occasionally I take some one else up with me, first the paymaster, then the intelligence officer and finally the M.O. None of them would care to insure my life. Then after I have taken on Henschel permanently and he has been transferred to the staff he is always furious if I leave him behind and some one else flies with me in his stead. He is as jealous as a little girl.

We are out again a number of times over the Gulf of Finland before the end of September, and we succeed in sending another cruiser to the bottom. We are not so lucky with the second battleship *Oktobrescaja Revolutia*. She is damaged by bombs of smaller calibre but not very seriously. When we manage on one sortie to score a hit with a two thousand pounder, on that particular day not one of these heavy bombs explodes. Despite the most searching investigation it is not possible to determine where the sabotage was done. So the Soviets keep one of their battleships.

There is a lull in the Leningrad sector and we are needed at a new key point. The relief of the infantry has been successfully accomplished, the Russian salient along the coastal strip has been pushed back with the result that Leningrad has now been narrowly invested. But Leningrad does not fall, for the defenders hold Lake Ladoga and thereby secure the supply line for the fortress.

# 5

# BEFORE MOSCOW

We carry out a few more missions on the Wolchow and Leningrad front. During the last of these sorties it is so much quieter everywhere here in the air that we conclude the balloon must be about to go up in some other part of the line. We are sent back to the central sector of the Eastern front, and as soon as we get there we begin to notice that the infantry is spoiling for action. There are rumours here of an offensive in the direction of Kalinin—Jaroslav. Over the air bases Moschna—Kuleschewka we by-pass Rshew and land at Staritza. Flight Lieutenant Pressler has replaced our late skipper as squadron commander. He comes from a neighbouring wing.

Gradually the cold weather sets in and we get a foretaste of approaching winter. The fall in the temperature gives me, as engineer officer of the squadron, all kinds of technical problems, for suddenly we begin to have trouble with our aircraft which is only caused by the cold. It takes a long time before experience teaches me the answer to the problems. The senior fitters, especially, now have their worries when every one is doing his utmost to have the maximum possible number of aircraft serviceable. Mine has an accident as well. He is unloading bombs from a lorry when one of them tips over and smashes his big toe with its fins. I am standing close by when it happens. For a long time he is speechless; then he comments, gazing ruefully at his toe: "My long-jumping days are over!" The weather has not yet become really cold. The sky is overcast, but there are warmer currents again with low clouds. They are of no help to us in our operations.

Kalinin has been occupied by our troops, but the Soviets are fighting back very bitterly and still holding their positions nearer the town. It will be difficult for our divisions to develop their advance, especially as the weather is of great assistance to the Russians. Besides, the incessant fighting has seriously reduced the strength of our units. Also our supply lines are not functioning any too smoothly, because the main communications road from Staritza to Kalinin runs right in front of the town in the hands of the enemy who exerts a continuous pressure from the East on our front line. I can soon see for myself how difficult and confused the situation is. Our effective strength in aircraft is at the moment small. The reasons are casualties, the effects of the weather, etc. I fly as No. 1—in the absence of the C.O.—in a sortie to Torshok, a railway junction N.W. of Kalinin. Our objectives are the railway station and the lines of communication with the rear. The weather is bad, cloud level only about 1800 feet. This is very low for a target with extremely strong defense. Should the weather deteriorate sufficiently to endanger our return flight we have been ordered to make a landing on the airfield near the town of Kalinin. We have a long wait for our fighter escort at our rendezvous. They fail to show up; presumably the weather is too bad for them. By waiting about in the air we have wasted a lot of petrol. We circuit round Torshok at a moderate altitude trying to discover the most weakly defended spot. At first it seems that the defense is pretty uniformly heavy, and then having found a more favourable spot we attack the railway station. I am glad when all our aircraft are in formation again behind me. The weather goes from bad to worse, plus a heavy fall of snow. Perhaps we have just enough petrol left to reach Staritza provided we are not forced to make too wide a detour because of the weather. I quickly decide and set course for the nearer Kalinin; besides, the sky looks brighter in the East. We land at Kalinin. Everybody is running round in circles in steel helmets. Aircraft from another fighter-bomber wing are here already. Just as I am switching off my ignition I hear and see tank shells fall on the airfield. Some of the aircraft are already riddled with holes. I hurry away in search of the operations room of the formation which has moved in here to obtain a more accurate picture of the situation. From what I learn we shall have no time to waste in overhauling our aircraft. The Soviets are attacking the airfield with tanks and infantry, and are less than a mile away. A thin screen of our own infantry protects our perimeter; the steel monsters may be upon us at any moment. We Stukas are a godsend to the ground troops defending the position. Together with the Henschel 123s of the fighter-bomber wing we keep up a steady

**Henschel 123**

attack on the tanks until late in the evening. We land again a few minutes after taking off. The ground personnel are able to follow every phase of the battle. We are well on the mark, for everybody realizes that unless the tanks are put out of action we have had it. We

spend the night in a barracks on the Southern outskirts
of the town. We are startled out of sleep by a grinding
noise. Is it one of our flak tractors changing position or is it Ivan with his tanks? Anything can happen here in Kalinin. Our infantry comrades tell us that
yesterday some tanks drove into the market square,
firing at everything that showed itself. They had broken
through our outposts and it took a long time to deal
with them in the town. Here there is an incessant thun-
der of gunfire; our artillery is in our rear shelling Ivan
above our heads.

The nights are pitch dark with a low blanket of
cloud. There is no air fighting except close to the
ground. As once again the supply road has been cut
the battle-weary ground troops are faced with many
shortages. Yet they never falter in their superhuman
task. A sudden cold snap of over forty degrees freezes
the normal lubricating oil. Every machine gun jams.
They say the cold makes no difference to the Russians;
that they have special animal fats and preparations. We
are short of equipment of every kind, the lack of which
seriously impairs our effective strength in this excessive
cold. A very slow trickle of supplies is coming through.
The natives cannot remember such bitter weather in
the last twenty or thirty years. The battle with the cold
is tougher than the battle with the enemy. The Soviets
could not have a more valuable ally. Our tank troops
complain that their turrets refuse to swivel, that everything is frozen stiff. We remain at Kalinin for some
days and are in the air incessantly. We soon get to know
every ditch. The front line has been pushed forward
again a few miles to the East of our airfield, and we return to our base at Staritza where we have long been
expected back. From here we continue operations, also
in the direction of Ostaschkow, and then we are ordered to move to Gorstowo near Rusa, about fifty miles
from Moscow.

Our divisions which have been thrown in here are
pushing forward along the motor road through Mosh-

aisk towards Moscow. A narrow spearhead of our tanks advancing through Swenigorod—Istra is within six miles of the Russian capital. Another group has also thrust even further Eastwards and has established two bridgeheads to the North of the city on the East bank of the Moscow—Arctic canal; one of them at Dimitrov.

It is now December and the thermometer registers 40-50 degrees below zero (centigrade). Huge snow-drifts, cloud cover generally low, flak intense. Plt./Off. Klaus, an exceptionally fine airman and one of the few left of our old companions, is killed, probably a chance hit from a Russian tank. Here, as at Kalinin, the weather is our chief enemy and the saviour of Moscow. The Russian soldier is fighting back desperately, but he, too, is winded and exhausted and without this ally would be unable to stem our further advance. Even the fresh Siberian units which have been thrown into the battle are not decisive. The German armies are crippled by the cold. Trains have practically stopped running, there are no reserves and no supplies, no transportation for the wounded. Iron determination alone is not enough. We have reached the limit of our strength. The most needful things are lacking. Machinery is immobil-ized, transport bottle-necked; no petrol, no ammunition. Lorries have long since been off the roads. Horse-drawn sleighs are the only means of locomotion. Tragic scenes of retreat recur with ever greater frequency. We have few aircraft. In temperatures like these engines are short-lived. As previously when we had the initiative we go out in support of our ground troops, now fighting to hold the attacking Soviets.

Some time has passed since we were dislodged from the Arctic canal. We are no longer in possession of the big dam N.W. of Klin in the direction of Kalinin. The Spanish Blue Division after putting up a gallant resis-tance has to evacuate the town of Klin. Soon it will be our turn.

Christmas is approaching and Ivan is still pushing on towards Wolokolamsk, N.W. of us. We are billeted with the squadron staff in the local school and sleep on the floor of the big schoolroom; so every morning when I get up my nocturnal ramblings are repeated to me. One finds out that five hundred operational sorties have left their mark. Another part of our squadron is quartered in the mud huts common here. When you enter them you can imagine you have been translated to some primitive country three centuries ago. The living room has the definite advantage that you can see practically nothing for the tobacco smoke. The male members of the family smoke a weed which they call Machorka and it befogs everything. Once you have got used to it you can make out the best piece of furniture, a huge stone stove three feet high and painted a dubious white. Huddled round it three generations live, eat, laugh, cry, procreate and die together. In the houses of the rich there is also a little wooden-railed pen in front of the stove in which a piglet romps in pursuit and evasive combat with other domestic animals. After dark the choicest and juiciest specimens of bug drop onto you from the ceiling in the night with a precision that surely makes them the Stukas of the insect world. There is a stifling frost; the Pans and Paninkas —men and women—do not seem to mind it. They know nothing different; their forebears have lived like this for centuries, they live and will go on living in the same way. Only this modern generation seems to have lost the art of telling stories and fairy tales. Perhaps they live too close to Moscow for that.

The Moskwa flows through our village on its way to the Kremlin city. We play ice hockey on it when we are grounded by the weather. In this way we keep our muscles elastic even if some of us are somewhat damaged in the process. Our adjutant, for example, gets a crooked nose with a slight list to starboard. But the game distracts our thoughts from the sad impressions over the front. After a furious match on the Moskwa I always go to the *Sauna*. There is one of these Finnish steam baths in the village. The place is, however, unfortunately so dark and slippery that one day I trip over the sharp edge of a spade propped against the wall and come a cropper. I escape with a nasty wound.

The Soviets have by-passed us to the North; it is therefore high time we pulled out to some airfield further to the rear. But we cannot do this; for days the clouds have hung so low above the forest towards Wiasma in the West that flying is out of the question. The snow lies deep on our airfield. Unless we are extremely lucky Ivan will arrive on our door step at the same time as Santa Claus. The Russian units which have by-passed us are certainly unaware of our presence, otherwise they would have bagged us long ago.

So we spend Christmas still in our schoolhouse at Gorstowo. When dusk falls a brooding silence descends on many of us, and we prick our ears at every clanking noise outside. But after our Christmas sing-song the gloom is soon dispelled. A couple of glasses of the copious vodka buck up even the moodiest among us. In the afternoon the Wing Commander pays us a short visit to distribute decorations. In our squadron I am first to receive the German Golden Cross. On the first Christmas holiday we vainly issue an invitation to our sporting colleagues in Moscow to come over for a Christmas match. So we have our own game of ice hockey on the Moskwa by ourselves. The bad weather continues for days.

As soon as it improves we start to pull out, flying back above the vast forests and along the motor road in the direction of Wiasma. No sooner are we airborne than the weather deteriorates, we fly in close formation skimming the tree tops. Even so it is difficult not to lose sight of one another. Everything is one grey blur, a swirling blend of fog and snow. Each aircraft is dependent on the skill of the flight leader. This kind of flying is more strenuous than the hottest sortie. It is a black day for us; we lose several crews in the squadron who are not equal to the task. Over Wiasma we turn off N. to starboard and fly in the direction Sytchewka —Rhew. We land in deep snow at Dugino, about twelve miles South of Sytchewka, and billet ourselves on a *Kolchose*. The merciless cold continues and now at last suitable equipment and clothing arrive by air. Transport aircraft land daily on our airfield bringing fur clothing, skis, sledges and other things. But it is too late to capture Moscow, too late to bring back our side the comrades who have been killed by the frost; too late to save the tens of thousands who have had to be sent back from the offensive with frozen toes and fingers; too late to give new impetus to the irresistibly advancing army which has been forced into dug-outs and trenches by the pitiless fist of an inconceivably hard winter.

We are now flying in areas with which we are familiar from last summer: in the region of the source of the Volga W. of Rhew, near Rhew itself, and along the railway line near Olinin and to the South. The deep snow sets our troops a colossal task, but the Soviets are quite in their element. The cleverest technician now is the one who uses the most primitive methods of work and locomotion. Engines no longer start, everything is frozen stiff, no hydraulic apparatus functions, to rely on any technical instrument is suicide. There is no starting our engines in the early mornings at these temperatures although we keep them covered up with straw mats and blankets. The mechanics are often out in the open all night long, warming up the engines at intervals of half an hour in order to make sure of their starting when we take off. Many cases of frostbite are due to spending these bitterly cold nights looking after the engines. As engineer officer I am always out and about between sorties so as not to lose any chance of getting one extra aircraft serviceable. We are seldom frozen in the air. We have to fly low in bad weather and the defence is heavy so that one is too keyed up to notice the cold. That does not of course exclude the chance of discovering symptoms of frostbite on our return to the warmth of our billets.

At the beginning of January General von Richthofen lands on our airfield in a Fieseler-Storch and in the name of the Führer invests me with the Knight's Cross

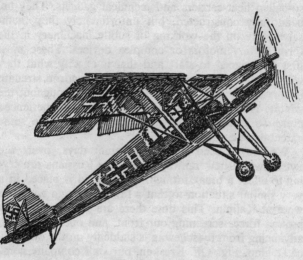

**Fieseler-Storch**

of the Iron Cross. The citation specially mentions my successful ship and bridge destructions last year.

An even more intense cold increases the difficulty of keeping aircraft serviceable for the next day's operations. I have seen desperate mechanics try to warm up their engines with a naked flame in the hope of inducing them to start. One of them said to me:

"They'll either start now or be burnt to a cinder. If they won't they're no use to us anyway."

All the same this strikes me as a rather drastic method of solving our problem and I hit upon another. A petrol can makes a tin oven. A sort of chimney protrudes from the top with a perforated cowl to stop the sparks from flying. We place this whole contraption underneath the engine and light a fire in it, pointing the stove-pipe towards the priming pump round which the heat now radiates. We maintain the heat until we get a result. It is primitive, but just the thing for the Russian winter. We receive deliveries of complicated, so-called heat-carriers and technical gadgets. They are beautifully constructed, but unfortunately they themselves rely on the working of subtle machinery in the form of tiny motors or complex devices. These must first be induced to start and that is exactly what they will not do because of the cold. Our squadron strength in serviceable aircraft is therefore small throughout the winter. These few are mostly flown by old, experienced crews so that the disadvantage in quantity is to some extent compensated by quality.

We have been out for some days over the Sytschewka-Rhew railway where the Russians are trying to effect a breakthrough. Our airfield is placed in a very similar situation to that a few weeks ago when we were at Kalinin. This time there are no battle-worthy ground forces screening our front, and one night Ivan, advancing from Sytschewka is suddenly on the outskirts of Dugino. Flg./Off. Kresken, our staff company commander, gets together a fighting party drawn from our ground personnel and those of the nearest units, and holds the airfield. Our gallant mechanics spend their nights, turn and turn about, manning trenches with rifles and hand grenades in their hands, and during the day return to their maintenance duties. Nothing can happen in daylight, for we still have a store of petrol and bombs on our airfield. For two successive days it is attacked by cavalry units and ski battalions. Then the situation becomes critical and we drop our bombs close to the perimeter of our airfield. The Soviet losses are heavy. Then Kresken, one time athlete, assumes the offensive with his combat group. We hover above him with our aircraft, shooting and bombing down all opposition to his counter-attack. So the whole fore-field of our station is cleared of the enemy again. Our Luftwaffe soldiers at the beginning of the war certainly never saw themselves being used in this way. An armoured unit of the army now expands our gains, recaptures Sytschewka and establishes its H.Q. there. So the situation is more or less stabilized again and a new front built up on the line Gschatsk—Rhew covering our sector. The days of monotonous retreat are over.

The foxes stand the cold better than we do. Every time we fly back from Rhew at low level above the snow-covered plains we can see them crawling through the snow. If we whizz over them at six or ten feet they duck and blink timidly up at us. Jäckel has still a few rounds left in his M.G. and takes a pot shot at one. He hits him too. Then Jäckel flies back to the spot in a Storch with skis. Master Reynard's pelt is however completely riddled with holes.

I am disagreeably surprised by the news that in view of my high total of operational flights I am to be sent home immediately. My instructions are to proceed to Graz in Steiermark at the end of a period of leave where I am to take over command of a Reserve Flight and give new crews the benefit of my most recent experiences. Repeated asseverations that I do not need a rest, that I do not want to leave the Stukas, even pulling strings, avail me nothing. My orders are final. It is hard to say goodbye to the comrades with whom chance has thrown me together. Flt./Lt. Pressler is going to ask for me back the moment I am in my new job and a little grass has grown over the incident. I clutch at every straw.

One morning I am on my way West; in a transport aircraft over Witebsk—Minsk—Warsaw to Germany. I spend my leave skiing in the Riesengebirge and in the Tyrol and try to assuage my fury by exercise and sunshine. Gradually the peace of this mountain world which is my home and the beauty of its glittering snow-capped peaks relaxes the tension of day-in day-out operational flying.

# 6

## TRAINING AND PRACTICE

Before taking over the job of training new crews I get married. My father is still Rector of his church and performs the ceremony in our little country village to which I am attached by so many happy memories of my scape-grace boyhood.

. Then off to Graz, this time not as a learner but as an instructor. Formation flying, diving, bombing, gunnery. I often sit in the aircraft eight hours in the day, as for the time being I have hardly any help. In bad weather or when technical duties are on the schedule there are military exercises or sport. Crews are sent to me for further training from the Stuka schools after which they proceed to the front. When they have passed on I shall meet some of them again in days to come; perhaps have them in my own unit. If for no other reason, it pays to spare no trouble with their training. In my leisure hours I keep in training by athletics; I play tennis, swim, or spend my time in the magnificent country round Graz. After two months I get an assistant. Pilot Officer Jäckel of the 3rd Flight has just been awarded the Knight's Cross of the Iron Cross, and has at the same time been seconded for less exacting work. We carry out exercise operations against peaceful targets, as though at the front. I have two Messerschmitt aircraft on my flight strength so that we are also able to represent enemy interception. The training is stiff and arduous, but I believe the crews who stand up to it and do what is required of them are learning a lot.

Physical toughness and endurance is fostered by sport. Almost every Monday morning I take the flight for a six mile run; it does them all a world of good. In the afternoon we go to Andritz for a swim and tests of nerve. They all qualify as pole jumpers and there is keen competition for the swimming certificate.

Jäckel is a few years younger than I and still quite a boy. One cannot be angry with him no matter how awkward a situation arises. He is gay and full of fun; he takes life in his stride. On Sunday afternoons I usually go off into the mountains. There is a bus stop in front of the guard room and I board it there on my way into the town. The shadow of the bus travels with us at the side of the road and I suddenly become aware of figures which form part of this shadow apparently perched on the roof of the bus. They are "cocking snooks" and in other ways playing the fool, especially when girls happen to be passing. I can guess who they are by their caps. They are soldiers belonging to our station, but they cannot be men of my unit because strict orders have repeatedly been issued forbidding all service men to climb on the top of the buses. Rather pointedly I remark to a lieutenant of a ground unit sitting next to me:

"Those chaps up there must be yours."

With a faintly superior edge to his voice he retorts:

"You will laugh. They are yours!"

When the soldiers alight in Graz I order them to report to me at 11 A.M. on the Monday morning. When they troop in to receive what is coming to them I say:

"What the devil do you mean by it? You know you've been breaking an order. It's unheard of."

I can see by their faces that they want to say something and I ask if they have any excuse to offer.

"We only thought it was all right for us as Pilot Officer Jäckel was up there with us too."

I hastily dismissed them before I burst out laughing. Then I picture Jäckel perched on the roof of the bus. When I tell him what he has let me in for he puts on his innocent expression, and then I can keep a straight face no longer.

In Graz a few days later we narrowly escape another off-duty accident. A Glider Club had begged me to tow their glider with an ancient Czech biplane because they had no one else to pilot it. I do this and, being a private flight, it is an opportunity for me to take with me my wife who is very keen to fly. After 2½ hours I ask how much petrol we are likely to have left; the petrol gauge does not show this. They tell me the machine has enough for four hours; I can carry on flying without the least anxiety. I accept this assurance and fly back towards the aerodrome. As we are flying at low level above the middle of a potato field the engine conks out. I have only time to yell out: "Hold tight," for I know that my wife is not strapped in, before I come down in the furrows. The aeroplane bounces over a ditch and then comes safely to a standstill in a cornfield. We fetch some petrol and then I take off again from a field path for the aerodrome two miles away.

How many of my colleagues, especially in the Luftwaffe, come through battles with the enemy unscathed only to crack up in some utterly stupid "civilian" accident! This trivial incident once again confirms the necessity for the apparently silly rule by which we are obliged to be at least as careful when we have left the operational front as we are in the keenest attack. Similarly when in action with the enemy we are not allowed to accept unnecessary risks even if we are not inhibited or deterred by the thought of our lives during an operation.

When I land again on the aerodrome with the ancient biplane I learn that the reserve flight of another squadron has been transferred to Russia. In that case it should soon be our turn. For a long time it has been preying on my mind that I have been home now for several months, and all of a sudden I realise how I have been fidgeting to get to the front. I constantly fret at being kept out of it for so long, and I feel this restlessness particularly strongly when I sense that too long an absence from the front line might well be dangerous to me. For I am only human, and there are many instincts in me which would gleefully exchange the intimate fellowship of death for the more intimate fellowship of life. For I want to live, the desire is stronger every time—I feel it in the throbbing of my pulses whenever I escape death once again in an attack, but I am also conscious of it in the exhilaration of a head-long rush down a steep Alpine slope. I want to live. I love life. I feel it in every deep drawn breath, in every pore of my skin, in every fibre of my body. I am not afraid of death; I have often looked him in the eye for a matter of seconds and have never been the first to lower my gaze, but each time after such an encounter I have also rejoiced in my heart and sometimes cried out with a whoop of jubilation trying to overshout the roar of the engines.

All this I think of as I mechanically chew down my supper in the Mess. And then already my mind is firmly made up. I will doggedly pull every possible string until they take me out of this rut and send me back again to a fighting formation at the front.

I do not accomplish my real object, but it is not long before we are all ordered to the Crimea. Sarabus, close to Sinferopol, is our new station and there, at any rate, we are closer to the front than we were before. We solved the transport problem by using our Ju 87's as tug aircraft for freight gliders. Over Kracow—Lemberg—Proskurow—Nicolajew we are soon at our destination. The aerodrome there is a very large one and suitable for training purposes. Our makeshift quarters are not very different from those of the front, but where there is a will there is a way. We resume our routine training as at Graz. We specially enjoy it when we practise landings on other airfields, for then sometimes we land in the morning in the west on the shore of the Black Sea, and perhaps in the afternoon in the northwest near the sea of Asow. We bathe for at least half an hour on the lovely beaches in the broiling sunshine. There are no hills except near Kertsch, and in the south where the Jaila range of about 5,000 feet runs along the south coast of the Crimea. All the rest of the country is flat; vast steppes, in the middle of them huge tomato plantations. A very narrow coastal strip stretches between the sea and the Jaila mountains: the Russian Riviera. We are often there and fetch kindling with lorries; there is no timber where we are stationed. The comparison with the Riviera turns out to be rather feeble. I see a few palm trees at Jalta—so far so good —but two or three of these trees are far from making a Riviera. From a distance the buildings gleam brightly in the sun, especially when one is flying at low level along the coast. It makes a surprisingly good impression; but if you walk through the streets of Jalta and get a close view of everything the general primitiveness and vulgarity of this Soviet watering place is a tremendous disillusion. It is no different in the neighbouring towns of Aluschta and Alupka. My men are delighted by the many vineyards between these two places; the vintage season is just beginning. We sample the grapes on every hillside and often arrive home late with a prodigious bellyache.

I have been chafing now for some considerable time at not being sent back to the war. I ring up the General of the Air Command in the Caucasus and offer him my Stukas as an operational unit; most of the crews are ready for the front. I point out that it will be splendid training for all of them, and that the Wing may consider itself lucky to get crews which have already had experience. First, we receive an order to move to Kertsch. It appears that Soviet supply trains often travel along the south coast. From here we would be able to attack them. But it gets no further than "would"! For hours together we stand by waiting for the supply trains, but nothing happens. Once I want to try my luck with my Messerschmitt fighter; my objective being enemy reconnaisance aircraft. But the blighters at once sheer off far out to sea setting a course for Tuapse—Suchum, and I can no longer overtake them because, naturally, I cannot take off until after I have spotted them. Soon afterwards, however, I succeed in effecting our transfer to Beloretschenkaja, near Maikop, where another wing is stationed. Here we shall get proper operational flying again, for we are to be used together in support of the advance in the direction of Tuapse.

Overnight we have now become a busy frontal formation. We are in the air from early to late in the area where the army is attacking up the Psich valley by way of Chadykenskaja—Nawaginskaja, over the Goitsch pass in the direction of Tuapse. It is not exactly easy for us because in our training unit we use only relatively old and obsolete aircraft, and the Wing operating here, with which we frequently fly together, has the very latest type. When flying in formation at high altitudes this puts us at a noticeable disadvantage.

Fighting in the narrow valleys is a thrilling experience. We are often unwarily enticed by our eagerness for a fight into a trap, if we pursue the enemy or try too persistently to discover his hiding places. If in our search we fly into one of these narrow valleys we are frequently unable to manoeuvre at all. Sometimes, however, a mountain suddenly looms up at the end of such a valley, rising sheer and blocking the way ahead. Then we have to make a quick reaction, and time and again we owe our escape to the good performance of our aircraft. But that is still child's play compared with the situation we find ourselves in when 600 feet above us the mountains are wreathed in dense cloud.

The mountain crests here are between 3,500 and 4,500 feet. It is easier after we have been into every valley a few times and know which valleys have exits, and behind which mountain it is possible to get out into open country. This is all guess work in bad weather and with low lying clouds. When we make low level attacks on some valley road occasionally the defence fires down at us from above because the mountain sides on either side of us are also occupied by the Ivans.

Our numerically weak mountain troops are putting up a stubborn fight against a far superior enemy lodged in strong mountain positions. We are in close liaison with the ground forces and do our best to answer their every call for attack and support. The battles in the mountain forests are particularly difficult; it is fighting blind-fold. If our Operations Officer gives us permission to attack a certain belt of forest we carry out his instructions even when we are unable to see it clearly. It is on such occasions as these that the Army commends our usefulness and the effectiveness of our attack.

The Geimamberg, the neighbouring heights, are in German hands. By stiff fighting we are pushing forward to the south west. Less than thirteen miles separate our comrades from Tuapse. But the casualties in the mountain fighting are too high and there are practically no reserves available. So the assault on the Goitsch pass is abandoned and final success is denied us.

There is a ding-dong battle for the Goitsch railway station.

A Soviet armoured train hurls its heavy stuff into our thin attacking line. This armoured train is crafty. It belches fire and then, like a dragon, retires into its lair. This dragon's lair is a mountain tunnel in the neighbourhood of Tuapse. If we fly up it streaks back like lightning at our approach into the shelter of the tunnel and we only glimpse its tail. Once we catch it napping—nearly. We have "crept up on it," but at the last minute it must have received a warning. It is hit, but the damage cannot have been serious; a couple of days later it has been repaired and re-appears. But now this steel monster is extremely wary; we never once catch sight of it again. Then we make the following decision: if we are unable to get to close quarters with this armoured train we will make its guardian angel its fatality! We block the exit from the tunnel with a special bomb, thereby preventing the armoured train from any excursion and giving our comrades on the ground, at least for a time, a sorely needed respite. "Give and take is the whole philosophy of life," says my rear gunner with a grin.

We also attack the port of Tuapse, which, like all ports, is strongly defended by flak. The town and the harbour itself, behind the chain of mountains, is still in Soviet hands. If we fly at an altitude of 9,000 feet the light flak reaches us long before we approach the target. A.A. guns are sited on the mountains for the last few miles of our approach. To avoid the flak we fly at an altitude of only 2,500 feet, for the mountain ridges rise perpendicularly from the sea to a height of 4,500 to 5,000 feet. Our attacks are directed against the dock yards, port installations and ships lying in the harbour, principally tankers. Generally everything mobile starts to career in circles in order to avoid our bombs. If they were not so already, my crews are now fully fledged operational airmen. The flak over the port is not at all comparable with the defence at Kronstadt; it is nevertheless impressively heavy. It isn't possible to fly straight back over the mountains because they are much too high. We usually dive very low on to the harbour and then sheer off seawards at our maximum ceiling and so escape relatively quickly out of the range of the defence. Out at sea, however, the Soviet pursuit aircraft are already waiting for us. We have now to climb to a good 9,000 feet in order to get back home with a margin of at least 3,000 feet above the mountain flak because in air battle it is easy to lose altitude.

The conditions under which we attack are much the same as the Gelendshik area where we also occasionally participate in attacks on airfields or naval targets in the bay of the same name. The Soviets have soon located our station at Beloretschenskaja; at first they bomb it day and night. Small as is the material damage, they nevertheless inflict a serious blow on the wing whose guests we are. Their C.O., Squadron Leader Orthofer, is killed in one of these raids. I choose this very moment to land and taxi in; bombs are dropping to port and starboard. My aircraft is hit by many splinters and becomes unserviceable, but I escape unhurt.

General Pflugbeil, who is in command of all the Luftwaffe formations here, is often present at our dispersal. He brings us the news that we are to move further east to an airfield near Terek. Here another push is in progress and we are to support it. It is aimed in the direction Grossny—Caspian Sea. At the time the move takes place our tank spearhead has reached a point just short of Okshokodnice. Over Georgiewski— Piatigorsk and Mineralnya Wody where one can look down on the vast and magnificent Elbruz mountains we fly to our new base at Soldatskaja. We make a short half way landing at Mineralnya Wody and rest. Here there is a real plague of mice. In palliasses, in cupboards and crannies, in every hold and corner they patter—everywhere mice. They jump out of our haversacks, they eat up everything. It is impossible to sleep, one can hear them rustling even in one's pillow. I open everything in order to scare them away. Then there is a few minutes quiet, but immediately the noise begins again as loud as before. At Soldatskaja we are rid of this plague of mice. Presumably Ivan's constantly falling bombs soon frightened them away from here. We have few A.A. guns. We do not now operate, as was originally intended, in support of the tank spearhead to the east, but our first mission is in the south. A few days later Naltschik is captured by German and Rumanian troops. The panorama as we approach our objective to the south is glorious. Ahead of us the snow peaks of the 15,000 feet range, glittering in the sunshine in all imaginable colours, below us green meadows spotted with yellow, red and blue. These spots are plants and flowers. Above us a brilliant blue sky. When approaching the target I often forget entirely the bombs I am carrying and the objective. Everything makes such a soothing, peaceful and beautiful impression. The mountain world of which the Elbruz is the centre has such a

gigantic and overpowering effect; in this or that valley
here one could easily tuck away several of the Alps.

After the capture of Naltschik we make a few more
sorties eastwards to the Terek front, beyond Mosdok.
Then, quite unexpectedly comes the withdrawal to Beloretschenskaja in the battle zone of Tuapse where bitter fighting is still going on for the old key areas. It is
getting on for November. I fly my 650th operational
sortie and for some weeks I have not been feeling any
too fit. Jaundice! I have guessed it for some time, but I
hope that it will pass and that I shall not be taken out
of operations because of this. The whites of my eyes
are yellow, my skin the same colour. Always I deny
that anything is wrong with me to anyone who asks,
especially to General Pflugbeil who has been trying for
quite a while to order me to bed. Malicious persons
say that I have been eating too much whipped cream.
Perhaps there is some truth in this. The General had
brought along a case of champagne to celebrate my
600th operational flight and was quite astonished when
I told him I was sure my outfit would appreciate his
gift and explained that my own particular weakness
lay in another direction. A few days later several large
cakes arrived with two pails full of whipped cream, not
too difficult a problem in view of the number of cows
in these parts. For two days we practically ate nothing
but these sweets; the next day hardly a single crew was
fit to fly. As I am now as yellow as a quince a Messerschmitt 108 arrives with the General's orders that I
am to be taken, by force if necessary, to hospital at
Rostow. I succeed in persuading him to let me stop
off to report to my Wing at Karpowa near Stalingrad.
We fly there on a northerly course over Elistra. I immediately move heaven and earth to stay with the
Wing and from here hand over my flight to someone
else. It doesn't work, but the Wing Commander promises me No. 1 Flight in which I began the Russian
Campaign.

"But into hospital first!"

Then in the middle of November I am shut up in the hospital at Rostow.

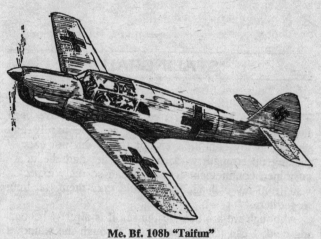

**Me. Bf. 108b "Taifun"**

# 7

## STALINGRAD

This lying in hospital gets on my nerves. I have been here now for almost a week, I can see hardly any change in my condition except that I am not exactly picking up strength with the strict diet and the unaccustomed confinement to bed. I can scarcely expect a visit from my colleagues; it would take them too long to get here.

Although we are near to the sea it is already becoming cold; I can tell by the breeze through the windows which are paned less with glass than with the lids of packing cases.

The doctor in charge of my case is an excellent fellow but he has lost patience with me, and so he becomes the "case" the day he enters my room and informs me offhandedly:

"There is an ambulance train leaving for Germany the day after tomorrow; I am arranging for you to go by it."

"I shall do no such thing."

"But you simply must go home for treatment. What are you thinking of?"

His professional wrath is aroused.

"But I can't be sent out of the line for so ludicrous an illness. This is a very nice hospital, but I have had enough of lying in bed."

In order to leave no doubt in his mind that I mean what I say:

"I must fly back to my squadron right away."

Now the doctor really is angry; he opens his mouth, snaps it shut again, and finally delivers himself of this vehement protest:

"I accept no responsibility—you understand, no responsibility whatever."

He is silent for a moment, then he adds energetically:

"Moreover, I shall make an endorsement to that effect on your discharge sheet."

I pack my things, I get my discharge sheet from the office and—off to the aerodrome. Here there is working a fitter who has often overhauled aircraft of my Wing. One only needs to have luck on one's side. An aircraft has just this moment come out of the repair shop; it so happens that it has to be flown up to the front to the Wing at Karpowo, ten miles from Stalingrad. I cannot say that I feel very strong and fit, I bumble around as if I were walking in my sleep. I do not, however, attribute this so much to my illness as to the sudden fresh air.

Exactly two hours later I am on the airfield at Karpowo after having flown past Tazinskaja—Surwikino and lastly Kalatsch on the Don. The runway is packed with aircraft, mostly Stukas of our Wing and those of a neighbouring squadron. The airfield itself offers no opportunities for camouflage, it lies right in the open country. It slopes away gently on one side.

After landing I go off to find the signboards. Exact orientation within the unit area has always been one of our special fads. Even if nothing or very little else indicates our presence the signboards are certain to be there. So I very soon discover the Wing orderly room. It is bang in the centre of the aerodrome in a hole in the ground, described in military parlance as a bunker. I have to wait a while before I can report to the C.O.; he has just gone out on a short operational flight with my friend Kraus. When he comes in I report my return; he is more than surprised to see me back so soon:

"You do look a sight! Your eyes and everything are yellow as a quince."

There is no talking myself out of this without a white lie, so I brazenly reply,

"I am here only because I have been discharged as fit."

It works. The C.O. looks at the M.O. and says with a shake of his head:

"If he is fit, then I understand more about jaundice than all the doctors. Where are your medical papers by the way?"

A ticklish question. On the aerodrome at Rostow I had had desperate need of some paper and had put my doctor's cunningly worded certificate to a more profitable and appropriate use. I have to think quickly and reply in the same tone of voice:

"I understand that the medical papers are being sent by courier."

In accordance with the promise made to me ten days before, I take over the command of my old flight.

We have few operational missions; they have been out only once over a Volga harbour in the vicinity of Astrachan. Our main task is to deliver attacks within the city area of Stalingrad. The Soviets are defending it like a fortress. My squadron commander gives me the latest news. There has been practically no change in the ground personnel. From armourer Götz to Sen./ Fitter Pissarek all are still there. The flying personnel necessarily presents a different picture because of casualties, but the new crews I have trained have all been posted to the reserve squadron. Living quarters, offices, etc., are all underground. In a very short time I have found my feet again and feel at home. The next day we fly a sortie over Stalingrad, where approximately two thirds of the city is in German hands. It is true the Soviets hold only one third, but this third is being defended with an almost religious fanaticism. Stalingrad is Stalin's city and Stalin is the god of these young Kirgises, Usbeks, Tartars, Turkmenians and other Mongols. They are hanging on like grim death to every scrap of rubble, they lurk behind every remnant of a wall. For their Stalin they are a guard of fire-breathing war-beasts, and when the beasts falter, well-aimed revolver shots from their political commissars nail them, in one way or the other, to the ground they are defending. These Asiatic pupils of integral communism, and the political commissars standing at their backs, are destined to force Germany, and the whole world with her, to abandon the comfortable belief that communism is a political creed like so many others. Instead they are to prove to us first, and finally to all nations, that they are the disciples of a new gospel. And so Stalingrad is to become the Bethlehem of our century. But a Bethlehem of war and hatred, annihilation and destruction.

This is the thought which occupies our minds as we fly sortie after sortie against the Red fortress. The section of the city held by the Soviets borders immediately on the west bank of the Volga, and every night the Russians drag everything needed by the Red Guardsmen across the Volga. Bitter fighting rages for a block of houses, for a single cellar, for a bit of factory wall. We have to drop our bombs with painstaking accuracy because our own soldiers are only a few yards away in another cellar behind debris of another wall.

On our photographic maps of the city every house is distinguishable. Each pilot is given his target precisely marked with a red arrow. We fly in, map in hand, and it is forbidden to release a bomb before we have made sure of the target and the exact position of our own troops. Flying over the western part of the city far behind the front, one is struck peculiarly by the quiet prevailing there and by the almost normal traffic. Everyone, including civilians, go about their business as if the city were far behind the front. The whole western part is now in our hands, only the small eastern quarter of the city towards the Volga contains these Russian nests of resistance and is the scene of our most furious assaults. Often the Russian flak dies down in

the afternoon, presumably because by then they have
used up the ammunition brought up across the river
the night before. On the other bank of the Volga the
Ivans take off from a few fighter airfields and try to
hamper our attacks on the Russian part of Stalingrad.
They seldom push home the pursuit above our positions, and generally turn back as soon as they no
longer have their own troops below them. Our airfield
lies close to the city, and when flying in formation we
have to circuit once or twice in order to gain a certain height. That is enough for the Soviet air intelligence to warn their A.A. defence. The way things are
going I dislike the idea of being away from my flight
for a single hour; there is too much at stake, we feel
that instinctively. This time I am physically at bend or
breaking point, but to report sick now means the loss
of my command, and this fear gives me additional
stamina. After a fortnight in which I feel more as if I
were in Hades than on earth, I gradually recover my
strength. In between we fly sorties in the northern sector north of the city where the front joins the Don. A
few times we attack targets near Beketowa. Here especially the flak is extraordinarily heavy, the sorties are
difficult. According to statements taken from captured
Russians the A.A. guns here are served exclusively by
women. When the day's mission takes us here our crews
always say: "We've a date with the flak girls to-day."
This is in no way derogatory, for all of us who have
already been there know how accurately they fire.

At regular intervals we attack the northern bridges
over the Don. The biggest of these is near the village of
Kletskaja and this bridgehead on the west bank of the
Don is most vigilantly defended by flak. Prisoners tell
us that the H.Q. of a command is located here. The
bridgehead is constantly being extended and every day
the Soviets pour in more men and material. Our destruction of these bridges delays these reinforcements,
but they are able to replace them relatively quickly

with pontoons so that the maximum traffic across the river is soon fully restored.

Up here on the Don the line is mainly held by Rumanian units. Only in the actual battle area of Stalingrad stands the German 6th Army.

One morning after the receipt of an urgent report our Wing takes off in the direction of the bridgehead at Kletskaja. The weather is bad: low lying clouds, a light fall of snow, the temperature probably 20 degrees below zero; we fly low. What troops are those coming towards us? We have not gone more than half way. Masses in brown uniforms—are they Russians? No. Rumanians. Some of them are even throwing away their rifles in order to be able to run the faster: a shocking sight, we are prepared for the worst. We fly the length of the column heading north, we have now reached our allies' artillery emplacements. The guns are abandoned, not destroyed. Their ammunition lies beside them. We have passed some distance beyond them before we sight the first Soviet troops.

They find all the Rumanian positions in front of them deserted. We attack with bombs and gun-fire—but how much use is that when there is no resistance on the ground?

We are seized with a blind fury—horrid premonitions rise in our minds: how can this catastrophe be averted? Relentlessly I drop my bombs on the enemy and spray bursts of M.G. fire into these shoreless yellow-green waves of oncoming troops that surge up against us out of Asia and the Mongolian hinterland. I haven't a bullet left, not even to protect myself against the contingency of a pursuit attack. Now quickly back to remunition and refuel. With these hordes our attacks are merely a drop in the bucket, but I am reluctant to think of that now.

On the return flight we again observe the fleeing Rumanians; it is a good thing for them I have run out of ammunition to stop this cowardly rout.

They have abandoned everything; their easily defended positions, their heavy artillery, their ammunition dumps.

Their cowardice is certain to cause a debacle along the whole front.

Unopposed, the Soviet advance rolls forward to Kalatsch. And with Kalatsch in their hands they now close a semi-circle round our half of Stalingrad.

Within the actual area of the city our 6th Army holds its ground. Under a hail of concentrated artillery fire it sees the Red assault waves surge up incessantly against them. The 6th Army is "bled white," it fights with its back to a slowly crumbling wall: nevertheless it fights and hits back.

The front of Stalingrad runs along a plateau of lakes from north to south and then joins the steppe. There is no island in this ocean of plain for hundreds of kilometres until the fair-sized town of Elistra. The front curves East past Elistra.

A German infantry motorized division based on the town controls the mighty waste of steppe. Our allies also hold the gap between this division and the 6th Army in Stalingrad. The Red Army suspects our weakness at this point, especially in the northern sector of the lake district, the Soviets break through westwards. They are trying to reach the Don! Another couple of days and the Russians are on the river. Then a Red thrust forces a wedge in our lines to the northwest. They are trying to reach Kalatsch. This plainly spells the impending doom of the 6th Army. The two Russian attacking forces join hands at Kalatsch and then the ring round Stalingrad is closed. Everything happens with uncomfortable speed, many of our reserves are overwhelmed by the Russians and trapped in their pincer movement. During this phase one deed of anonymous heroism succeeds another. Not one German unit surrenders until it has fired its last revolver bullet, its last hand grenade, without carrying on the fighting to the bitter end.

We are now flying in all directions over the pocket

wherever the situation seems most threatening. The Soviet pressure on the 6th Army is maintained, but the German soldier stands firm. Wherever a local penetration is successful it is sealed off and the enemy thrown back again by a counter-attack. Our comrades do the impossible to stem the tide; they stand their ground, knowing that their retreat is cut off because cowardice and treachery have come to the aid of the Red Army. Our airfield is now frequently the target of Soviet airforce attack in low and high level raids. In proportion to the great expenditure of force we sustain very little damage. Only now we are running so short of bombs, ammunition and petrol, that it no longer seems prudent to leave all the squadrons within the pocket. So everything is flown out in two or three detachments and afterwards no support from the air will be possible from this airfield. A special flight under Pilot Officer Jungklausen remains in the pocket in order to give uninterrupted support to the hard-pressed 6th Army for as long as it is still able to take off. All the rest of our flying personnel moves back out of the pocket to Oblivskaja, just over 100 miles west of Stalingrad.

Fairly strong German forces now go in to the attack from the area of Salsk in co-operation with two newly arrived armoured divisions. These divisions have been out of the line and we know that they are elite troops thoroughly refreshed. The attack is a thrust from the southwest in a northeasterly direction with the ultimate aim of re-establishing the broken communications with Stalingrad and thereby relieving the 6th Army. We support this operation daily from dawn till dusk. It must succeed if the encircled divisions are to be freed. The advance goes rapidly forward, soon our comrades have overrun Abganerowo a bare 19 miles south of the pocket. By hard fighting they have gained nearly 40 miles.

Despite stiffening opposition we are still steadily advancing. If it were now possible for the 6th Army to exert pressure from the inside on the south rim of the pocket the operation could be accelerated and simplified, but it would hardly be able to do this even if the order were given. The 6th Army has long since succumbed to physical exhaustion; only an iron determination keeps it going. The debilitation of the encircled army has been aggravated by the lack of the barest necessities. They are now without food, ammunition or petrol. The temperature, generally between 20 and 30 degrees below zero, is crippling. The chance of their breaking out of the ring containing them depends on the successful execution of the plan to fly in the barest minimum of supplies into the pocket. But the weather god is apparently on the side of the enemy. A prolonged spell of continuous bad weather prevents us from flying in adequate supplies. In previous battles in Russia these operations have been so invariably successful that a pocket could always be relieved. But this time only a fractional part of the indispensable supplies is able to reach its destination. Later on, landing difficulties arise and we are compelled to rely on jettison drops. In this way again a part is lost. Notwithstanding, we fly with supplies in the thickest snow storms and under these conditions some of the precious freight falls into the Soviet lines.

Another calamity comes with the news that the Soviets have forced a huge gap in the sector of the front line held by our allies in the south. If the breakthrough is not pinned down it may bring disaster to the whole of the southern front. There are no reserves available. The break-through must be sealed off. The assault group intended for the relief of Stalingrad from the south is the only one available. The most effective elements are taken out of it and despatched to the new danger zone. We have daily been flying over the spearheads of the German attack and we know the strength of the opposition. We also know that these German divisions would have reached the pocket and so relieved the encircled army there.

As they now have to divide up their potential, it is all over. It is too late to free the 6th Army; its tragic fate is sealed. The decision not to let the strongly concentrated assault group continue its advance on Stalingrad must be a sad blow; the weak residue of this force can no longer do it alone.

At two decisive places our allies have yielded to Soviet pressure. Through no fault of the German soldier the 6th Army has been lost. And with it Stalingrad. And with Stalingrad the possibility of eliminating the real dynamic centre of the Red armies.

# 8

# WITHDRAWAL

Jungklausen has just flown out the last remaining stores of bombs and petrol and is back with the Wing. He has done an excellent job under difficult circumstances, but even here in Oblivskaja the conditions in which he finds us are anything but quiet. One morning there is musketry fire on the far side of the aerodrome. As we discover later, the ground staff of another unit is engaged in a battle with the regular Soviet troops. The met. flier gives the alert by firing a succession of red Vereys. I immediately take off with the squadron and close to the airfield I see horses, their dismounted riders beside them, all Ivans. To the north, an incalculable army of horses, men and material. I climb, knowing the condition of our defences and wanting to make a preliminary survey of the general situation. It does not take me long: a Russian cavalry division is advancing and there is nobody to stop them. North of us there is, as yet, no coherent front, so that the Soviets have infiltrated unnoticed through a newly created gap. Their main force is two to three miles distant from our airfield with its spearhead on its periphery. There are no ground forces in this area; this is therefore the direst emergency. The first thing we do is to destroy their artillery with bombs and cannon fire before they can take up positions; then we attack the other constituents. A dismounted cavalry unit is immobilized and loses its fighting efficiency. Therefore we have no choice but to shoot down all their horses.

Without intermission we take off and land; we are all in feverish haste. Unless we can wipe them all out before dusk our airfield will be threatened by nightfall.

In the afternoon we spot a few Soviet tanks. They are rolling at top speed in the direction of the aerodrome. We must destroy them, otherwise we are hopelessly lost. We go in with bombs. They manoeuvre to avoid them. The sheer urgency of self-defence gives us a precision we have never had before. After the attack we climb and fly back to the airfield by the shortest route, well satisfied with the good job we have done and with the success of our defensive measures. Suddenly I see straight in front of me . . . right on the edge of the airfield . . . it is surely impossible! The last Soviet tank has escaped from the helter-skelter caused by our bombardment and is intent on carrying through its task. Alone it can shoot our whole airfield with everything on it to blazes. So into a dive, and the well aimed bomb hits the tank a few yards from the runway.

In the evening, I fly my seventeenth sortie of the day and we take a good look at the battlefield. It is quiet, everything is wiped out. Tonight we shall certainly sleep undisturbed. During the last sorties our A.A. on the airfield has left its sited positions and is forming a kind of protective screen in the forefield, in case any of the surviving Ivans should take it into his head to run in the wrong direction during the night. I personally think it unlikely. The few who have escaped will be more inclined to report back to some rear H.Q. that their late cavalry unit will not return and must be written off.

Shortly before Christmas we are at Morosowskaja, a little further to the west. Here much the same thing happens to us. Ivan is lurking a few miles away from the airfield at Urjupin. The weather hampers every take-off. We do not want to be surprised by Ivan during the night without the prospect of any means of hitting back from the air. On the 24th December we are, in any case, to retire to another airfield in the southeast. The continuous bad weather forces us to turn back during our flight and to spend Christmas, after all, as best we can at Morosowskaja. On Christmas Eve we are all aware that our sentries may sound the alarm at any moment. In that case we shall have to defend the airfield and all our aircraft. No one feels any too comfortable; it is more noticeable in some than in others. Although we sing the Christmas hymns, the proper Christmas atmosphere eludes us. Pissarek has had one over the eight. He seizes Jungklausen in a bear-like hug and whirls him round the room. The sight of the teetotaller dancing lady to the waltzing bear does something to liven things up. It amuses the men and dispels all gloomy thoughts and breaks the ice of unconviviality. Come what may, we are all conscious of the sense of fellowship.

The following day we learn that on Christmas Eve the Soviets have overrun the neighbouring airfield at Tazinskaja, 30 miles west, where a transport squadron of our command is stationed. The Soviets have behaved shockingly; the corpses of some of our colleagues are completely mutilated, with eyes gouged out and ears and noses cut off.

We have now a clear demonstration of the full extent of the Stalingrad débâcle. During Christmas week we are engaged with forces north of Tazinskaja and near our own airfield. Gradually operational Luftwaffe units are brought up from the rear and also fresh units are being assembled from reserve organisations. In this way a light combatant screen is built up covering our airfields. Optimists may call it a front; but there is no real fighting power until seasoned divisions can again be put into the line who can retrieve the situation for which they are not to blame. But till that happens the going is hard and there is much need of improvisation. Owing to the new situation, we are no longer able to continue the support we have been giving to the Tschir front along the river of the same name, in the areas Nishtschirskaja and Surwikino.

This front is the first newly created barrier in an east-westerly direction against the enemy attacking from the north. The country is perfectly flat and offers no sort of obstacles in the way of terrain. Everything is steppe as far as the eye can reach. The only possible cover is in so-called *Balkas,* clefts in the surface of the earth, or gulleys, the bottoms of which lie some 30 feet below the surrounding plain. They are relatively wide so that vehicles can be parked in them, not only one behind the other but also side by side. The whole country stretches like this for many hundreds of miles from Rostow to Stalingrad. If the enemy is not encountered on the march, he is always to be found in these hiding places.

In fine, cold weather there is a good deal of fog in the early hours of the morning, but it frequently does not come up until we are already in the air. During one flight to the Tschir front we have just started on our way back when it suddenly thickens. I immediately make a landing with my flight on a large field. There are none of our own troops to be seen. Henschel goes off with some of the gunners to reconnoitre. They are back in three hours, they can find us again only by shouting for the last few hundred yards. I can hardly see my hand before my face. Shortly before mid-day the fog lifts a little, and a bit later we land smoothly on the airfield.

The month of January is quickly past and we pitch our H.Q. temporarily at Tazinskaja before moving to Schachty. The fighting from here is mainly against those enemy forces which are threatening the Donetz area. For sorties further north my squadron uses the airfield at Woroschilowgrad. It is not far from here to the Donetz; possible attempts to cross the river can be more easily countered from here. Because of the uninterrupted sorties and the stiff fighting we have done since Stalingrad, we are greatly reduced in the number of aircraft we can daily put in the air. The whole squadron has at the moment scarcely more than enough aircraft to form one strong flight. To fly on separate missions is seldom profitable, we fly in formation the leadership of which usually devolves on me. The whole Donetz area is full of industrial installations, chiefly mines. If the Soviets once get among these plants it will be difficult to throw them back; here they can find good cover and camouflage. Low level attacks among chimneys and mine shafts have generally only limited success, the pilots have to pay too much attention to their surroundings and the obstacles to be avoided, and cannot concentrate on the objective.

On one of these days Flying Officers Niermann and Kufner celebrate their birthday. Northwest of Kamensk we look for the enemy, especially tanks, and the individual aircraft have separated somewhat from each other. On the tail of Kufner's aircraft, with Niermann aboard it, flies a Lag 5. I warn them and Niermann asks "Where?" He doesn't see it because the Lag has sneaked up from behind. Now it has already opened fire at close range. I had immediately turned back though without much hope of getting there in time. In the nick of time I shoot him off their tail before he realises what is happening. After this Niermann no longer claims that he is infallible in spotting every fighter.

Such a "birthday celebration" is quite good fun, and many practical jokes are played; so also on this occasion. We have with us an acting M.O. Our airmen say that he cannot stand the "noise of firing." In the small hours of the morning Jungklausen goes to the telephone and gets this doctor out of bed. Jungklausen pretends to be his superior officer in the Air Medical Corps:

"You are to prepare immediately to be flown into the pocket."

"Would you repeat that please?"

"You are to prepare immediately to be flown into the pocket of Stalingrad. You are to relieve a colleague there."

"I don't think I understand."

The doctor lives only on the floor below; we wonder that he does not hear Jungklausen's loud voice from the room above. He must be too excited.

"But you know that I have a bad heart."

"That is beside the point. You are to take off for the pocket immediately."

"But you know I have recently had an operation. Wouldn't it be better to give this assignment to a colleague?"

"You can't mean that seriously! I cannot imagine that you are trying to wriggle out of this assignment. What sort of a hole should we be in if we cannot even count on you?"

We are splitting our sides with laughter. The next day the doctor runs around in a terrible stew, but he boasts to anyone who is willing to listen to him that perhaps he is going to be required for this highly dangerous assignment. A few days later he has tumbled to the joke and is transferred. Better for us, better for him.

In these days for quite a short time we use the airfield at Rowenki and then we move to Gorlowka, not far from Stalino, the centre of the Donetz industrial region. Heavy snowstorms hamper our flying activity: it is always a slow business getting the whole squadron into the air.

Pilot Officer Schwirblat is sent to me as replacement officer, and on his first operational flight he has to fly alone with me into the Artemowsk area. I have flown some way ahead because apparently he has had difficulty taxying on the snow. Then after he becomes airborne, instead of taking a short cut to join me he follows my track without closing up on me. Some Lags have fun with him and use him for target practice. It is a marvel that he is not shot down; he flies straight on without taking any defensive action; obviously he thinks that is the correct thing to do. I have

to turn back and come in behind him; whereupon the
fighters sheer off. After landing he discovers holes in
his fuselage and tail unit. He says to me:

"The flak peppered me properly; it must have been
flak, for I never even saw a fighter."

I say with a touch of sarcasm:

"I must warmly congratulate you on the excellence
of your rear gunner who was presumably determined
to see nothing—not even when the Lags were using
him for target practice."

Later, however, Schwirblat is to prove himself the
best man in the Wing, of an exemplary toughness. Everyone in the outfit speaks of him only as my shadow;
for when on operations he sticks to me like a burr. In
addition, he joins me in all my sporting activities with
the same keenness, and he never smokes or drinks. It
is not very long before he gives proof of his flying skill.
He nearly always flies as my No. 2 and we often go
out alone. We cannot let up for a moment because the
Soviets are attempting a westward thrust across the road
from Konstantinowska to Kramatorskaja in the direction of Slawiansk to our north. In one of these attacks
my record of operational sorties reaches the 1000 mark.
My colleagues offer their congratulations by presenting
me with a lucky chimney sweep and a pig. Despite stubborn recalcitrance on my part, my 1001st operational
flight ends for some months to come my employment at
the front.

# 9

## STUKA VERSUS TANK

I am first to go home on leave; but I am determined to
fly to Berlin before I begin it, to find out what they
mean to do with me. A special mission awaits me and
therefore I have to report to a department of the Air
Ministry. The high total of my operational flights is the
sole reason for all this. If this is the sort of thing it lets
me in for I shall not let them keep count any longer.

In Berlin no one knows anything.

"In that case I can at once resume my command; my
Wing has presumably made a mistake."

In ministries and departments, however, mistakes are
denied on principle. After much telephoning I am instructed to proceed, on the expiration of my leave, to
Rechlin where experiments are being carried out in the
use of anti-tank weapons from aircraft. The Officer
Commanding, Flt./Lt. Steppe, is an old acquaintance
of mine. Afterwards the establishment is going to
Briansk in order to confirm theory in practice. This
sounds rather better, but all the same it is not an
operational command. I am congratulated on my promotion to Flight Lieutenant.

I spend the next fortnight skiing at St. Anton. A big
ski tournament is being held here. As an active com-
petitor and senior ranking officer, I am at the same time
captain of the Luftwaffe team competing. There are a
lot of bigshots present: Jennewein, Pfeifer, Gabel and
Schuler; for they also belong to the Luftwaffe. It is a

pleasant holiday and at the end of the fortnight my batteries are recharged.

I wish I could get out of going first to Rechlin. I
would rather go straight to Briansk. The anti-tank experimental unit has already assembled and has conducted its preliminary tests. We have here Ju. 88 type
aircraft with 7.5 cm. cannon installed under the pilot's
seat, and Ju. 87 Stukas like those I have always flown,
fitted with a 3.7 flak cannon under each wing. They
use a special ammunition with a Wolfram centre, supposed to penetrate any armour likely to be encountered. These shells do not explode until after they have
penetrated the protective armour. The Ju. 87, which
is not any too fast of itself, now becomes even slower
and is unfavourably affected by the load of the cannon it carries. Its manoeuvrability is disadvantageously
reduced and its landing speed is increased considerably. But now armament potency is a prior consideration over flying performance.

Experiments with Ju. 88s armed with a large calibre
cannon are soon abandoned as the difficulties which
arise hold out no promise of success. Also one operational flight undertaken with Ju. 87s results only in
losses. The majority of our establishment is sceptical;
what impresses me is the possibility of being able to
shoot with an accuracy of within 20-30 cm. If this is
attainable one should be able to hit the easily vulnerable parts of the tank provided one could get within
close enough range—that is my conviction. From vis-
ual models we learn to recognize infallibly the various
types of Russian tank and are taught where the most
vulnerable parts are located: engine, petrol tank, ammunition chamber. Merely to hit a tank is not enough
to destroy it, it is necessary to hit a particular spot (i.e.
petrol or ammunition) with incendiary or explosive
stuff. So a fortnight passes; then the Ministry wishes
to know whether we are ready for an immediate
transfer to the Crimea. The Soviets are exerting heavy
pressure and there we shall certainly have a wider and

better field for the practical test of our theories.

To fly in at low level and then open fire from a few yards above the ground is impossible on a stabilized front with strong A.A. emplacements; we know that much because the losses are greater than the results. We shall only be able to use this weapon, if at all, where the front, and consequently the A.A. defence, is on the move. Flt./Lt. Steppe stays behind at Briansk and will follow us later. I fly over Konotop and Nikolajew with all serviceable aircraft to Kertsch on the Crimean peninsula. At Kertsch I meet up with my wing and it wrings my heart to see the old faces again and for the time being no longer to be one of them. They are bombing the hotly contested bridgehead at Krymskaja. Comrades tell me that Soviet tanks which have broken through are advancing not more than a mile or so beyond the old main battle line. This means then that we shall have to attack them while they are still covered by the sited, and therefore heavy, flak defence of their own front line.

The A.A. in this battle area is concentrated in a very restricted space. After the end of the fighting near the oilfields not far from the Caspian Sea where the Soviet oil centre lies, practically all their A.A. artillery has been brought up from those distant areas and concentrated here. They have travelled up through Mosdok—Piatigorsk—Armawir—Krasnodar. On one of the first days after our arrival we already make the first test south of Krymskaja. Tanks which have broken through are located 800 yards in front of their own main line. We find them at once and are eager to see what can be done. It is mightly little, for I am still flying above our own front line when I receive a direct hit by flak. Other aircraft fare no better. Now in addition enemy fighters arrive on the scene, an old production series of Spitfires. This is the first time I have met this type of aircraft in Russia. One of our young pilot officers is brought down in an orchard. He turns up the same evening with fruit and diarrhoea.

After this beginning and the feeble results of our first test the outlook is none too rosy. We are the object of commiseration wherever we appear, and our sympathizers do not predict a long lease of life for any of us. The heavier the flak, the quicker my tactics develop. It is obvious that we must always carry bombs to deal with the enemy defence. But we cannot carry any on our cannon-carrying aircraft as the bomb load makes them too heavy. Besides, it is no longer possible to go into a dive with a cannon-carrying Ju. 87 because the strain on the wing planes is too great. The practical answer is therefore to have an escort of normal Stukas.

A fresh Soviet assault offers us the opportunity to initiate this important new departure. N.E. of Temjruk the Soviets are endeavouring to turn the Kuban front. They begin to ferry parts of two divisions across the lagoons in the hope of bringing about by this manoeuvre the collapse of the Kuban front. We have only isolated strongpoints with a very thin support line holding the marshland and the lagoons N.E. of Temjruk. Naturally their striking power is limited, and in no way a match for this new Soviet operation.

Our reconnaissance confirms the presence of a strong assembly of boats in the harbour of Jeisk and near Achtary. These are attacked by our Stukas. The targets are so small and the boats so numerous that these attacks alone cannot deflect the Russians from their plan. Now at all hours of the day and night they swarm across the lagoons. The total distance they have to travel is something like thirty miles. The lakes are connected by little canals, and so the Russians edge nearer and nearer to Temjruk, behind the Kuban front and far in our rear. They pause at intervals to rest under cover of the tall reeds and on the eyots. When they keep themselves hidden in this way they are hard to locate and recognize. Yet if they wish to resume their advance they have again to travel across open water. We are in the air every day from dawn till dusk, racing above the water and the reeds in search of boats. Ivan

comes on in the most primitive craft; one rarely sees a
motor boat. Besides rifles he carries with him hand
grenades and machine guns. He glides across in the little boats with a load of five to seven men; as many as
twenty men are packed on board the larger craft. In
dealing with them we do not use our special anti-tank
ammunition, for a high potency is not required here.
On the other hand one must have a useful explosive
effect on hitting the wood, in this way the boats are
most quickly smashed. Normal flak ammunition with
a suitable fuse proves the most practical. Anything trying to slip across the water is as good as lost. Ivan's
losses in boats must be serious for him. I alone with my
aircraft destroy seventy of these vessels in the course
of a few days.

Gradually the strength of the defence increases, but
that does not stop us.

Flying Officer Ruffer, an excellent gunner belonging
to a neighbouring anti-tank squadron flying H.129s, is
brought down and lands like Robinson Crusoe on an
island in the middle of the lagoons. He is lucky. He is
rescued by a company of German assault troops. Soon
the Soviets realize that they must write off this plan, for
with these losses success is no longer attainable.

It is now about the 10th of May and I receive the
news that the Führer has awarded me the Oak Leaves;
I am to leave immediately for Berlin for the investiture.
The next morning, instead of my usual excursion flying
my cannon-carrying aircraft at low level over the straits
of Kertsch on the search for boats, I am on my way to
Berlin in a Me. 109. En route, I puzzle out a plan of
campaign to wangle an early return to my Wing. In the
Reichskanzlei I learn from Wing-Commander von Below, the adjutant of the Luftwaffe, that some twelve
soldiers are to receive the decoration at the same time
as myself. They are members of all the services of different ranks. I tell Wing-Commander von Below that
I intend to explain to the Führer that I am tired of being seconded to the experimental unit and wish to be
allowed to resume command of my old front squadron

in the Immelmann Stuka Wing. Only on this condition will I accept the decoration. He urges me not to, and gives me his promise to deal with the matter himself. I say nothing of the steps I have already taken in memos addressed to the Air Command.

**Me. 109**

Shortly before we report to the Führer, von Below brings me the welcome news that he has just fixed everything. I get back to my old squadron, with the proviso that I shall continue to study the usefulness of the experimental aircraft. I gladly agree, and now at last I can really be happy over the Oak Leaves.

The Führer pins the medal on our chests. He talks to us for over an hour about the military situation, past, present, and future plans. He touches on the first winter in Russia and Stalingrad. All of us who were there at the front are amazed at his unerring grasp of detail. He does not blame the German soldier at the front, but sees things exactly as we up there have experienced them. He is full of ideas and plans, and absolutely confident. Again and again he stresses that we must win the victory over Bolshevism, as otherwise the world will be plunged into an appalling chaos from which there is no way out. Therefore, Bolshevism must be smashed by us, even though for the present the Western Allies refuse to recognize how disastrous is their policy for themselves and the rest of the world. He radiates a calmness which infects us all. Each of us goes away to his task revitalized, and so two days later I am back with my Wing at Kertsch. I take over the command of my old squadron.

# 10

# ON THE KUBAN AND AT BJELGOROD

I have taken a cannon-carrying aircraft with me and I introduce my squadron to the new machine. Wherever I see a chance of an operation for the experimental unit it takes off together with mine. Later it is reformed into an anti-tank squadron which operates independently, but in action it is subordinate to my supervision and command. The Briansk establishment now also follow us; Captain Steppe likewise returns to the squadron formation.

There is work enough for us Stuka bombers, for the Soviets have got across the Black Sea and behind our front. They have landed and formed beach-heads on the hilly coast east and southwest of Noworossisk. These are now frequently the target of our attacks. Reinforcements and material continue to arrive at the landing quays. The A.A. defence is as furious as at other crucial points of the Kuban bridgehead. Many of my comrades make their last flight here. My squadron commander bails out over the beach-head; he is lucky, the wind carries him over our lines. So we fly back and forth between the beach-head and Krymskaja. I generally dive with my flight almost to ground level and then fly off in a low level flight out to sea near the beach-head, or over the marshland further north where the defence is weaker. The small release height of the bomb improves the bombing results, and also the defence is not yet accustomed to our very low level tactics.

If, as we approach Krymskaja above the tobacco-growing ravine, the flak begins and many a new crew gets windy, they are soon calmed down again when they hear the "old sweats" having their fun over the R/T with a joke or a snatch of song. Someone calls out: "Maximilian, get cracking!" This refers to the skipper of the second squadron; he keeps on circuiting in the flak, eternally delaying his dive, so that the aircraft behind lose their sense of direction. This self-confident coolness then soon infects the tyros. Not infrequently I do a loop, a roll or some other stunt; I wonder if the A.A. gunners think I am having a lark with them?

The weather here does not hamper operations. Almost invariably a bright blue sky and glorious sunny summer weather. Any day there is no flying we go off to the sea for a bathe, either to the Sea of Azow or the Black Sea; parts of the coast have magnificent beaches. If Schwirblat and I feel like diving we go into the harbour of Kertsch where there are cranes and walls of sufficient height.

The aerodrome at Kertsch is so crowded that we move with our squadron to Kertsch-Bagerowo, six miles to the west; we billet ourselves in a 'Kolchose.' As there is plenty of timber available we soon set about building ourselves a shack for our mess. Petrol is rationed at the moment and we fly only if it is absolutely necessary. So during these weeks we get a whole series of free days which each one of us spends in his own fashion. Schwirblat and I take our almost daily six mile run and so get to know the whole district, not only from the air.

Every night we receive a visit from Soviet P2s and old DBIIIs: they chiefly bomb the railway station, harbour and airfield in Kertsch IV. We have some A.A. sited there, occasionally also a few night fighters. We generally watch them coming and going, for almost ev-

ery attack a few come down in flames. Our adversaries
are not very skilled at night fighting; they evidently
need much practice. They have an occasional stroke of
luck every now and again. A bomb drops on an ammunition train standing in a siding and for hours explosions light up the night sky with a ghostly light, the
earth trembles from the detonations. Very soon these
raids become a part of our daily routine, and we generally stay in bed and sleep; otherwise we feel the effect of the lack of sleep on our own raids the following day, and that can be disastrous.

We are in the last days of June and nearing the end
of our time in the Crimea. Minister Speer is here on
a visit in connection with a vast construction project
on the road from Kertsch; at the same time the Wing
is visited by the Japanese.

At this time, too, Squadron Leader Kupfer, the skipper of our Wing, has his birthday; there is sufficient
reason to celebrate. The beautiful garden of the summer
quarters of the Wing is presently enlivened by the music of the gay but slightly out of tune band of an army
unit. They play all the request items the musical clam-
our for. Everyone has his choice. In hours like these
one forgets that home is so far away and that a war is
going on. All are carried away out of time and space
into an invisible world of beauty and of peace, where
there is no Krymskaja, no beach-head, no bombs and
no misery. Such hours of relaxation and reverie hearten
all of us.

By the beginning of July the Soviet pressure has
slackened and the German front is stabilized. It stands
between Krymskaja and Moldawanskoje, a retirement
of only a few yards. We never have the house-warming
of our shack, for on the 4th July we receive urgent
orders to move. Nobody knows exactly where we are
going; at all events we are to fly today to Melitopol;
there we are to receive further orders tomorrow. We
take off northwards above the blue waters.

Melitopol is a town on the lines of communication
far behind the front. The aerodrome is occupied by a

bomber formation with Heinkel IIIs; our colleagues let out that today of all days a German entertainment party is giving a performance, a ballet troop of ten pretty girls between the ages of 18 and 20. In less than no time the aircraft are under cover and overhauled for the following day. Cupid lends everyone wings. Everyone tidies up at lightning speed and literally flies to the theatre. The sight of pretty German girls after so long a time cannot fail to cheer the heart of every soldier from the Russian front, old and young alike. That inveterate clown, Pilot Officer Jäckel, uproots the plants in front of the theatre with the intention of offering them later as bouquets. In duty bound to the honour of their regiments the army units do not easily yield ground, and we are involved in the keenest competition with them. I am not quite sure whether we shall succumb to the feminine glamour or whether after years in Russia we shall find the girls more or less pretty. Schwirblat is also dubious. Finally he says it would have been better if we had gone for our usual six mile run, we should then have been spared this misgiving.

In the morning the engines again hum their familiar song. We now know our destination: Charkow. We land on the airfield to the north and are billeted outside the city. The city itself does not make too bad an impression and is doubtless one of the show places of Soviet Russia, such as we have seldom seen. A skyscraper in the Red Square is a typical specimen of Soviet architecture and, damaged though it is, is still a much gaped-at object of Ivan's pride; otherwise the buildings date back to the Tsarist era. The city has parks, a wide network of thoroughfares, cinemas and a theatre.

At the crack of dawn the next morning we take off in the direction of Bjelgorod, our operational area for the ensuing few weeks. On the ground we meet old acquaintances from the East Front, crack divisions, for whom we are happy to fly. We know that here we are going forward and there will be no unpleasant surprises. Besides armoured divisions, the Guards divisions *Totenkopf* and *Grossdeutschland* are in the line. This offensive is a northward thrust with Kursk, occupied by very formidable Soviet forces, as its objective. We are pushing diagonally into the bulge of the Russian front which extends westwards to Konotop and hinges on Bjelgorod in the south and is bounded on its northern side by the open country south of Orel.

The ideal would be to establish a main front line between Bjelgorod and Orel; will the units thrown in be able to achieve this? We shall not let them down. We are in the air from dawn till dusk in front of our tank spearheads, which have soon gained 25 miles and have reached the outskirts of Obojan.

The Soviet resistance is strong, even in the air. On one of the first mornings when approaching Bjelgorod I see half to port an He. III formation flying above me. The flak opens up on them, one aircraft explodes in the air, and is blown to smithereens. Such experiences harden one. Our comrades' sacrifices must not be made in vain. Afterwards we attack in the area of the same Soviet A.A. positions; during low level attacks I often catch sight of the wreckage of the shot-down Heinkel glittering in the sun. In the afternoon a Luftwaffe Flight Lieutenant comes to me and informs me that my cousin has been killed that day. I reply that my cousin must have been shot down this morning N.W. of Bjelegorod in a Heinkel III. He wonders how I can tell him so exactly what happened. My cousin is the third son of my uncle to be killed in the family; he himself will later also be reported missing.

The next weeks deal us severe blows in the Wing. My training school friend, Flight Lieutenant Wutka, skipper of the 8th Flight, is killed; so too is Flying Officer Schmidt whose brother had recently been killed in the air fighting over Sicily. In the cases of Wutka and Schmidt it is not quite clear whether their aircraft exploded when coming in to dive or when operating the bomb release. Is it possible that a short circuit was due to some act of sabotage which caused the explosion? Again some months later this idea occurs to us when similar things happen; at the moment, in spite of the most thorough investigation, we can establish no definite proof.

Great tank battles rage below us during these operations, a picture such as we have rarely had the chance of witnessing since 1941. The tank masses face each other on open plains. The enemy anti-tank defences have sited themselves in the rear with their guns camouflaged. Sometimes also the tanks themselves are dug in defensively, especially when they have been immobilized but otherwise still retain their fighting efficiency.

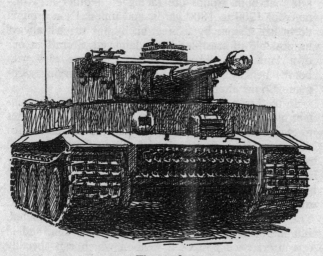

**Tiger tank**

Numerically the Soviets' tanks are always vastly superior to ours, qualitatively one immediately recognizes the superiority of our tanks and armament. Here for the first time our Tiger tank is used in larger formations. All our tank types invariably have a more rapid rate of fire and their gunnery is more accurate. The chief reason for this is the better quality of our weapons, but the decisive factor is the superior quality of the men who handle them.

More dangerous for our tanks is the Soviet heavy and very heavy anti-tank artillery which appears at every key point of the battle area. As the Russians are masters of camouflage their Pak is only spotted and neutralized with difficulty.

The sight of these masses of tanks reminds me of my cannon-carrying aircraft of the experimental unit, which I have brought with me from the Crimea. With this enormous target of enemy tanks it should be possible to try it out. It is true the flak defences covering the Soviet tank units are very heavy, but I say to myself that both groups are facing each other at a distance of 1200 to 1800 yards, and unless I am brought down like a stone by a direct hit by flak it must always be possible to crash-land the damaged aircraft in our own tank lines. The first flight therefore flies with bombs behind me in the only cannon-carrying aeroplane. So the attempt is made.

In the first attack four tanks explode under the hammer blows of my cannons; by the evening the total rises to twelve. We are all seized with a kind of passion for the chase from the glorious feeling of having saved much German bloodshed with every tank destroyed.

After the first day the fitters have their hands full, for the aircraft have been heavily damaged by flak. The life of such an aeroplane will always be limited. But the main thing is: the evil spell is broken, and in this aircraft we possess a weapon which can speedily be employed everywhere and is capable of dealing successfully with the formidable numbers of Soviet tanks. There is great rejoicing in the flight, the squadron, the wing and the group over this newly-gained discovery and its practical confirmation. In order to secure supplies of this aircraft a signal is immediately sent to all sections of the anti-tank experimental unit, asking for all serviceable aircraft to be flown here at once with crews. So the anti-tank flight is formed. For operational purposes it is under my command.

The succeeding days and battles complete the picture and further successes are not denied us. While the cannon-carrying aircraft go in to attack, a part of the bomber formation deals with the ground defences; the rest circle at a fairly low level like a broody hen round her chickens in order to protect the anti-tank aircraft from interception by enemy fighters.

Little by little I discover all the tricks. Skill is often the result of getting hurt. We lose aircraft in weakly defended areas because we are cruising in the middle of an artillery duel. The air space in the line of the artillery trajectory must be avoided, otherwise there is the danger of being shot down "by accident."

After some time the Soviets have managed fairly successfully to cope with our air attacks against their tanks. If it is at all possible they move up their A.A. guns with the leading tanks. The tanks also are equipped with smoke shells to create a fog screen or to imitate a conflagration in the hope that their pursuers may veer off in the belief that they have achieved their purpose. Experienced crews soon get wise to this manoeuvre and are no longer deceived by it. A tank which is really on fire will show very bright flames, and to simulate such flames is far too risky a business. In many cases the tank will blow up as the fire catches the ammunition normally always carried in every tank. It is very uncomfortable for us if the explosion is instantaneous and our aircraft is flying at an altitude of 15-30 feet above the tank. This happens to me twice in the first few days when I suddenly fly through a curtain of fire and think: "This time you are for it."

I come out, however, safe and sound on the other side even though the green camouflage of my aircraft is scorched and splinters from the exploding tank have riddled it with holes.

Sometimes we dive onto the steel monsters from behind, sometimes from the side. The angle of attack is not too steep to prevent us flying in quite close to the

ground, and so also when pulling out from getting into
any trouble in case the aircraft overshoots. If it overshoots too far it is hardly possible to avoid contact
with the ground with all its dangerous consequences.

We have always to try to hit the tank in one of its
most vulnerable places. The front is always the strong-
est part of every tank; therefore every tank invariably
tries as far as possible to offer its front to the enemy.
Its sides are less strongly protected. But the best target
for us is the stern. It is there that the engine is housed,
and the necessity for cooling this power centre permits
of only a thin armour plating. In order to further assist
the cooling this plating is perforated with large holes.
This is a good spot to aim at because where the engine
is there is always petrol. When its engine is running a
tank is easily recognizable from the air by the blue
fumes of the exhaust. On its sides the tank carries petrol
and ammunition. But there the armour is stronger than
at the back.

The tanks frequently carry infantry; if we are in
sectors where we are already known these tank rifle-
men jump off, even when travelling at full speed. They
all think their hour has come and that they have only
a second before we are upon them. And Ivan prefers
to meet the attack on terra firma.

In the second half of July the resistance in front of
the German divisions stiffens; hedgehog after hedgehog
has to be overcome and progress is only very slow. We
take off daily from morning till night, and support the
spearheads of the attack which have advanced northwards across the Pskoll river far along the railway from
Bjelgorod.

One morning on dispersal we are surprised by a
strong formation of IL II bombers which has ap-
proached our aerodrome unobserved flying at a low
level. We take off in all directions in order to get away
from the airfield; many of our aircraft are still taxiing
up to the take-off in the opposite direction. Miraculous-
ly, nothing happens; our A.A. guns on the airfield open

up for all they are worth and this evidently impresses the Ivans. We can see normal 2cm flak ricocheting off the armour of the Russian bombers.

Only very few places are vulnerable to this ammunition, but with 2cm armour-piercing ammo. our light flak can bring down the armoured Ivans.

Quite unexpectedly at this time we receive the order to move to Orel, on the other side of the bulge where the Soviets have gone over to the offensive and are threatening Orel. A few hours later we arrive at the aerodrome north of Orel over Konotop. We find the situation around Orel roughly corresponding to the rumours we have already heard at Charkow. The Soviets are attacking the town from the north, east and south.

Our advance has been halted all along the front. We have seen too clearly how this has happened: first the landing in Sicily and afterwards the Putsch against Mussolini, each time our best divisions have had to be withdrawn and speedily transferred to other points in Europe. How often we tell one another during these weeks: the Soviets have only their Western Allies to thank that they continue to exist as a militarily effective force!

It is a hot August for us in every sense of the word; to the south there is bitter fighting for the possession of Kromy. In one of our first attacks in this area directed against the bridge in this town a very odd thing happens to me. As I am diving, a Russian tank just starts to cross the bridge; a moment before the bridge was clear in my sights. A 500 kg. bomb aimed at the bridge hits him when he is half-way across it; both tank and bridge are blown to smithereens.

The defences here are unusually strong. A few days later in the northern area, west of Bolchow, I get a direct hit in my engine. I receive a full burst of splinters in the face. I think first of bailing out, but who can tell where the wind will carry the parachute? There is very little hope of coming down safely, especially as Jaks are in this area. I succeed, however, in making a forced landing in the very front German line positions with my engine cut off. The infantry unit occupying this part of the line takes me back to my base in a couple of hours.

I take off at once on a fresh sortie and in the same region, too. It is a peculiar feeling to return a little later to the same place where one has been shot down a short while before. It stops one from becoming hesitant and brooding over the risks one is running.

We are about to take up positions. I have climbed rather too high and observe the heavy flak; it is now directing its fire on our formation, and the gun positions are recognizable from the flash of the guns. I immediately attack them and order the aircraft accompanying me to drop their bombs at the same time on the Russian gun-sites. I fly home relieved with the comforting feeling that they too must now be sweating hard.

Russian aircraft raid our airfield in the Orel sector every night. At first we are under canvas, later in stone buildings on the airfield. There are slit-trenches alongside the tents; we are supposed to take cover in them as soon as the raiders appear. Some of us, however, sleep through the raids because, in view of the uninterrupted all day flying, a good night's rest is indispensable if we are to be fit to go out again the next day. In any case Ivan generally keeps up his bombing all night. My friend, Walter Kraus, then skipper of the 3rd Squadron, is killed in one such raid. After his training period with me in the Reserve-Flight at Graz, being a former reconnaissance pilot, he soon found himself at home in the new sector and was a great asset to our Wing. He had just been promoted to Squadron Leader and awarded the Oak Leaves. We mourn the loss of a friend and comrade with bitter grief; his death is a staggering blow. How many hard blows of incomprehensible destiny must we yet experience?

I am relieved of the command of the first flight, and given the 3rd Squadron instead. I know it inside out from earlier on; was I not its old Squadron engineer officer? As far as new faces have appeared I know them all from my visits to the squadron. It is not difficult to knock them into shape as Squadron Leader Becker is there. We have nicknamed him Fridolin. There is nothing he does not know; he is the soul and the mother of the ground personnel. Our medical care is in the hands of Stabsarzt Gadermann, who is also the friend and counsellor of everybody. Soon the 3rd Squadron Command consists of a kind of family in which all orders are given and carried out in the best cooperative spirit. In the air this means no sort of reorganisation because during the last year I have often led the squadron formation.

Here I soon fly my 1200th operational flight. I have as escort a fighter squadron to which, incidentally, the famous skier Jennewein belongs. Between sorties we often chat about our native mountains and, of course, about skiing. He fails to return from one joint mission with our squadron and is reported missing. Apparently he was hit, then, according to the account of his colleagues, he transmitted over the R/T: "Got a hit in the engine, am flying into the sun." At the time, however, the sun was already almost due west. So for once he could not have chosen a more unfavourable course because in the break-through area north of us, at Bolchow, the objective of our attack, the Soviets have succeeded in pushing a funnel-shaped wedge through our front from east to west. If, therefore, he flew west he was over the middle of the break-through area, and must have come down on Russian territory. A few miles to the south would have been enough to reach our own lines as the funnel is very narrow. Here at Orel there is no changing our run of bad luck. The staff captain of my 9th Flight is flying with his rear gunner, Flying Officer Hörner; he has the Knights Cross of the Iron Cross and is one of the senior officers in our squadron. After being hit by flak in the area northeast of Orel he nose-dives and makes a belly-landing in No Man's Land. He and his aircraft remain there, lying on the slope of a small gulley. At first I believe he has made a forced landing although it seemed as if he had been badly hit already in the air; also the impact was too

violent when his aircraft struck the ground. After flying
over the spot several times at low level I can perceive
no movement in the aircraft. Our Medical Officer goes
forward and with the help of the army reaches the
wreck, but it is too late to save any of the crew. He
has taken a priest with him and so our two comrades
are laid to their eternal rest.

There is very little conversation in our squadron for
the next few days, only the most necessary exchanges;
the bitterness of these days oppresses us all. It is not
very different in other units. In a dawn attack on important Soviet artillery emplacements east of Orel the
flights of the 1st Squadron fly with mine, the second
flight led by Flying Officer Jäckel. He has become a
magnificent airman and has a pet stunt which he does
habitually. Wherever he sees a fighter he attacks it even
though it is far superior to his aircraft in speed and
armament. Already on the Kuban front he has given us
many a laugh. He always contends that his Ju. 87 is
particularly fast; that at full throttle he can leave the
others standing. This cheery soul often brings down
a fighter; he reminds one of a stag roaming the forest
in search of a hunter and when he finds one instantly
charging him with lowered antlers. He is the life and
soul of his flight; without repeating himself he can tell
jokes from nine in the evening till four o'clock in the
morning. 'Bonifacius Kiesewetter' and other ballads of
course belong to his repertoire.

On this particular morning he has, with his flight,
attacked a neighbouring battery and we are returning
to base. We are just flying over our front line when
someone yells: "Fighters!" I can see them, a long distance away; they show no signs of attacking us. Jäckel
turns round and joins issue with them. He shoots one
of them down but even fat Jensch, his at other times
dependable rear-gunner, appears to be looking round
instead of in front of him. There is apparently another
Lag 5 coming up behind him. I see his aircraft go into a
kind of backward dive from a height of 600 feet and

burst into flames. I can only imagine that in his eagerness for battle Egbert forgot how low he was flying and that he had no business to indulge in such acrobatics. So we lose this dear comrade also.

The thought occurs to many of us: "Now when one after the other of the old-timers goes, I can almost reckon by the calendar when my own number will be up." Every jinx must come to an end sooner or later; we have long been waiting for our bad luck to change. To live in constant danger induces fatalism and a certain callousness. None of us any longer gets out of bed when the bombs are dropping at night. Dead tired from being in the air without intermission all day and every day we hear, half awake and half asleep, the bombs bursting close at hand.

In the east to west break-through area north of us things go from bad to worse; now Kareitschew, northwest of us, is threatened. In order to reach this target area more quickly and the Shisdra sector further to the north, we move to the airfield at Kareitschew. Much of the fighting is developing in the forest regions which are very hard to see into clearly from above. They make it easy for the Reds to camouflage their positions and our attacks are very difficult. I hardly ever catch sight of a tank; so I mostly fly with a bomber. Since I took over the command of the squadron the anti-tank flight has been more closely incorporated in my squadron, and the staff work, both technical and tactical, has quickly been adapted to the employment of the cannon-carrying aircraft I introduced.

Our stay at Kareitschew is not a long one. There has been talk again for some days of another move to the south where the situation is critical. After several sorties based on Briansk we do indeed move back again to Charkow. But this time our operational base is the aerodrome on the south side of the city.

# 11

# BACK TO THE DNIEPER

Here also at Charkow there have been all sorts of changes in the few months since we left. On our side full strength divisions have been withdrawn, and the Soviets have gone over to the offensive. We have not been here more than a day or two when Soviet shells begin falling in the city. Our airfield has no large stores of petrol or bombs for us to use, and so another transfer to a more favourable airfield does not come as a surprise. It lies 100 miles to the south, close to the village of Dimitriewka. As it is a considerable distance from here to the present front we use two take-off airfields, one at Barwenkowo for the front on the Donetz at Isjum, the other at Stalino for missions on the Mius front. Each of these airfields has a small detachment to service us during the day. We take our first shift and armourer personnel up with us every morning. Both at Isjum on the Donetz and at Mius a stable defensive line has been established, and is under heavy attack by strong Soviet forces. Often our operations officer assigns us the same old target: the same wood, the same ravine. We can soon dispense with map readings and all the rest of it. As Steen used to say: "We are big boys now."

On one of our first sorties in the Isjum sector somebody calls over the R/T: "Hannelore!"—that is my call-sign—"Aren't you the bloke who used to crack nuts?" I do not reply, and now he keeps on repeating his question over and over again. Suddenly I recognize the voice as that of an Int. Ops. Officer with whom we have often co-operated and with whose division we always got on splendidly. It is of course a breach of security regulations, but I cannot resist answering that I did indeed use to crack nuts and that he was a keen footballer. He admits it delightedly and all the air crews who have been listening to the conversation, amused by the episode, give the cold shoulder to the furiously barking flak. This Flg./Off. of the Air Intelligence service, Epp by name, is one of the best Vienna centre forwards. Since he is with a unit in the thick of the battle I shall have frequent occasions to meet him.

Flg./Off. Anton who took over the command of the 9th Flight after Hörner's death is killed on the Mius. His whole aircraft blows up as he is coming in to dive, in the same inexplicable way as has happened several times before. Again another of our old-timers gone, a Knight of the Iron Cross. Among our air crews there is a constant come and go, never any settling down—the remorseless rhythm of war.

Autumn is already in the air when we receive orders to include the Dnieper front in our operations. So further westward. For days we go out on missions from the airfield N.W. of Krasnoarmaiskoje. Here the Soviets are pushing into the Donetz industrial area from the east and the northeast. Apparently this is a large scale operation; they are everywhere. Besides, they raid our airfield uninterruptedly with Boston bombers: a nuisance, because maintenance work is held up and so we are late in getting into action. During these raids we squat in slit trenches behind our aircraft and wait there till Ivan has had his bit of fun. Luckily our losses in aircraft and material are small.

No one tells us that the army units which pass our airfield are almost the last, and that Ivan is on their heels. It will not be long before we find it out for ourselves. We have taken off from the western airfield and are flying over the town and gaining height. Our mission is to attack enemy forces about 25 miles N.E. On the other edge of the town I see obliquely and at some

distance six to eight tanks; they are camouflaged and
otherwise very similar to ours. Their shape, however,
strikes me as rather odd. Henschel interrupts my reflections:

"Let's take a look at those German tanks on the way
back."

**Douglas A20 Boston**

We fly on towards our objective. Considerably further west I meet a strong enemy force; there is no
longer any sign of German troops.

Now we fly back and take a closer look at the tanks.
They are all T 34s—Russians. Their crews are standing
beside them studying a map:a briefing. Startled by our
approach they scatter and crawl back into their tanks.
But at the moment we can do nothing because we
have first to land and remunition. In the meantime the
Soviets drive into the town. Our airfield lies on the
other side of it. In ten minutes I am ready to take off
again and search for them among the houses. When
they are being attacked the tanks dodge round the
buildings, and in this way are quickly out of our sights.

I hit four of them. Where can the rest have got to? They may appear on our airfield at any minute. We cannot evacuate it because some of our personnel are in the town and we have to wait till they get back. Now, too, I remember that I have sent a car with one of our Q.M. staff to the Army Q.M. stores in the eastern section of the town. Unless he has extraordinary luck he is for it. Later it transpires that a T 34 came round the corner of the Q.M. stores just as our car drove up. With an open throttle and his knees knocking together he got clear away.

I go out once more. The squadron cannot fly with me, otherwise we shall not have enough petrol for the now inevitable move to Pawlowka. I can only hope that by the time I return all my men will be back at the airfield. After a long search I spot two tanks in the western part of the town and knock them out. Apparently they were headed for us, to smoke out the hornets' nest of Stukas. But it is already high time to pull out, and after first setting fire to all unserviceable aircraft which have to be left behind we take off. While we are making a circuit of the airfield preparatory to taking up squadron formation I see tank shells burst on the perimeter. So they have got there, but we are there no longer.

The compass points W.N.W. After a while we fly off at low level over a road. Intense flak comes up at us from a long motorized column travelling through below us with an escort of tanks. We break our close formation and circle round the vehicles: Soviet tanks and lorries, mostly of American origin, therefore Russian. I admit I am puzzled as to how these beggars have suddenly turned up here so far west, but they must be Russians. We gather height and I give the order to engage the flak, which must be neutralized first so that we can come in for a low level attack undistracted.

After we have for the most part silenced the flak we split up into sections over the length of the column and shoot it up. The daylight is slowly fading; the whole road looks like a fiery serpent; a jam of burning motor vehicles and tanks which have not had time to drive off the road to right or left. We spare hardly one, and the material loss to the Soviets is again considerable. But what is this? I fly ahead above the first three or four vehicles, they all carry our flags on their radiators. These lorries are of German manufacture. For two hundred yards further on white Verys are being fired from the ditches at the side of the road. That is the signal of our own troops. It is a long time since I have had such a sickening feeling in my stomach. I would willingly crash my aircraft somewhere here on the spot. Can it have been a German column after all? Everything is ablaze. But why then were we subjected to such a heavy fire from the lorries? . . . How come that they are American-made trucks? . . . Besides, I actually saw men running in brown uniforms! Sweat breaks out at every pore and a stupefying sense of panic overcomes me.

It is already fairly dark when we land at Pawlowgrad. None of us utters a word. Every one is preoccupied with the same thought. Was it a German column? The uncertainty chokes us. I cannot find out by telephone from any Luftwaffe or Army unit what column it could have been. Towards midnight some soldiers arrive. My operational officer wakes me out of an exceptionally restless sleep, he tells me it is something important. Our comrades of the army wish to thank us for helping them to make their escape today. They tell us that their lorries were overtaken by a Russian column. They just managed to put on a spurt of a few hundred yards in order to find cover from the Russian fire in the ditches at the side of the road. It was at this moment that we appeared on the scene and shot up Ivan. Our chaps took immediate advantage of the situation and sprinted on for another two hundred yards. This is a load off my mind, and I share the elation of my brothers in arms.

A short time after this incident we are at Dnjepropetrowsk. Our station is the airfield on the east bank of the Dnieper, it is a long way to our billets in the centre of the town. For a Russian city the place makes a good impression, like Charkow. Soviet bombers or ground attack aircraft make almost daily raids on the bridge over the Dnieper in the middle of the city. The Reds hope by destroying it to cut off the line of retreat for the German troops and material, and to make it impossible to bring up supplies and reserves to this army group. Up to now we have not seen them have any success in their attacks on the bridge. Perhaps it is not big enough. The civilians are exultant. As soon as the Soviet raiders have gone they rush down to the Dnieper with buckets because they have noticed after a raid quantities of dead fish floating on the surface of the river. Certainly so much fish has not been eaten in the town for many a long day. We fly alternatively N.E. and S. as the Soviets are driving forward from the Don in order to prevent us from establishing a line on the Dnieper and consolidating our positions there. At the same time as we move our base from Dnjepropetrowsk to Bolschaja Costromka, 80 miles further W., I lose Becker. He is transferred to the Wing staff. I fight his transfer for a long time as he belongs to our "family circle," but it is useless and after a good deal of palaver the decision is final.

# 12

# FURTHER WESTWARD

Bolschaja Costromka is a typical Russian village, with all the advantages and disadvantages these adjectives imply; for us Central Europeans mostly disadvantages. The village is scattered and mainly consists of mud houses, few buildings are of stone. One cannot speak of a layout of streets, but the village is criss-crossed by unpaved lanes at the most peculiar angles. In bad weather our vehicles sink axle-deep into the mud and it is impossible to get them out. The airfield lies on the northern edge of the village on the road to Apostolowo, which is generally unusable for motor traffic. Therefore our personnel have lost no time in adapting ourselves to the use of horses and ox-drawn carts so as to retain our mobility for all contingencies. The air crews often have to ride to their aircraft on horseback; they then dismount on to the wing planes, for the runway itself is not much better. In the prevailing weather conditions it resembles a sea of mud broken by tiny islands, and if it were not for the broad tyres of the Ju. 87 we should never become airborne. One can tell how close we are to the river Dnieper. Our billets are scattered all over the village; the squadron staff is quartered in and near the schoolhouse at the southern end of it. We have a common room, a kind of "officers' mess," in the so-called H.Q. building.

The square in front of this building is frequently under water and when it freezes, as it sometimes does, we play ice hockey in front of the house. Ebersbach and Fickel never miss the chance of a game. Recently however both of them have become rather sceptical as a result of the many bruises on their shins. In the worst weather the ice hockey goal posts are occasionally erected indoors, only the shortening of the field always makes it even more uncomfortable for the goal-keepers. The furniture cannot possibly suffer any damage because there isn't any.

The Russians are dumbfounded by the many little things our soldiers carry on their person. They think the snapshots of our homes, our rooms, our girls, are propaganda. It takes a very long time to convince them that they are genuine, that all Germans are not cannibals. They presently even doubt the truth of the indoctrinated catchword: *Germanski nix Kultura.* In a few days time, here as elsewhere, the Russians come and ask if they may be allowed to hang up again their icons and their crucifixes. Previously under the Soviet régime they have had to keep them hidden away because of the disapproval of a son, a daughter, or a commissar. That we raise no objection to their displaying them evidently impresses them. If you tell them that there are any amount of crucifixes and religious pictures to be seen in our country they can hardly believe it. Hastily they re-erect their holy niches and repeatedly assure us of their hope that this permission will not be revoked. They live in terror of their commissars, who keep the village under surveillance and spy on its inhabitants. This office is often undertaken by the village schoolmaster.

At the moment we are having a muddy spell and consequent difficulties in getting up supplies, even our rations. When flying low over the Dnieper I have often seen both our own and the Russian ground troops tossing hand-grenades into the water and by this means catching fish. We are at war, the Dnieper is a battle zone, every possibility of feeding the troops must be exploited. So one day I decide to try my luck with a little hundred pound bomb. Gosler, our Q.M., is sent out ahead with a small fatigue party to the Dnieper.

I show him on the map beforehand the exact stretch of
the river where I intend to drop my bomb inshore.
After waiting until I have identified our chaps I drop
my missile from between sixty and ninety feet. It falls
into the river very near to the bank and explodes after
a short delay. The anglers down below must have been
a bit scared by the explosion, for they all suddenly fall
flat on their stomachs. A few smart alecks who are already out in midstream in an ancient boat, so as to be
quick off the mark in picking up the fish, are almost
capsized by the wave caused by the explosion and the
resultant fountain of water. From above I can see the
white bellies of the dead fish floating on the surface.
The soldiers join in the scramble to haul the lot in as
quickly as possible. The native fishermen come out
from their hiding places and also pull into the bank
as many fish as they can. The lorry with the fishing
party returns from the Dnieper a few hours after me;
they bring back with them several hundredweight of
fish. Among the catch are some monster specimens
weighing 60 to 80 pounds; mostly sturgeon and a kind
of river carp. For ten days we have an orgy of fish and
find this an excellent diet. Particularly the sturgeon,
smoked or boiled, tastes delicious; even the huge carp
have no slimy taste at all. A couple of weeks later a
fresh fishing operation is carried out with equal success.

Our almost daily sorties take us in the most different
directions. To the east and the southeast the Soviets are
continuously battering against our bridgehead at Nikopol, chiefly from the Melitopol area. The names of the
key points on the map are many of them German:
Heidelberg, Grüntal, Gustavfeld. They are the homes of
German settlers whose forebears colonized this district centuries ago. Further north the front runs eastward along the other bank of the Dnieper beyond
Saporoschje and after crossing the river, into the Krementschuk sector. Dnjepropetrovsk lies behind the Russian lines. As so often, the Soviets exert pressure at different points and frequently succeed in making local

penetrations of our front. The situation is restored by counter-attacks, generally by armoured divisions. The industrial town of Kriwoi-Rog, which is in the front zone to our north, has a concrete runway, but we are not able to use it.

One morning one of the Soviet thrusts reaches Kriwoi-Rog and the airfield. The brunt of the Soviet attack comes from the north from the direction of Piatichatki. Here Flg./Off. Mende is reported missing. Despite the most strenuous search we fail to find this good comrade swallowed up in the vastness of Russia. The situation here is also restored by a counter-attack, and the front pushed back a few miles north. Supply traffic feeding this group is rolling forward uninterruptedly, so we attack the Dnieper bridges. Our target is then generally between Krementschuk and Dnjepropetrovsk. One morning, because of a fresh advance by the Russians pressing forward from the north, I have to go out in bad weather. My mission is to obtain an overall picture of the enemy dispositions and to assess the chances under prevailing met. conditions of attacking with a larger formation. Before taking off I am told that a certain village in the battle area is still held by our troops, but that they are being very hard pressed and urgently need relief. Operational contact is to be made with the unit in question and an operations officer is on the spot.

With low cloud cover we fly in threes into the target area, and presently I hear the voice of an operations officer I know; at all events I hope he is the one I have been told to contact and not another. I should mention that every one wants our support for his own division. We always have to insist on being given the call sign of the unit. The demands on us are so heavy that to satisfy them all we should need twenty times as many men and aircraft. Judging by the voice it is once again the footballer Epp speaking from the ground, but without waiting for his message I have already made out strong enemy concentrations 1½ to 2 miles ahead. I am still flying over our lines and banking round when

I observe the flash of many flak batteries. I cannot see the shell bursts up in the air because they are hidden in the clouds, but now something hits the cockpit and the engine. I have flak splinters in my face and in my hands. The engine is likely to stop at any minute. It putters for another couple of minutes and then conks out. During this interval I discover a meadow west of the village. I feel sure that I have not yet been spotted by the Russians. I bring off a smooth landing on this meadow. Quickly Fickel brings his aircraft down beside me. We have no idea how long this area will remain in our possession; therefore Henschel and I take out the most essential things, our weapons, clock and parachutes and climb into Fickel's machine. The third in the section has already flown home and reported the incident. Not long afterwards we, too, make a safe landing at Costromka. In these days Flg./Off. Fritsche also has a stroke of luck. After being hit by fighters S.E. of Saparoschje, near Heidelberg, he bails out without mishap, although in the act of jumping he smashes something on the empennage. This grand flight leader and Knight of the Iron Cross is back in operations after a short convalescence.

But we are not always so lucky. Once on our way back from a battle area to the N.E. we are already close to the airfield and preparing to come in singly after flying low above it. In the last phase of our fly-in our flak suddenly opens fire. High above us are Russian fighters. They show absolutely no direct intention of attacking, but the flak looses off at them, trying of course to fire in between our aircraft. And Flg./Off. Herling, leader of the 7th flight and Flg./Off. Krumings, the squadron engineer officer, are both hit, and crash. A bit later Flg./Off. Fritsch is also killed. Three of my friends who have been as inseparable as a four leaved clover, all three decorated with the Knight's Cross of the Iron Cross, lay down their lives for their country. We are stunned by their loss as by a mean and furtive blow. They were first rate airmen and good comrades to their men. Sometimes there are periods here at the front when one is under a jinx and there seems to be no breaking the run of bad luck.

In November a radio message is received: I have been awarded the Knight's Cross with Oak Leaves and Swords and am to report at once for the investiture to

**Knight's Cross with Oak Leaves and Swords**

the Führer's H.Q. in East Prussia. It is about this time that I destroy my hundredth tank. Personally I am glad of this new decoration, not least because it is a tribute to my squadron's achievement, but at the same time I am distressed that sanction for my recommendation of Henschel's Knight's Cross has not come through. It must be held up somewhere. I therefore decide in any case to take my rear gunner with me when I report. Henschel has just completed his thousand operational sorties, and with a recent bag of several Soviet fighters is easily our best gunner. We fly to East Prussia, over Winiza, Proskurow, Lemberg and Krakau, to the Führer's H.Q. near Goldap.

First we land at Lötzen. I report to Wing Commander von Below. He tells me that Sqdn./Ldr. Hrabak is to receive the Oak Leaves at the same time as I; he is due to report with me. I have brought Henschel along with me and ask Below whether Henschel's recommendation has reached his office. He tells me it has not, but immediately promises to find out from the Reichsmarschall how the matter stands. There also the papers cannot be found. They suppose they have been submitted to the Reichsmarschall for sanction. This obtained by word of mouth from Goering himself by von Below, who goes straight to the Führer and reports to him that I have brought Henschel with me for the aforementioned reasons, and that the Commander-in-chief of the Luftwaffe has approved the award. The answer is: "Henschel is to come with the others." This is a great occasion for my faithful rear-gunner. Only a few receive the Knight's Cross at the Führer's hands, as personal investiture by the Commander-in-Chief begins with the Oak Leaves.

And so Sqdn./Ldr. Hrabak, Henschel and I stand in the presence of the Führer. First he pins on our decorations and then drinks tea with us in his study. He speaks of past operations in the East and of the lessons to be learnt from them; he tells us about the creation of new units now in progress which will certainly be needed to meet the coming invasion by the Western Allies. The country will still be able to raise a large number of divisions and our industry can equip them with sufficient armament. Meanwhile German inventive genius, he informs us, is still working on stupendous projects, and we must succeed in wresting victory from Bolshevism. Only the Germans are in a position to do this, he affirms. He is proud of his Eastern Front soldiers, and he knows their tremendous exertions and the difficulties they face. He is looking well; and is full of ideas, and of confidence in the future.

On leaving Lötzen we must make a slight detour over Hohensalza to Görlitz where we give our gallant Ju. 87 a two days' rest. Henschel's home in Saxony is not very far from here, and he goes on by train to rejoin me two days later for our return to the front. We then fly over

Vienna, Krakau, Lemberg and Winiza to Kirowograd in filthy weather. The further east we get, the more we feel the imminence of winter. Low lying clouds with densely driving snow hamper our flight and make it difficult for us to keep our course. We feel much happier when as dusk is falling our kite taxies in on the frozen airfield at Costromka and we are home again with our comrades. It is already cold here, but we have no reason to grumble at that because the frost improves the condition of the roads in the village. Large open spaces are solid ice and it is not always the easiest thing to cross them without skates. When we are grounded by bad weather we restart our ice hockey games. Even the least sportingly inclined becomes infected by the enthusiasm of the rest. We use every conceivable implement from regulation hockey sticks to old brooms and shovels. The most primitive Russian skates compete with special footgear fitted with proper hockey blades. Many just lumber about in airman's fur boots. It is all one, it is the exercise that matters.

Here in South Russia we get occasional warm days which turn everything back into an inconceivable quagmire. Perhaps it has something to do with the influence of the Black Sea or the Sea of Azov. Our airfield cannot stand up to such vagaries of climate, and we always clear out of it and move over to the runway at Kirowograd. One of these muddy spells coincides with Christmas and New Year. Consequently units are compelled to celebrate these holidays in isolation instead of in a general squadron party. Father Christmas has brought a surprise for every soldier, and to look at their faces no one would guess that this is already the fifth winter of our campaign.

At the beginning of 1944 the hard weather really sets in and operational activity is increased. The Soviets push forward to the west and southwest from the area W. of Dnjepropetrovsk, and for a short time cut road communications between Krivoi Rog and Kirowograd. A counter-offensive by our old friends, the 14th and 24th armoured divisions, is very successful. Besides taking a large number of prisoners and a mass of captured material, we manage to bring about a lull, at least temporarily, in this sector. We fly continually from Kirowograd and are billeted quite close to the airfield. The Wing staff is quartered near by. The day they move in they have a most uncomfortable surprise. The Wing adjutant, Squdn./Ldr. Becker, alias "Fridolin," and the engineer officer, Flt./Lt. Katschner, are not quite conversant with the local heating arrangements. Carbon monoxide gas is generated in their rooms during the night, and Katschner wakes up to find Fridolin already unconscious. He staggers out into the fresh air dragging Fridolin with him, thus saving both their lives. For a soldier to lose his life as the result of a silly accident instead of by enemy action is particularly tragic. Afterwards we see the funny side of it and their mishap becomes a standing joke; both have to put up with many a leg-pull.

In the course of our operations during this period we witness a most unusual drama. I am out with the anti-tank flight S. and S.W. of Alexandrija; after firing off all our ammunition we are homeward bound for Kirowograd to refuel and remunition for another sortie. We are skimming the almost level plain at a low altitude half way to Kirowograd and I am just above a dense hedgerow. Behind it twelve tanks are on the move. I recognize them instantly: all T 34s heading N. In a twinkling I have climbed and circled round the quarry. Where on earth have they come from? They are Soviets beyond all doubt. Not one of us has a round of ammunition left. We must therefore let them rumble on. Who knows where they will get to by the time we can return with fresh ammunition and attack them.

The T 34s pay no attention to us and proceed on their way behind the hedge. Further north I see something else moving on the ground. We fly over at low level and recognize German comrades with type IV tanks. They gaze up at us from their tanks, thinking of anything else but the nearness of an enemy and a possible skirmish. Both lots of tanks are travelling towards each other, separated only by this tall line of bushes. Neither can see the other because the Soviets are moving in sunken ground below a railway embankment. I fire red Vereys, wave and drop a message in a container in which I inform my tank colleagues who and what are coming in their direction two miles away, assuming they both keep to the same course. By dipping my aircraft towards the spot where the T 34s are travelling at

**PZKW IV**

the moment I tip them off to the nearness of the enemy. Both parties drive steadily on. Circling low we watch for what is going to happen. Our tanks halt at a point where there is a gap of a few yards in the hedge. At any minute now they may both be suddenly surprised by the sight of the other at point blank range. I wait tensely for the second when both will get the shock. The Russians have closed down their turret-tops; perhaps they suspect something from our astonishing manoeuvres. They are still rolling in the same direction, travelling fast. The lateral distance separating the two parties is not more than fifteen or twenty yards. Now!

The Russians in the sunken ground have reached the gap and see the enemy in front of them on the other side of the hedge. It takes exactly two seconds for the first IV tank to set his opposite number on fire at a range of twenty yards; bits and pieces pepper the air. In another few seconds—up till then I have not seen a shot fired from the rest of the T 34s—six Russian tanks are ablaze. The impression is that they have been taken completely by surprise and have not yet grasped what is happening even now. Some T 34s move in closer under cover of the hedge, the rest try to escape over the railway embankment. They are immediately picked off by the German tanks which have meanwhile got a field of fire through the gap. The whole engagement lasts one minute. It is in its way unique. Without loss to ourselves every one of the T 34s have been destroyed. Our comrades on the ground are proudly elated at their success; we are not less delighted. We throw down a message of good wishes and some chocolate, and then fly home.

After a series of comparatively uneventful sorties it is not usually very long before we get another jolt. We get one now. Three of us go out, Flg./Off. Fickel and Flg./Off. Stähler escorting me with bombers on a tank hunt. We have no fighter escort with us and have just flown past one of our own armoured units when 12 to 15 Aircobras appear with very aggressive intentions. They have all red noses and look as if they belong to a good unit. A wild helter-skelter begins close to the ground and I am glad when I have brought my two colleagues safely home, even though our aircraft are not entirely undamaged. Our experience is often the topic of evening arguments and reminiscences. Fickel and Stähler think that we had a pretty narrow squeak. At the same time the discussion is a useful lesson to our newcomers in correct evasive action in aerial combat.

Our One Squadron has been stationed for some time at Slynka, N. of Nowo Ukrainka, W. of us. My III Squadron also receives orders to transfer there with all flying personnel, while our ground personnel proceeds by road to Pervomaisk on the Bug. Notification of my promotion to the rank of Squadron Leader comes through at the end of our time at Kirowograd.

At Slynka it begins to look as if winter had really set in. A bitter East wind blows almost every day. Temperatures fall to 20-30 degrees below zero. The effect of the cold is perceptible in the number of serviceable aircraft, for maintenance and repair in the open at these temperatures is a specialized business. It is particularly bad luck, because a spearhead of the Russian offensive N. of Kirowograd has just made a penetration into the neck of the Marinowka valley. They are bringing up very strong reserves in order to consolidate the positions won as a springboard for a fresh advance. Every half-serviceable aircraft on the airfield is used for low level attacks. On one sortie to the east, Flg./ Off. Fickel is forced down after being badly shot up. The terrain is not unfavourable, and I am able to make a landing quite close beside him and take him on board my aircraft with his rear-gunner. In a short time we are back on our airfield, the poorer by yet another aircraft.

The Russian tanks rarely deliver night attacks, but during the next few days we—our colleagues N. of us in particular—get a taste of them. At midnight my Int. Ops. Officer wakes me in some agitation and reports that some men belonging to a fighter squadron stationed at Malaja Wisky have just turned up with a request that I take off immediately: the Soviets have driven onto their airfield in among the aircraft and their billets in the village. A cloudless starry night. I decide to have a word myself with the refugees. Malaja Wisky is 19 miles to the N. and several Luftwaffe formations with their aircraft have been accommodated on this airfield.

"All we can tell you is that there was a sudden racket while we were asleep and when we looked out Russian tanks were going past with infantry perched on top of them." Another describes the tanks' invasion of the

airfield. It all happened very quickly and it is evident
that they were taken completely by surprise, for they
have nothing on but their pyjamas.

I weigh up the situation and conclude that for me to
take off there and then is impossible and also pointless, because to hit a tank I must have relatively good
visibility. It is not enough that it is a clear and starry
sky. We shall have to wait till sunrise. It is useless to
consider dropping a few bombs simply to put the wind
up the infantry passengers, because the place is occupied by German units. They are supply organizations,
more or less helpless against the Soviet tanks.

We must take off at the crack of dawn; unluckily, on
the return flight we shall have to contend with fog, for
it looks suspiciously like it even now. We approach the
airfield at low level and see our heavy flak in action on
the ground. They have already knocked out some of
the most venturesome of the steel monsters; the rest
have retired to cover and are out of range. All the personnel of the air formations are at their posts. As we
fly over the airfield they perform a regular war dance,
for they have no doubt that we shall get them out of
their predicament. One T 34 has driven into the flying
control hut and stands there drunkenly, lopsidedly
among the wreckage. Some have concealed themselves
in a factory area. Here the approach is hampered by
the tall chimneys. We have to be devilish careful not to
fly into them. Our cannons reverberate in every corner
of the village. We also drop bombs outside the place;
at least those Ivans who have come on the farthest now
perceive that it is better to beat a retreat. For the most
part they make for the eastern exit from the village
where a number of deep gulleys offer cover. Here, too,
their supply lorries with ammunition and petrol are
parked. They hope to hold us off with light and medium flak, but we plaster their A.A. guns with bombs
and follow up with cannon. Now they are completely
silenced. Shortly afterwards the lorries catch fire and
blow up.

The Ivans are in flight across the snow towards the

East. Our most troublesome job today is the landing at Slynka, as the fog on the airfield refuses to lift and only allows a very short field of view when coming in to land.

By nightfall we have been back and forth seven times with the squadron while I, with one other aircraft, have been out fifteen times. Malaja Wisky has been cleared of the enemy with the loss of sixteen tanks destroyed from the air.

Not long after this episode our flying personnel leaves to join our ground personnel at Pervomaisk North. The airfield there has a small concrete runway, but it is of no use except to park aircraft on so as to keep them from sinking into the mud. It is practically impossible to take off, land or taxi; the whole place is a quagmire. Near the airfield is a hamlet in which we are billeted. After the last sortie of the day, or on days when no flying is possible, Gadermann must have his exercise. After finishing up with a long cross country run we always take a hot and cold tub, and end with a roll in the snow in front of the house *in puris naturalibus*. One's feeling of fitness after this routine is indescribable; it is like being born again. Some Pans and Paninkas, who take a poor view of water in any case, happen to be passing at a distance from the house and gape at us all in amazement. I am sure that our antics are a fresh confirmation of their propaganda cliché: *"Germanski nix Kultura."*

Without met. reconnaissance it has proved a waste of time to make a dawn sortie with a larger formation in this sector. The target area may be obscured by fog and then an attack is impossible. To go out for no purpose is a waste of precious petrol, to say nothing of the fact that these met. conditions may be fatal to larger formations and inexperienced crews. Therefore a standing order has been issued that a met. flyer is to be sent out at daybreak, and his report on weather conditions in the area of our proposed target for that day determines whether we take off or not. The task is usually

too important for me to pick anyone indiscriminately
for this patrol; Fickel has to go out with him, or some
one else if Fickel needs a rest.

One morning we are heading towards the front at
dawn. I have taken advantage of the weather and we
have taken off before it is fully daylight. I concentrate
on memorizing the whole front in this sector. In the
twilight I see clearly the enemy's artillery fire. From its
volume one can draw one's conclusions for the coming
day. The artillery positions, once spotted, are instantly
marked on my map. In less than no time they will be
unrecognizable, and very likely a few hours later may
be under bombardment by our Stukas. This reconnaissance information is also of great interest to our colleagues on the ground. If I have flown low over the
front in the early morning I can give the army exact
intelligence of enemy concentration points. In this way
any surprises for the coming day are eliminated. It is
an impressive picture, and to me, up there the flash of
the many guns in the semi-darkness, resembles a vast
railway station in which the lights flicker or are being
constantly switched on and off. Fiery strings of bright
and darkly coloured beads reach up at me and form a
sort of connecting line with the ground. The enemy
defence has spotted us. Gaily coloured Vereys shoot up
from down below, pre-arranged signals between units
on the ground. Gradually on our regular early morning visits we have begun to get too close for Ivan's liking. This is a special nuisance, because in the early
hours we often catch his tanks unawares. They, too,
like to take advantage of the first daylight in order to
effect a surprise and are now shot up by me. One
cannot be sore with Ivan for sending his Red Falcons
up to scour the front soon after dawn. We often have a
skirmish with the Red Falcons. It is not exactly agree-
able for the two of us to manoeuvre against a superior number without fighter protection.

During this phase Fickel looks very wan and Gadermann advises me to let him knock off for a good while

fairly soon or at least to relieve him of these sorties alone with me. Even though Fickel speaks half in jest when he says after making a landing with a badly damaged aircraft: "That has taken another few years off my life," I can see for myself that he is no athlete, and that even his stamina is not inexhaustible. But I appreciate that he does not suggest not coming with me, and at moments like these I always feel this comradeship is something very fine.

Our present dawn reconnaissance is focussed at points W.N.W. and S.W. of Kirowograd, where the Soviets are making repeated attempts to break through with their inexhaustible masses. If any kind of flying weather prevails we take off with the whole squadron on a fresh sortie half an hour after our first landing, to attack the important targets which have just been reconnoitred. Now in winter a thick veil of mist makes all observation more or less guess work, and we take off without any certainty that we shall be able to land here again in another hour's time. Dense fog comes up quite suddenly and then often hangs for several hours, impenetrable. When it is like this a car would be more useful than an aeroplane.

On one occasion I am out with Fickel; we have completed our reconnaissance and made some low level attacks in the Kirowograd area. It is already daylight and we are flying west on our way home. We have still more than half way to go, and have reached Nowo Ukrainka when suddenly we fly into a densely gathering fog. Fickel keeps very close to my aircraft so as not to lose sight of me entirely. The ground is now barely visible. Above the place just mentioned I perceive some tall chimneys in the very nick of time. The fog bank rises to a great height so that we cannot possibly fly above it. I shall have to come down again somewhere or other. Who knows for how far these weather conditions stretch? To keep to a westward course for as long as our petrol holds out and trust to luck, and then perhaps to make a landing in a partisan area, is no solution either. It cannot be long before we shall reach our lines, and I shall be urgently needed. Besides, our petrol is very low after our long reconnaissance patrol, so the only thing to be done is to stay close to the ground and try to reach our airfield with minimum visibility. Everything is one grey blur. No horizon. Flg./Off. Fickel's aircraft has disappeared. I haven't caught sight of him since Nowo Ukrainka. Perhaps he hit a chimney after all.

As long as the terrain remains level we can fly on through this wall of fog. As soon as an obstacle looms up, telegraph poles, trees or rising ground, I have to pull on the joy stick and instantly run into an impenetrable pea-souper. To grope my way slowly at haphazard out of this fog would be an irresponsible risk. The ground is only visible from ten or twelve feet, but at this level some obstacle may suddenly emerge from the fog. I am flying only by compass, and judging by the clock I should be twenty flying minutes from my airfield at Pervomaisk. Now either the plain gives place to hills or the fog becomes denser; the slightest pull on the stick and I am right in the thick of it. I have just been hard put to it to clear some high poles. Now it is too much of a good thing.

"Henschel, we are coming down to land."

Where I have no idea, for I can see next to nothing, only a grey opacity. I lower my landing flaps and throttle back. I hold the aircraft at low speed and feel my way on the ground. No overshoot. We come to a standstill. Henschel pulls back the canopy roof and jumps out with a grin all over his face.

"We were lucky that time."

Visibility on the ground is a bare fifty yards. We are apparently on a knoll from which the fog is still drifting downwards. I tell Henschel to walk back a little way; I can hear what I take to be the sound of motor vehicles. Perhaps a road. Meanwhile I sit tight in my trusty Ju. 87 and once again rejoice to be alive. Henschel comes back. My guess was right; a road runs behind us. Army drivers have told him that it is a good twenty five miles to Pervomaisk and that the road leads

straight to it. We restart the engine and taxi towards
the road. Visibility is still little more than thirty, at most
forty, yards. We taxi along the very broad highway as if
we were driving a car, obeying the usual traffic regulations and allowing heavy lorries to pass. Where the
traffic is congested I stop to avoid the risk of an accident in case the lorry drivers should fail to see my aircraft until they are right on top of us. Many of them
think they are seeing a ghost plane. So I taxi on for two
hours, uphill, downdale. Then we come to a level
crossing; there is no way of getting through it with my
wings however I tack and manoeuvre. Here I ditch my
aircraft at the side of the road. Only 7½ miles to
Pervomaisk. With a lift from a passing army car I am
quickly back on our dispersal. Meanwhile Henschel
stands guard over our machine and is relieved by the
first shift. Our comrades have been worried about us,
because the time our petrol could be expected to last
has elapsed, and also because in the meantime we had
not rung up from anywhere, and they are overjoyed
at our return.

There is still no sign of Fickel. We are very concerned. By midday the fog lifts, I drive back to my aircraft and take off from the road. A few minutes later
she is once again on our airfield at Pervomaisk and the
faithful mechanics gaze at her as at a prodigal returned.
Another sortie in the afternoon. When I come in Gadermann tells me that Fickel has rung up from Nowo
Ukrainka. Both he and his rear-gunner have found their
way safely out of the fog. He lost me when it became
thickest and landed at the same time. Now our joy is
great.

Very soon after this the focal point of our operations
shifts further north. A German force is encircled in
the Tscherkassy area, and a relief operation is to be
undertaken with freshly brought-up reserves. The relief
attack is delivered mainly from the S. and S.W. We
generally support the 11th and 13th armoured divisions which, thrusting northward W. of Nowy Mirgo-

rod, have reached a sector of the river. The Soviets are very strongly entrenched behind it. Here there are plenty of good targets for us; air activity on both sides is intense, the Iron Gustavs in particular trying to emulate us by attacking our tank divisions and their supply units. With our slow Ju. 87s we always do our best to break up and chase away these IL II formations, but they are a little bit faster than we are because, unlike ourselves, they have a retractable undercarriage. Besides, being more strongly armoured, they are considerably heavier. This is noticeable when coming in to attack; they can pick up speed very much more quickly. But as we usually have our hands full with low level attacks to try to overtake them is anyhow out of the question.

During this phase I am lucky in one encounter with Iron Gustavs. My flights are out on a bombing mission against Soviet prepared positions in a wood. I am circling round above them because I am flying the cannon-carrying aircraft and have not yet succeeded in finding any tanks to attack. A IL II formation flies past diagonally ahead of us, 900 feet below on a S.E. course, escorted by Lags and Airocobras. My No. 2 is carrying bombs. I tell him that we are attacking the IL formation. We are already losing height. When I have got to within three hundred feet of them I see that I cannot gain on them any more and that the Iron Gustavs are again travelling faster than I am. Moreover, the fighters are becoming interested in me. Two of them have already banked round behind me. It is a longish shot, but I get one of the ungainly birds into my sights and loose off a round of anti-tank ammunition from each of my slow-firing cannons. The Gustav becomes a ball of flame and disintegrates into a rain of fiery particles. The rest appear to have got the wind up properly; they streak away downwards even faster and the distance between us increases visibly. Besides, it is high time for me to start weaving, for the fighters are hard on the tail of the miscreant. My evasive tactics bring me closer to my squadron, whereupon the Russians turn away. No doubt they guess that our fighter escort is not far off so that it will not be so easy to shoot me down. In the afternoon Flg./Off. Kunz fails to return from a sortie in the same sector; with seventy claims he topped the list of tanks destroyed. His run of luck began in the Bjelgorod and Charkow area, since when he has gained a great deal more experience. His loss is a great blow to us and makes one more gap in our circle of comrades.

The general offensive for the relief of the force encircled in the Tscherkassy area is successful, and our shock troops are able to create a kind of lane into the pocket. Once the link-up is established the front here is withdrawn together with the bulge. We move back in consequence from Pervomiask to Rauchowka, and as far as we are concerned the Nowo Mirgorod area is left far behind the Russian lines.

A short time after this American bomber formations flying east after accomplishing their missions over Germany land at Nowo Mirgorod, where their aircraft are overhauled by their allies for a fresh sortie. Their operational base as with many American formations is the Mediterranean.

South of us meanwhile the situation has also changed, and our bridgehead at Nikopol has been abandoned. The Soviets press forward in the Nikolajew area, and the German divisions N.W. of it find themselves engaged in very heavy fighting.

# 13

## RETREAT TO THE DNIESTER

In March 1944 our southern front is on the defensive, fiercely contesting the efforts of strong Russian forces to effect a decisive southward breakthrough so as to liquidate the whole German front in the South. My Stuka squadron is operating from Rauchowka, 125 miles N. of Odessa, in support of our army units. We are in the air from dawn till dusk, doing our utmost to relieve our hard-pressed comrades on the ground by destroying tanks and attacking artillery and Stalin "barrel-organs." Our efforts are successful in preventing any decisive breach of our front. Moreover the army, as a result of this victorious delaying action, is able a few weeks later to retire in good order to new positions further west.

One day during this battle we go out W.N.W. along the Dniester on a reconnaissance patrol. The river below us makes an elbow to the N.W. Urgent signals from the Rumanians have reported large convoys of Red motorized and armoured formations on the move round and west of Jampol. On the face of it the report seems rather incredible, because if it is true it must mean that the Soviets have broken through to the north at the same time as they launched their offensive in the south and would already be 125 miles in our rear in Bessarabia. I carry out the reconnaissance with another aircraft for company. These fears are unfortunately confirmed. Strong Soviet concentrations of all

132

arms are massing in the Jampol area, furthermore a large bridge is under construction.

One cannot help wondering how it is possible that this operation has hitherto been unobserved. It is nothing strange for us, we have had the same experience too often during the Russian campaign. Our East Front is always very thinly held; frequently whole areas between the momentary key points are only patrolled. Once this chain of outposts is breached the enemy advances into an undefended zone. Far behind the line perhaps he may come across a baking company, of some non-belligerent supply unit. The vastness of the country is Russia's most valuable ally. With his inexhaustible man power he can easily pour his masses into any such weakly defended vacuum.

Although the situation in the Jampol area is menacing we do not regard it as absolutely hopeless because this sector, being the gateway to their own country, has been entrusted to the Rumanians. So in my briefing for this reconnaissance I have been told to expect the presence of Rumanian covering divisions on the Dniester, and have therefore been warned to be careful of the effects of any attack. Merely by their uniforms it is not easy to distinguish the Rumanians from the Russians from the air.

The strategical objective of the Soviet offensive is clear: a still wider encirclement of our forces in the south and a simultaneous thrust by way of Jassy into the Ploesti oilfields. As the intervention of my squadron in the Nikolajew area is still daily required, it is not possible at first for us to fly more than one or two sorties in this sector. For all our operations we are using the advance airfield at Kotowsk, S. of Balta. So now, unusually, this mission takes us west. Our main targets are troop concentrations in the neighbourhood of Jampol, and the bridge which is being built there. After every attack the Soviets immediately replace the damaged pontoons and hurry on with the completion of the bridge. They try to smash our attacks by intense

flak and fighter interception, but not once do we allow them to drive us back with our mission unaccom-
plished.

Our successes are corroborated by picked-up Russian
radio messages. These chiefly consist of complaints
against their own fighters, the Red Falcons, charging
them with cowardice and enumerating their losses in
men, arms and building material caused by their pol-
troonery. We are often able to listen in to Russian R/T
conversations between their ground units and the Red
Falcons. There is a Russian-speaking officer in my
squadron who tunes in his wireless set to their wave
length and instantly makes a verbatim translation. The
Russians often yell wildly over the R/T in order to interfere with our reception. The Russian frequency is
generally practically the same as ours. The Soviets frequently try to give us target alterations during flight.
Of course the new targets lie inside the German lines.
These pretended corrections are issued in fluent German, but we very soon see through this trick and once
I am wise to it if ever I receive one of these fake corrections when in the air I invariably come down to
make sure that the amended target is really an enemy
objective. Often we hear a warning shout: "Cancel attack. Target occupied by our own troops." The speaker
is, needless to say, a Russian. His last words are then
usually drowned by the noise of our bombs. We get
many a good laugh when we overhear the ground control cursing the Russian fighters.

"Red Falcons, we shall report you to the Commissar
for cowardice. Go on in and attack the Nazi swine. We
have again lost our building material and a whole lot
of equipment."

We have long been familiar with the bad morale of
the bulk of the Red fighter pilots; only a few crack
units are an exception to the rule. These reports of losses
of material are a valuable confirmation of our success.

A few days before the 20th March, 1944, we are
hampered by vile weather with heavy rain storms. In

airman's lingo we say: "Even the sparrows have to walk." Flying is impossible. While this weather lasts the Soviets are enabled to continue their advance and push on with their crossing of the Dniester unmolested. There is no prospect of forming a defensive front against this threat on the ground; not even a single company can be spared from the Nikolajew sector and no other reserves are available. In any case we assume that our Rumanian allies will defend their own country with the fanatical fury of self-preservation and so compensate for our numerical weakness.

On the 20th March, after seven sorties in the Nikolajew and Balta area, I take off with my squadron on the eighth of the day, our first mission for five days against the bridge at Jampol. The sky is a brilliant blue and it can be taken for granted that after this prolonged respite the defence will have been considerably strengthened by flak and fighter protection. As my airfield and Rauchowka itself is a quagmire our fighter squadron has moved to the concrete airfield at Odessa. We, with our broad tires, are better able to cope with the mud and do not immediately become bogged down in it. We fix a rendezvous by telephone for a certain time about thirty miles from the target at 7500 feet above a conspicuous loop of the river Dniester. But apparently difficulties have also cropped up at Odessa. My escort is not at the rendezvous. The target is clearly visible, so naturally we attack. There are several new crews in my squadron. Their quality is not as good as it used to be. The really good men have by this time been long since at the front, and petrol for training purposes has been strictly rationed to so many gallons per man. I firmly believe that I, had I been restricted to so small an allowance, could not have done any better than the new trainees. We are still about twelve miles from our objective when I give the warning: "Enemy fighters." More than twenty Soviet Lag 5s are approaching. Our bomb load hampers our manoeuvrability. I fly in defensive ellipses so as to be able at any moment to come in myself behind the fighters, for their purpose is to shoot down my rear aircraft. In spite of the air battle I gradually work round to my objective. Individual Russians who try to shoot me down by a frontal pass I disappoint by extremely mobile tactics, and then at the last moment dive through the midst of them and pull out into a climb. If the new crews can bring it off today they will have learnt a lot.

"Prepare for attack, stick together—close up—attack!"

And I come in for the attack on the bridge. As I dive I see the flash of a host of flak emplacements. The shells scream past my aircraft. Henschel says the sky is a mass of cotton wool, his name for the bursting flak. Our formation is losing its cohesion, confound it, making us more vulnerable to the fighters. I warn those lagging behind:

"Fly on, catch up, we are just as scared as you are."

Not a few swear words slip past my tongue. I bank round, and at 1200 feet see my bomb nearly miss the bridge. So there is a wind blowing.

"Wind from port, correct to port."

A direct hit from our No. 3 finishes off the bridge. Circling round I locate the gun sites of the still aggressive flak and give the order to attack them.

"They are getting hell very nicely today," opines Henschel.

Unfortunately two new crews have lagged slightly behind when diving. Lags cut them off. One of them is completely riddled and zooms past me in the direction of enemy territory. I try to catch up with him, but I cannot leave my whole squadron in the lurch on his account. I yell at him over the R/T, I curse him; it is no use. He flies on to the Russian bank of the Dniester. Only a thin ribbon of smoke rises from his aircraft. He surely could have flown on for another few minutes, as the other does, and so reached our own lines.

"He lost his nerve completely, the idiot," comments Fickel over the R/T. At the moment I cannot bother about him any more, for I must try to keep my ragged formation together and manoeuvre back eastward in ellipses. After a quarter of an hour the Red fighters turn off defeated, and we head in regular formation for our base. I order the skipper of the seventh flight to lead the formation home. With Pilot Off. Fischer, flying the other staff aircraft, I bank round and fly back at low level, skimming the surface of the Dniester, the steep banks on either side. A short distance ahead in the direction of the bridge I discern the Russian fighters at 3000 to 9000 feet. But here in the bed of the river I am difficult to see, and above all my presence is not expected. As I climb abruptly over the scrub on the river bank I spot our aircraft two or three miles to the right. It has made a forced landing in a field. The crew are standing near it and they gesticulate wildly as I fly over at a lower level. "If only you had paid as much attention to me before, this delicate operation would not have been necessary," I mutter to myself as I bank round to see whether the field is suitable for a landing. It is. I encourage myself with a breathed: "All right then . . . get going. This lot today will be the seventh crew I shall have picked up under the noses of the Russians." I tell Plt./Off. Fischer to stay in the air and interfere with the fighters in case they attack. I know the direction of the wind from the bombing of the bridge.—Flaps down, throttle back, I'll be down in a jiffy.—What is happening? I have overshot—must open up and go round again. This has never happened to me before at such a moment. Is it an omen not to land? You are very close to the target which has just been attacked, far behind the Soviet lines!—Cowardice?— Once again throttle back, flaps down—I am down . . . and instantly notice that the ground is very soft; I do not even need to brake. My aircraft comes to a stop exactly in front of my two colleagues. They are a new crew, a corporal and a L.A.C. Henschel lifts the canopy and I give them a sign to hop in and be quick about it. The engine is running, they climb in behind with Henschel. Red Falcons are circling overhead; they have not yet spotted us.

"Ready, Henschel?"

"Yes." I open the throttle, left brake—intending to taxi back so as to take off again in exactly the same way as I landed. My starboard wheel sticks deep in the ground. The more I open my throttle, the more my wheel eats into it. My aircraft refuses to budge from the spot. Perhaps it is only that a lot of mud is jammed between the mud-guard and the wheel.

"Henschel, get out and take off the mud-guard, perhaps then we can make it."

The fastening stud breaks, the wheel casing stays on; but even without it we could not take off, we are stuck in the mud. I pull the stick into my stomach, ease it and go at full throttle into reverse. Nothing is of the very slightest use. Perhaps it might be possible to pancake, but that does not help us either. Plt./Off. Fischer flies lower above us and asks over the R/T:

"Shall I land?"

After a momentary hesitation I tell myself that if he lands he too will not be able to take off again and reply:

"No, you are not to land. You are to fly home."

I take a look round. There come the Ivans, in droves, four hundred yards away. Out we must get. "Follow me," I shout—and already we are sprinting southward as fast as our legs can carry us. When flying over I have seen that we are about four miles from the Dniester. We must get across the river whatever we do or else we shall fall an easy prey to the pursuing Reds. Running is not a simple matter; I am wearing high fur boots and a fur coat. Sweat is not the word! None of us needs any spurring on; we have no mind to end up in a Soviet prison camp which has already meant instant death to so many dive bomber pilots.

We have been running for half an hour. We are putting up a pretty good show; the Ivans are a good half a mile behind. Suddenly we find ourselves on the edge of almost perpendicular cliffs at the foot of which flows the river. We rush hither and thither, looking for some way of getting down them . . . impossible! The Ivans are at our heels. Then suddenly a boyhood recollection gives me an idea. We used to slide down from bough to bough from the tops of fir trees and by braking our fall in this way we got to the bottom safely. There are plenty of large thorny bushes, like our dog-rose, growing out of the stone face of the cliff. One after the other we slide down and land on the river bank at the bottom, lacerated in every limb and with our clothes in ribbons. Henschel gets rather jittery. He shouts:

"Dive in at once. Better to be drowned than captured by the Russians."

I advise common sense. We are aglow from running. A short breather and then strip off as many garments as we can. The Ivans have meanwhile arrived panting at the top. They cannot see us because we are in a blind angle of their field of vision. They rush up and down unable to imagine where we have disappeared to. It is a cinch they think it impossible that we have leapt over the precipice. The Dniester is in flood; the snows are thawing out, and here and there a lump of ice drifts past. We calculate the breadth of the river as six hundred yards, the temperature as 3-4 degrees above freezing. The three others are already getting into the water; I am just divesting myself of my fur boots and fur jacket. Now I follow them, clad only in shirt and trousers; under my shirt my map, in my trousers pockets my medals and my compass. As I touch the water, I say to myself: "You are never going in here"—then I think of the alternative and am already striking out.

In a very short while the cold is paralysing. I gasp for breath, I no longer feel that I am swimming. Concentrate hard, think of the swimming strokes and carry out the motions! Only imperceptibly the far bank draws nearer. The others are ahead of me. I think of Henschel. He passed his swimming test with me when we were with the reserve flight at Graz, but if he goes all out today under more difficult conditions he will be able to repeat that record time, or perhaps get very near it. In mid-stream I am level with him, a few yards behind the gunner of the other aricraft; the corporal is a good distance in front, he seems to be an excellent swimmer.

Gradually one becomes dead to all sensation save the instinct of self-preservation which gives one strength; it is bend or break. I am amazed at the others' stamina, for I as a former athlete am used to overexertion. My mind travels back. I always used to finish with the 1500 metres, often glowing with heat after trying to put up the best possible performance in nine other disciplinary exercises. This hard training pays me now. In sporting terms, my actual exertion does not exceed ninety per cent of my capability. The corporal climbs out of the water and throws himself down on the bank. Somewhat later I reach the safety of the shore with the L.A.C. close after me. Henschel has still another 150 yards to go. The other two lie rigid, frozen to the bone, the gunner rambling deliriously. Poor chap! I sit down and watch Henschel struggling on. Another 80 yards. Suddenly he throws up his arms and yells: "I can't go on, I can't go on any more!" and sinks. He comes up once, but not a second time. I jump back into the water, now drawing on the last ten per cent of energy which I hope is left me. I reach the spot where I just saw Henschel go down. I cannot dive, for to dive I need to fill my lungs but with the cold I cannot get sufficient air. After several fruitless attempts I just manage to get back to the bank. If I had succeeded in catching hold of Henschel I should have remained with him in the Dniester. He was very heavy and the strain would have been too much for almost any one. Now I lie sprawled on the bank . . . limp . . . exhausted . . . and somewhere a deep-seated misery for my friend Henschel. A moment later we say a Paternoster for our comrade.

The map is sodden with water, but I have everything in my head. Only—the devil only knows how far we are behind the Russian lines. Or is there still a chance that we may bump into the Rumanians sooner or later? I check up on our arms; I have a 6.35 mm. revolver with six rounds, the corporal a 7.65 with a full magazine, the L.A.C. has lost his revolver whilst in the water and has only Henschel's broken knife. We start walking southward with these weapons in our hands. The gently rolling country is familiar from flying over it. Contour differences of perhaps six hundred feet, few villages, 30 miles to the south a railway running E. to W. I know two points on it: Balti and Floresti. Even if the Russians have made a deep penetration we can count on this line still being free of the enemy.

The time is about 3 p.m., the sun is high in the S.W. It shines obliquely in our faces on our right. First we go into a little valley with moderately high hills on either side. We are still benumbed, the corporal still delirious. I advise caution. We must try to skirt any inhabited places. Each of us is allotted a definite sector to keep under observation.

I am famished. It suddenly strikes me that I have not had a bit to eat all day. This was the eighth time we had been out, and there had not been time for a meal between sorties. A report had to be written out and despatched to the group on our return from every mission, and instructions for the next one taken down over the telephone. Meanwhile our aircraft were refuelled and rearmed, bombs loaded and off again. The crews were able to rest between whiles and even snatch a meal, but in this respect I did not count as one of them.

I guess we must now have been going for an hour; the sun is beginning to lose its strength and our clothes are starting to freeze. Do I really see something ahead of us or am I mistaken? No, it is real enough. Advancing in our direction out of the glare of the sun—it is hard to see clearly—are three figures three hundred yards away. They have certainly seen us. Perhaps they were lying on their stomachs behind this ridge of hills. They are big chaps, doubtless Rumanians. Now I can see them better. The two on the outside of the trio have rifles slung over their shoulders, the one in the middle carries a Tommy-gun. He is a young man, the other two are about forty, probably reservists. They approach us in no unfriendly manner in their brown-green uniforms. It suddenly occurs to me that we are no longer wearing uniforms and that consequently our nationality is not immediately evident. I hastily advise the corporal to hide his revolver while I do likewise in case the Rumanians become jittery and open fire on us. The trio now halts a yard in front of us and looks us over curiously. I start explaining to our allies that we are Germans who have made a forced landing and beg them to help us with clothing and food, telling them that we want to get back to our unit as quickly as possible.

I say: "We are German airmen who have made a forced landing," whereupon their faces darken and at the same moment I have the three muzzles of their weapons pointing at my chest. The young one instantly grabs my holster and pulls out my 6.35. They have been standing with their backs to the sun. I have had it in my eyes. Now I take a good look at them. Hammer and sickle—ergo Russians. I do not contemplate for a second being taken prisoner, I think only of escape. There is a hundred to one chance of pulling it off. There is probably a good price on my head in Russia, my capture is likely to be even better rewarded. To blow my brains out is not a practical consideration. I am disarmed. Slowly I turn my head round to see if the coast is clear. They guess my intention and one of them shouts "Stoy!" (Halt!) I duck as I make a double turn and run for it, crouching low and swerving to right and left. Three shots crack out; they are followed by an uninterrupted rattle of quick fire. A stinging pain in my shoulder. The chap with the Tommy-gun has hit me at close range through the shoulder, the other two have missed me.

I sprint like a hare, zig-zagging up the slope, bullets whistling above and below me, to right and to left. The Ivans run after me, halt, fire, run, fire, run, fire, run. Only a short while ago I believed I could hardly put one leg in front of the other, so stiff was I with cold, but now I am doing the sprint of my life. I have never done the 400 yards in faster time. Blood spurts from my shoulder and it is an effort to fight off the blackness before my eyes. I have gained fifty or sixty yards on my pursuers; the bullets whistle incessantly. My only thought: "Only he is lost who gives himself up for lost." The hill seems interminable. My main direction is still into the sun in order to make it more difficult for the Ivans to hit me. I am dazzled by the glare of the sun and it is easy to miscalculate. I have just had a lesson of that. Now I reach a kind of crest, but my strength is giving out and in order to stretch it still further I decide to keep to the top of the ridge; I shall never manage any more up and down hill. So away at the double southward along the ridge.

I cannot believe my eyes: on the hill top twenty Ivans are running towards me. Apparently they have seen everything and now mean to round up their exhausted and wounded quarry. My faith in God wavers. Why did He first allow me to believe in the possible success of my escape? For I did get out of the first absolutely hopeless corner with my life. And will He now turn me over unarmed, deprived of my last weapon, my physical strength? My determination to escape and live suddenly revives. I dash straight downhill, that is, down the opposite slope to that by which I came up. Behind me, two or three hundred yards away, my original pursuers, the fresh pack to one side of me. The first trio has been reduced to two; at the moment they cannot see me, for I am on the far side of the hill. One of them has stayed behind to bring in my two comrades who stood still when I took to my heels. The hounds on my left are now keeping a parallel course, also running down hill, to cut me off. Now comes a ploughed field; I stumble and for an instant have to take my eyes off the Ivans. I am dead tired, I trip over a clod of earth and lie where I have fallen. The end cannot be far off. I mutter one more curse that I have no revolver and therefore not even the chance to rob the Ivans of their triumph in taking me prisoner. My eyes are turned towards the Reds. They are now running over the same ploughland and have to watch their step. They run on for another fifteen yards before they

look up and glance to the right where I am lying. They
are now level with me, then diagonally in front, as they
move forward on a line 250 yards away. They stop and
look about them, unable to make out where I can have
got to. I lie flat on the slightly frozen earth and scratch
myself with my fingers into the soil. It is a tough proposition; everything is so hard. The miserable bits of
earth I manage to scrape loose I throw on top of me,
building up a fox-hole. My wound is bleeding, I have
nothing to bandage it with; I lie prone on the ice cold
earth in my soaking wet clothes; inside me I am hot
with excitement at the prospect of being caught at any
moment. Again the odds are a hundred to one on my
being discovered and captured in less than no time. But
is that a reason to give up hope in the almost impossible,
when only by believing that the almost impossible is
possible can it become so?

There now, the Russians are coming in my direction,
continually lessening the distance between us, each of
them searching the field on his own, but not yet me-
thodically. Some of them are looking in quite the wrong
direction; they do not bother me. But there is one
coming straight towards me. The suspense is terrible.
Twenty paces from me he stops. Is he looking at me?
Is he? He is unmistakably staring in my direction. Is he
not coming on? What is he waiting for? He hesitates for
several minutes; it seems an eternity to me. From time
to time he turns his head a wee bit to the right, a wee
bit to the left; actually he is looking well beyond me. I
gain a momentary confidence, but then I perceive the
danger once more looming large in front of me, and
my hopes deflate. Meanwhile the silhouettes of my first
pursuers appear on the ridge, apparently, now that so
many hounds are on the scent, they have ceased to
take their task seriously.

Suddenly at an angle behind me I hear the roar of
an aeroplane and look up over my shoulder. My Stuka
squadron is flying over the Dniester with a strong
fighter escort and two Fieseler Storches. That means
that Flt./Off. Fischer has given the alarm and they are

searching for me to get me out of this mess. Up there they have no suspicion that they are searching in quite the wrong direction, that I have long since been six miles further south on this side of the river. At this distance I cannot even attract their attention; I dare not so much as lift my little finger. They make one circuit after another at different levels. Then they disappear heading east, and many of them will be thinking: "This time even he has had it." They fly away—home. Longingly I follow them with my eyes. You at least know that tonight you will sleep under shelter and will still be alive whereas I cannot guess how many minutes more of life will be granted me. So I lie there shivering. The sun slowly sets. Why have I not yet been discovered?

Over the brow of the hill comes a column of Ivans, in Indian file, with horses and dogs. Once again I doubt God's justice, for now the gathering darkness should have given me protection. I can feel the earth tremble under their feet. My nerves are at snapping point. I squint behind me. At a distance of a hundred yards the men and animals file past me. Why does no dog pick up my scent? Why does no one find me? Shortly after passing me they deploy at two yards' intervals. If they had done this fifty yards sooner they would have trodden on me. They vanish in the slowly falling dusk.

The last glow of evening yields to blue, feebly twinkling stars appear. My compass has no phosphorescent dial, but there is still light enough to read it. My general direction must remain the south. I see in that quarter of the sky a conspicuous and easily recognizable star with a little neighbour. I decide to adopt it as my lodestar. What constellation in the Russian firmament can it be? It is growing dark and I can no longer see anybody. I stand up, stiff, aching, hungry, thirsty. I remember my chocolate—but I left it in my fur jacket on the bank of the Dniester. Avoiding all roads, footpaths, villages, as Ivan is sure to have sentries posted there, I simply follow my star across country, up hill and down dale, over streams, bogs, marshes and stubbly harvested maize fields. My bare feet are cut to ribbons. Again and again in the open fields I stub my toes against big stones. Gradually I lose all feeling in my feet. The will to live, to keep my freedom, urges me on; they are indivisible; life without freedom is a hollow fruit. How deep is Ivan's penetration of our front? How far have I still to travel? Wherever I hear a dog bark I make a detour, for the hamlets hereabouts are certainly not inhabited by friends. Every now and again I can see gun-flashes on the distant horizon and hear a dull rumble; evidently our boys have started an artillery bombardment. But that means the Russian break-through has gone far. In the gullies which cut through the occasionally rising ground I often lose my footing in the darkness and slump into a ditch where the gluey mud stands knee-deep. It sucks me in so tightly that I have no longer the strength to pull myself out, and flop with the upper part of my body sprawled on the bank of the ditch—my legs deep in slime. Thus I lie exhausted, feeling like a battery gone dead. After lying there for five minutes I am faintly recharged and summon up the strength to crawl up the sloping bank. But remorselessly the same mishap is repeated very soon, at latest at the next uneven ground. So it goes on till 9 p.m. Now I am done in. Even after long-ish rests I cannot recover my strength. Without water and food and a pause for sleep it is impossible to carry on. I decide to look for an isolated house.

I hear a dog barking in the distance and follow the sound. Presumably I am not too far from a village. So after a while I come to a lonely farmhouse and have considerable difficulty in evading the yelping dog. I do not like its barking at all as I am afraid it will alarm some picket in the near-by village. No one opens the door to my knocking; perhaps there is no one there. The same thing happens at a second farmhouse. I go on to a third. When again nobody answers impatience over-comes me and I break a window in order to climb in. At this moment an old woman carrying a smoky oil lamp opens the door. I am already half way through the window, but now I jump out again and put my foot in the door. The old woman tries to shove me out. I push resolutely past her. Turning round I point in the direction of the village and ask: "Bolshewisti?" She nods. Therefore I conclude that Ivan has occupied the village. The dim lamplight only vaguely illumines the room: a table, a bench, an ancient cupboard. In the corner a grey-headed man is snoring on a rather lop-sided trestle bed. He must be seventy. The couple share this wooden couch. In silence I cross the room and lay myself down on it. What can I say? I know no Russian. Meanwhile they have probably seen that I mean no harm. Barefoot and in rags, the tatters of my shirt sticky with coagulated blood, I am more likely to be a hunted quarry than a burglar. So I lie there. The old woman has gone back to bed beside me. Above our heads the feeble glimmer of the lamp. It does not occur to me to ask them whether they have anything to dress my shoulder or my lacerated feet. All I want is rest.

Now again I am tortured by thirst and hunger. I sit up on the bed and put my palms together in a begging gesture to the woman, at the same time making a dumb show of drinking and eating. After a brief hesitation she brings me a jug of water and a chunk of corn bread, slightly mildewed. Nothing ever tasted so good in all my life. With every swallow and bite I feel my strength reviving, as if the will to live and initiative has been restored to me. At first I eat ravenously, then munching thoughtfully, I review my situation and evolve a plan for the next hours. I have finished the bread and water. I will rest till one o'clock. It is 9:20 p.m. Rest is essential. So I lie back again on the wooden boards between the old couple, half awake and half asleep. I wake up every quarter of an hour with the punctuality of a clock and check the time. In no event must I waste too much of the sheltering dark in sleep; I must put as many miles as possible behind me on my journey south. 9:45, 10 o'clock, 10:15, and so on; 12:45, 1:00 o'clock.—Getting up time! I steal out;

the old woman shuts the door behind me. I have already stumbled down a step. Is it the drunkenness of sleep, the pitch dark night or the wet step?

It is raining. I cannot see my hand before my face. My star has disappeared. Now how am I to find my bearings? Then I remember that I was previously running with the wind behind me. I must again keep it in my back to reach the South. Or has it veered? I am still among isolated farm buildings; here I am sheltered from the wind. As it blows from a constantly changing direction I am afraid of moving in a circle. Inky darkness, obstacles; I barge into something and hurt my shins again. There is a chorus of barking dogs, therefore still houses, the village. I can only pray I do not run into a Russian sentry the next minute. At last I am out in the open again where I can turn my back to the wind with certainty. I am also rid of the curs. I plod on as before, up hill, down dale, up, down, maize fields, stones, and woods where it is more difficult to keep direction because you can hardly feel the wind among the trees. On the horizon I see the incessant flash of guns and hear their steady rumble. They serve to guide me on my course. Shortly after 3 a.m. there is a grey light on my left—the day is breaking. A good check, for now I am sure that the wind has not veered and I have been moving south all right.

I have now covered at least six miles. I guess I must have done ten or twelve yesterday, so that I should be sixteen or eighteen miles south of the Dniester.

In front of me rises a hill of about seven hundred feet. I climb it. Perhaps from the top I shall have a panorama and shall be able to make out some conspicuous points. It is now daylight, but I can discover no particular landmarks from the top; three tiny villages below me several miles away to my right and left. What interests me is to find that my hill is the beginning of a ridge running north to south, so I am keeping my direction. The slopes are smooth and bare of timber so that it is easy to keep a look out for any one coming up them. It must be possible to descry any movement from up here; pursuers would have to climb the hill and that would be a substantial handicap. Who at the moment suspects my presence here? My heart is light, because although it is day I feel confident I shall be able to push on south for a good few miles. I would like to put as many as possible behind me with the least delay.

I estimate the length of the ridge as about six miles; that is interminably long. But—is it really so long? After all, I encourage myself, you have run a six mile race—how often?—and with a time of forty minutes. What you were able to do then in forty minutes, you must now be able to do in sixty—for the prize is your liberty. So just imagine you are running a marathon race!

I must be a fit subject for a crazy artist as I plod on with my marathon stride along the crest of the ridge—in rags—on bare, bleeding feet—my arm hugged stiffly to my side to ease the pain of my aching shoulder.

You must make it . . . keep your mind on the race . . . and run . . . and keep on running.

Every now and again I have to change to a jog-trot and drop into a walk for perhaps a hundred yards. Then I start running again . . . it should not take more than an hour . . .

Now unfortunately I have to leave the protective heights, for the way leads downhill. Ahead of me stretches a broad plain, a slight depression in exactly the same direction continues the line of the ridge. Dangerous because here I can be more suddenly surprised. Besides, the time is getting on for seven o'clock, and therefore unpleasant encounters are more likely.

Once again my battery is exhausted. I must drink . . . eat . . . rest. Up to now I have not seen a living soul. Take precautions? What can I do? I am unarmed; I am only thirsty and hungry. Prudence? Prudence is a virtue, but thirst and hunger are an elemental urge. Need makes one careless. Half left two farmhouses appear on the horizon out of the morning mist. I must effect an entry . . .

I stop for a moment at the door of a barn and poke my head round the corner to investigate; the building yawns in my face. Nothing but emptiness. The place is stripped bare, no harness, no farm implements, no living creature—stay!—a rat darts from one corner to another. A large heap of maize leaves lies rotting in the barnyard. I grub amongst them with greedy fingers. If only I could find a couple of corncobs . . . or only a few grains of corn. . . But I find nothing. . . I grub and grub and grub . . . not a thing!

Suddenly I am aware of a rustling noise behind me. Some figures are creeping stealthily past the door of another barn: Russians, or refugees as famished as I am and on the self-same quest? Or are they looters in search of further booty? I fare the same at the next farm. Here I go through the maize heaps with the greatest care—nothing. Disappointedly I reflect: if all the food is gone I must at least make up for it by resting. I scrape myself a hole in the pile of maize leaves and am just about to lie down in it when I hear a fresh noise: a farm wagon is rumbling past along a lane; on the box a man in a tall fur cap, beside him a girl. When there is a girl there can be nothing untoward, so I go up to them. From the black fur cap I guess the man is a Rumanian peasant.

I ask the girl: "Have you anything to eat?"

"If you care to eat this. . ." She pulls some stale cakes out of her bag. The peasant stops the horse. Not until then does it occur to me that I have put my question in German and have received a German answer.

"How do you come to know German?"

The girl tells me that she has come with the German soldiers from Dnjepropetrowsk and that she learnt it there. Now she wants to stay with the Rumanian peasant sitting beside her. They are fleeing from the Russians.

"But you are going straight in their direction." I can see by their faces that they do not believe me. "Have the Ruskis already reached the town over there?"

"No, that is Floresti."

This unexpected reply is like a tonic. The town must lie on the Balti-Floresti railway line which I know.

"Can you tell me, girl, if there are still any German soldiers there?"

"No, the Germans have left, but there may be Rumanian soldiers."

"Thank you and God speed."

I wave to the disappearing wagon. Now I can already hear myself being asked later why I did not "requisition" the wagon . . . the idea never entered my mind. . . For are the pair not fugitives like myself? And must I not offer thanks to God that I have so far escaped from danger?

After my excitement has died down a brief exhaustion overcomes me. For those last six miles I have been conscious of violent pain; all of a sudden the feeling returns to my lacerated feet, my shoulder hurts with every step I take. I meet a stream of refugees with handcarts and the bare necessities they have salvaged, all in panic-stricken haste.

On the outskirts of Floresti two soldiers are standing on the scarp of a sandpit; German uniforms? Another few yards and my hope is confirmed. An unforgettable sight!

I call up to them: "Come here!"

They call down: "What do you mean: come here! Who are you anyway, fellow?"

"I am Squadron Leader Rudel."

"Nah! No squadron leader ever looked like you do."

I have no identification papers, but I have in my pocket the Knight's Cross with Oak Leaves and Swords. I pull it out of my pocket and show it to them. On seeing it the corporal says:

"Then we'll take your word for it."

"Is there a German Kommandantur?"

"No, only the rearguard H.Q. of a dressing station."

That is where I will go. They fall in on either side of me and take me there. I am now crawling rather than walking. A doctor separates my shirt and trousers from my body with a pair of scissors, the rags are sticking to my skin; he paints the raw wounds of my feet with iodine and dresses my shoulder. During this treatment I devour the sausage of my life. I ask for a car to drive me at once to the airfield at Balti. There I hope to find an aircraft which will fly me straight to my squadron.

"What clothes do you intend to wear?" the doctor asks me. All my garments have been cut to ribbons. "We have none to lend you." They wrap me naked in a blanket and off we go in an automobile to Balti. We drive up in front of the control hut on the airfield. But what is this? My squadron officer, Plt./Off. Ebersbach opens the door of the car:

"Pilot Officer Ebersbach, in command of the 3rd Squadron advance party moving to Jassy."

A soldier follows him out carrying some clothes for me. This means that my naked trip from Floresti has already been reported to Balti from there by telephone,

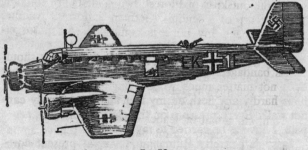

Ju. 52

and Ebersbach happened to be in the control hut when the message came through. He has been informed that his colleague who has been given up for dead will shortly arrive in his birthday suit. I climb into a Ju. 52, and fly to Rauchowka to rejoin the squadron. Here the telephone has been buzzing, the news has spread like wild fire, and the wing cook, Runkel, has already a cake in the oven. I look into grinning faces, the squadron is on parade. I feel reborn, as if a miracle had happened. Life has been restored to me, and this reunion with my comrades is the most glorious prize for the hardest race of my life.

We mourn the loss of Henschel, our best gunner with a credit of 1200 operational sorties. That evening we all sit together for a long while round the fire. There is a certain atmosphere of celebration. The Group has sent over a deputation, among them a doctor who is supposed to "sit by my bedside." He conveys to me the General's congratulations with an order that I am to be grounded and to be flown home on leave as soon as I am in a fit condition to travel. Once more I shall have to disappoint the poor general. For I am deeply worried in my mind. Shall we be able to hold the Soviets now advancing southward in force from the Dniester? I could not lie in bed for a single day.

We are due to move to Jassy with all personnel the next morning. The weather is foul, impossible to fly. If we all have to be idle perforce I may as well obey the doctor's orders and rest. The day after I fly with my squadron to Jassy, from where we have not so far to fly on our coming sorties over the Dniester. My shoulder is bandaged and I cannot move my arm, but that does not matter much when flying. It is worse that I have hardly any flesh on my feet and so naturally cannot walk. Every pressure on the controls involves acute pain. I have to be carried to my aircraft.

Jassy is a pretty Rumanian town, at present completely unscathed. To us a magnificent sight; it reminds us of home. We gape at the shop windows and are as delighted as children.

The next morning our reconnaissance discovers strong armoured and motorized formations already almost due N. of Balti, probably they have even reached the town. At first the weather is bad; the country is mountainous and the highest peaks are shrouded in mist. The situation is grave; there are no longer any troops covering our front. Motorized units can get here in half a day. Who is to stop them? We stand alone. Reconnaissance reports strong opposition by flak which the advancing Reds have brought up with them. Soviet Lag 5s and Aircobras continually fly above their armoured spearhead. Our southern front in Russia, the Rumanian oilfields, both factors of vital importance, are threatened. I am blind and deaf to all advice with regard to my physical condition. The Soviets must be checked; their tanks, the striking force of an army, destroyed. Another weeks goes by before our colleagues on the ground can build a defence line.

W.O. Rothmann, my loyal first shift, carries me to my aircraft. Six of the stiffest sorties in the worst of weather till three in the afternoon. Intense flak. I have to change aircraft after almost every sortie because of damage by flak. I am myself in pretty bad shape. Only the determination to halt the Soviets wherever I can still keeps me going. Besides, these are certainly the troops who tried to take me prisoner, and on the day I escaped the Moscow radio has already given out that they have captured Squadron Leader Rudel. Apparently they did not believe it possible for me to reach our lines. Have my colleagues who failed to make their escape betrayed the name of the one who did?

We attack tanks, supply convoys with petrol and rations, infantry and cavalry, with bombs and cannon. We attack from between 30 and 600 feet because the weather is execrable.

I go out with aircraft of my anti-tank flight carrying the 3.7mm. cannon on tank hunts at the lowest possible level. Soon all the rest of the flight are grounded because when my aircraft is hit I have to use another, and so one after the other gets a rest. If it takes too long to refuel the whole squadron I have my aircraft and another quickly refueled and remunitioned, and the two of us go out between sorties on one of our own. Generally there are none of our fighters there; the Russians realize their enormous numerical superiority

over us alone. Manoeuvring is difficult in these air
battles, for I am unable to operate the rudder controls,
I only use the stick. But up till now I have only been
hit by flak; in every sortie, however, and that is often
enough. On the last sortie of the day I fly with a normal Stuka (not a cannon-carrier) with bombs and two
2cm. calibre cannon. With this weapon one cannot
penetrate a moderately thickly armoured tank. Presumably the Reds are not expecting us to be out so late;
our only object is to locate their concentrations and to
obtain an overall picture of the general situation which
is of the very greatest importance for tomorrow. We fly
along the two roads running North in the direction of
Balti. The sun is already low on the horizon; half-left
huge clouds of smoke are rising from the village of
Falesti. Perhaps a Rumanian unit. I drop down below
the squadron and fly low over the village, and am met
by flak and strong opposition. I see a mass of tanks,
behind them a long convoy of lorries and motorized infantry. The tanks are, curiously, all carrying two or
three drums of petrol. In a flash it dawns upon me;
they no longer expected us and mean to dash through
tonight, if possible into the heart of Rumania, into the
oil region, and thereby cutting off our southern front.
They are taking advantage of the twilight and the darkness because by day they cannot move with my Stukas
overhead. This also accounts for the petrol drums on
board the tanks; they mean, if necessary, to push
through even without their supply columns. This is a
major operation and they are already under way. I now
see that perfectly plainly. We are alone to possess
this knowledge; the responsibility is ours. I give my
orders over the R/T:

"Attack of the most vital importance—"

"You are to drop every bomb singly—"

"Follow up with low level attack till you have fired
every round—"

"Gunners are also to fire at vehicles."

I drop my bombs and then hunt tanks with my 2cm.
cannon. At any other time it would be a sheer waste

of effort to fire at tanks with this calibre ammunition, but today the Ivans are carrying petrol drums; it is worth while. After the first bombs the Russian column stops dead in its tracks, and then tries to drive on in good order, covered by savage flak. But we refuse to let ourselves be deterred. Now they realise that we are in deadly earnest. They scatter in panic away from the road, driving at random into fields and spinning round in circles in every conceivable defensive manoeuvre. Every time I fire I hit a drum with incendiary or explosive ammunition. Apparently the petrol leaks through some joint or other which causes a draught; some tanks standing in the deep shadow of a hill blow up with a blinding flash. If their ammunition is exploded into the air the sky is criss-crossed with a perfect firework display, and if the tank happens to be carrying a quantity of Verey lights they shoot all over the place in the craziest coloured pattern.

Each time I come in to the attack I am sensible of the responsibility which rests on us and hope we may be successful. What luck that we spotted this convoy today! I have run out of ammunition; have just knocked out five tanks but there are still a few monsters in the fields, some of them even yet moving. I long to put paid to them somehow.

"Hannelore 7,1"—that is the call sign for the leader of the Seventh Flight—"you are to lead the way home after firing your last round."

I, with my No. 2, fly back at top speed to the airfield. We do not wait to refuel, we have enough petrol to last us; only more ammunition. The dusk is falling fast. Everything goes too slowly for my liking although the good chaps handling the bombs and shells are giving us all they have. I have tipped them off as to what is at stake and now they do not want to let down their comrades in the air. Ten minutes later I take off again. We meet the squadron returning; it is already approaching the airfield with position lights. It seems an age before I am back at last over my target. From a long way off I can see the burning tanks and lorries.

Explosions briefly illuminate the battle field with an eerie light. Visibility is now pretty poor. I head north, flying at low level along the road and catch up with two steel monsters travelling in the same direction, probably with the intention of carrying the sad news back to the rear. I bank and am on to them; I can only discern them at the very last second as I skim the ground. They are not an easy target, but as they, like their predecessors, carry the big drums, I succeed in blowing them both up, though I have to use up all my ammunition. With these two, a total of seventeen tanks for the day. My squadron has destroyed approximately the same number, so that today the Ivans have lost some thirty tanks. A rather black day for the enemy. Tonight at all events we can sleep quietly at Jassy, of that we can be sure. How far the general impetus of the offensive has been impaired we shall learn tomorrow. We make our final landing in the dark. Now gradually I become conscious of pain, as the tension slowly relaxes. Both the army and the air group want to know every detail. For half the night I sit by the telephone with the receiver to my ear.

The mission for tomorrow is obvious: to engage the same enemy forces as today.

We take off very early so as to be up in the forward area at the crack of dawn, for we can be certain that Ivan will also have made good use of the interval. The foulest weather, cloud ceiling 300-450 feet over the airfield. Once again, St. Peter is helping the other side. The surrounding hills are obscured. We can only fly along the valleys. I am curious as to what is in store for us today. We fly past Falesti; there everything is wreckage just as we left it yesterday. Due south of Balti we meet the first armoured and motorized convoys. We are greeted by fierce opposition, from both flak and fighter aircraft. It must have got round that we put up a good show yesterday. I should not much care to make a forced landing hereabouts today. We attack without intermission; on every sortie we are engaged in aerial

combat without protection, for in this sector there are
virtually none of our fighters available. In addition we
have plenty of trouble with the weather. Through having
to fly low all the time we are not without losses; but
we have to keep at it, for we are dealing with an emergency and it is in our own interest not to let up for an
instant. Unless we stay in the air it will not be long before Ivan occupies our airfield. It is unfortunate that I
no longer have Henschel with me on these difficult
sorties; with his gunnery experience the brave fellow
would have been able to make things a whole lot easier
for me. Today my rear-gunner is W.O. Rothmann. A
good chap, but he lacks experience. We all like flying
with him because we say: "Even if no one else gets back
you can bet old Rothmann will." On our return from
the first sortie I am again impatient at the delay and
sandwich in a "solo," accompanied by Plt./Off. Fischer.
We go out after tanks on the outskirts of Balti. We
have a rendezvous with a few fighters over the target.
We fly there as low as possible; the weather is worse
than ever, visibility not more than 800 yards. I look
for our fighters, climbing shortly before we reach the
town. There are fighters there—but not ours, all Russians.

"Look out, Fischer, they're all Aircobra. Stick to me.
Come in closer."

They have already spotted us. There are about twenty of them. We two alone are just their meat; they come
at us confidently, hell-for-leather. There is no air space
up above; we are flying at bottom level, taking advantage of every little gully in the effort to lose ourselves. I
cannot take any violent evasive action because I cannot kick the rudder-bar with my feet; I can only make
weary changes of direction by pulling my joy-stick.
These tactics are not good enough by a long chalk if I
have behind me a fighter pilot who knows the first
thing about his business. And the one now on my tail
knows all about it. Rothmann shows signs of the jit-
ters:

"They are shooting us down!"

I yell at him to shut up, to fire instead of wasting his breath. He gives a shout—there is a rat-a-tat-tat against my fuselage, hit after hit. I cannot shift the rudder-bar. A blind rage possesses me. I am beside myself with fury. I hear the impact of large calibre shells; the Aircobra is firing with a 3.7 cm. cannon in addition to its 2 cm. guns. How long will my faithful Ju. 87

**Bell P 39 Aircobra**

hold out? How long before my kite bursts into flames or falls apart? I have been brought down thirty times in this war, but always by flak, never yet by fighters. Every time I was able to use the rudder-bar and manoeuvre with the aid of it. This is the first and last time a fighter hits my aircraft.

"Rothmann, fire!" He does not answer. His last word is: "I am jammed—Ouch!" So now my rear defence is eliminated. The Ivans are not slow to grasp the fact; they become even more aggressive than before, coming in behind me and from port and starboard. One fellow comes at me again and again with a frontal pass. I take refuge in the narrowest ravines where there is barely room to squeeze through with my wings. Their marksmanship against their living target is not bad, they score one hit after another. The chances of my getting back are once again very small. But close to our own airfield at Jassy they abandon the chase; presumably they have run out of ammunition. I have lost Fischer. He was diagonally behind me all the time and I could not keep track of him. Rothmann, too, does not know what has happened to him. Has he made a forced landing or has he crashed? I do not know myself. The loss of the smart young officer hits the squadron particularly hard. My aircraft has been riddled by the 2 cm. guns and hit eight times by the 3.7 cannon. Rothmann would no longer insure my life for very much.

After such an experience one is mentally harassed and exhausted, but that cannot be helped. Into another aircraft and off again. The Soviets must be halted. On this day I knock out nine tanks. A heavy day. During the last sorties I have to peel my eyes to catch sight of a tank. This is a good sign. I believe that for the moment the main impetus of the enemy has been stemmed; infantry by itself without armour makes no great forward leaps.

Dawn reconnaissance the next morning confirms my supposition. Everything seems quiet, almost dead. As I land after the first sortie of the day a young aircraftsman springs onto the wing of my aircraft with wild gesticulations and congratulates me on the award of the Diamonds. A long distance message has just been received from the Führer, but it also includes an order forbidding me to fly any more. Some of his words are drowned by the noise of the running engine, but I guess the drift of what he is telling me. To avoid seeing this prohibition in black and white I do not go into the control room, but remain close to my aircraft until the preparations for the next take-off are completed. At noon the General summons me to Odessa by telephone. Meanwhile telegrams of congratulations have been pouring in from every point of the compass, even from members of the Reich government. It is going to be a hard fight to obtain leave to continue flying. The thought that my comrades are getting ready for another sortie and that I have to go to Odessa upsets me. I feel like a leper. This rider to the award disheartens me and kills my pleasure at the recognition of my achievement. In Odessa I learn nothing new, only what I already know and do not wish to hear. I listen to the words of congratulation absently; my thoughts are with my comrades who do not have this worry and can fly. I envy them. I am to proceed immediately to the Führer's headquarters to be personally invested with the Diamonds. After stopping off at Tiraspol we change over to a Ju. 87—if only Henschel were with me, now Rothmann sits behind. Over Foskani—Bucharest—Belgrade—Keskemet—Vienna to Salzburg. It is no every-day occurrence for the Head of the State to receive an officer reporting in soft fur flying boots, but I am happy to be able to move about in them, even though in great pain. Wing Commander von Below comes in to Salzburg to fetch me while Rothmann goes home by train, it being agreed that I shall pick him up in Silesia on my way back.

For two days I bask in the sun on the terrace of the Berchtesgadener Hotel, inhaling the glorious mountain air of home. Now gradually I relax. Two days later I stand in the presence of the Führer in the magnificent Berghof. He knows the whole story of the last fortnight down to the minutest detail and expresses his joy that the fates have been so kind, that we were able to achieve so much. I am impressed by his warmth and almost tender cordiality. He says that I have now done enough; hence his order grounding me. He explains that it is not necessary that all great soldiers should lay down their lives; their example and their experience must be safeguarded for the new generation. I reply with a refusal to accept the decoration if it entails the stipulation that I may no longer lead my squadron into action. He frowns, a brief pause ensues, and then his face breaks into a smile: "Very well, then, you may fly."

Now at last I am glad and happily look forward to
seeing the pleasure in the faces of my comrades when
they hear that I am back. We have tea together and chat
for an hour or two. New technical weapons, the strategic situation, and history are the staple of our conversation. He specially explains to me the V weapons
which have recently been tried out. For the present,
he says, it would be a mistake to overestimate their
effectiveness because the accuracy of these weapons is
still very small, adding that this is not so important, as
he is now hopeful of producing flying rockets which
will be absolutely infallible. Later on we should not rely
as at present on the normal high explosives, but on
something quite different which will be so powerful
that once we begin to use them they should end the
war decisively. He tells me that their development is
already well advanced and that their final completion
may be expected very soon. For me this is entirely vir-
gin ground, and I cannot yet imagine it. Later I learn
that the explosive effect of these new rockets is supposed to be based on atomic energy.

The impression left after every visit to the Führer is
enduring. From Salzburg I fly the short distance to
Görlitz, my home town. All the receptions given in my
honour are more of a strain than some operational
sorties. Once when I am lying in bed at seven o'clock
in the morning a girls' choir serenades me; it requires
a good deal of persuasion on the part of my wife to
make me say good morning to them. It is hard to explain to people that in spite of being decorated with the
Diamonds one does not want any celebrations or receptions. I want to rest and that is all. I spend a few
more days with my parents in my home village in an
intimate family gathering. I listen to the news bulle-
tins from the East on the wireless and think of the
soldiers fighting over there. Then nothing holds me back
any longer. I ring up Rothmann at Zittau and a Ju 87
flies over Vienna—Bucharest southwards to the Eastern Front once more.

## 14

# FATEFUL SUMMER 1944

A few hours later I land at Foscani in the North Rumanian zone. My squadron is now stationed at Husi, a little to the north. The front is very much more firmly held than it was a fortnight ago. It runs from the Pruth to the Dniester along the edge of the plateau north of Jassy.

The little town of Husi nestles among the hills. Some of these heights have extensive vineyard terraces. Are we in time for the vintage? The airfield is situated on the northern rim of the town, and as our billets are directly on the opposite side of it we have to go through the streets every morning on our way to dispersal. The population watches our activities with interest. When one talks to them they always show their friendliness. The representatives of the church especially maintain close contact with us, following the lead given by the bishop whose guest I often am. He is never tired of explaining that the clergy see in our victory the only possible chance of keeping religious liberty and independence, and that they long for it to come with the least possible delay. There are many tradesmen in the town, the place is full of little shops. This is very different from Soviet Russia which we have left so recently, where the middle class has vanished, swallowed up by the proletarian Moloch.

What especially strikes me as I walk through the town is the enormous number of dogs. To all appearances these hordes are masterless. They roam around and one meets them at every corner and on every square. I am temporarily quartered in a little villa with a vineyard, on one side of which flows a small stream where one can bathe. Whole processions of dogs wander through this vineyard in the night. They move in Indian file, in packs of twenty or thirty. One morning I am still abed when a huge mongrel looks in at my window with his forepaws on the sill. Behind him, likewise standing on their hind legs, are fifteen of his colleagues. They rest their forepaws on the back of the dog in front, all peering into my room. When I chase them away they slink off sadly and without barking, back to their restless prowling.

There is no shortage of food; we live well, for we receive our pay in leis, and even if there is not much worth buying there are always eggs. Consequently almost the whole of our pay is converted into eggs. Flg./ Off. Staehler holds the record of egg-consumption among the officers; he puts away astounding quantities. On days when shortage of petrol makes it impossible to fly this new source of energy is immediately put to the test; the whole squadron, to a man, takes some form of exercise, generally a long cross country run, gymnastics and, of course, a game of football.

I still find these exertions painful because the soles of my feet are not yet quite healed and my shoulder hurts me if I move it injudiciously. But for the squadron as a whole these ultra-routine sports are a splendid recreation. Some, and I am the keenest among them, take advantage of this extra leisure to stroll in the mountain woods or to practise some other sport.

Usually we drive to the airfield for the take off between 4 and 5 A.M. On the far side of the town we always run into a huge flock of sheep with a donkey walking in front. The donkey's eyes are almost completely covered by a long and straggling mane; we wonder how he can manage to see at all. Because of this mane we nickname him Eclipse. One morning as we squeeze past we tweak his tail in fun. The shock provides a whole series of reactions: first he lets fly with his hind-legs like a kicking horse, then remembering his asinine nature he stands stock still, and lastly his chicken heart begins to thump and he streaks off like the wind. The flock of sheep entrusted to his care of course understand nothing of this unusual contretemps, still less of the reason for his kicking and haring off. When they see that the donkey has left them in the lurch the air is filled with a pandemonium of bleating, and suddenly the sheep set off at a gallop in pursuit. . . Even if we meet with heavy opposition on our first sortie we do not care, for we still see the picture of this comic animal performance and our hearts are light with the joy of living. This gaiety robs the danger of the moment of its meaning.

Our missions now take us into a relatively stabilized sector where, however, the gradual arrival of reinforcements indicates that the Reds are preparing a thrust into the heart of Rumania. Our operational area extends from the village of Targul Frumos in the west to some bridgeheads over the Dniester S. of Tiraspol in the southeast. Most of our sorties take us into the area north of Jassy between these points; here the Soviets are trying to oust us from the high ground round Carbiti near the Pruth. The bitterest fighting in this sector rages round the ruins of the castle of Stanca on the so-called Castle Hill. Time and again we lose this position and always recapture it.

In this zone the Soviets are constantly bringing up their stupendous reserves. How often do we attack the river bridges in this area; our route is over the Pruth to the Dniester beyond Kishinew and further east. Koschnitza, Grigoriopol and the bridgehead at Butor are names we shall long remember. For a short period comrades of the 52nd Fighter Wing are stationed with us on our airfield. Their C.O. is Squadron Leader Barkhorn who knows his job from A to Z. They often escort us on our sorties and we give them plenty of trouble, for the new Yak 3 which has made its appearance on the other side puts up a show every now and then. A group advanced base is operating from Jassy, from where it is easier to patrol the air space above the front. The Group Captain is often up in the front line to observe the cooperation of his formations with the ground troops. His advance post has a wireless set which enables him to pick up all R/T interchanges in the air and on the ground. The fighter pilots talk to one another, the fighters with their control officer, the Stukas among themselves, with their liaison officer on the ground and others. Normally, however, we all use different wave lengths. A little anecdote which the Group Captain told us on his last visit to our dispersal shows the extent of his concern for his individual lambs. He was watching our squadron approaching Jassy. We were heading north, our objective being to attack targets in the castle area which the army wanted neutralised after making contact with our control. We were met over Jassy, not by our own fighters, but by a strong formation of Lags. In a second the sky was full of crazily swerving aircraft. The slow Stukas were ill-matched against the arrow-swift Russian fighters, especially as our bomb load further slowed us down. With mixed feelings the Group Captain watched the battle and overheard this conversation. The skipper of the 7th Flight, assuming that I had not seen a Lag 5 which was coming up from below me, called a warning: "Look out, Hannelore, one of them is going to shoot you down!" I had spotted the blighter a long time ago, but there was still ample time to take evasive action. I dislike this yelling over the R/T; it upsets the crews and has a bad effect on accuracy. So I replied: "The one who shoots me down has not yet been born."

I was not bragging. I only meant to show a certain nonchalance for the benefit of the other pilots because calmness in an awkward spot like this is infectious. The commodore ends his story with a broad grin:

"When I heard that I was no longer worried about you and your formation. As a matter of fact I watched the scrap with considerable amusement."

How often when briefing my crews do I give them

this lecture: "Any one of you who fails to keep up with me will be shot down by a fighter. Any one who lags behind is easy meat and cannot count on any help. So: stick closely to me. Flak hits are often flukes. If you are out of luck you are just as likely to be hit on the head by a falling slate from a roof or to fall off a tram. Besides, war is not exactly a life insurance."

The old stagers already know my views and maxims. When the new-comers are being initiated they hide a smile and think: "He may be right at that." The fact that they have practically no losses due to enemy fighter interception corroborates my theory. The novices must of course have some proficiency by the time they reach the front, otherwise they are a danger to their colleagues.

A few days later, for instance, we are out in the same operational area and are again attacking under strong enemy fighter interference. As the recently joined Plt./Off. Rehm follows the aircraft in front of him into a dive he cuts off the other's tail and rudder with his propeller. Luckily the wind carries their parachutes into our own lines. We spiral round them until they reach the ground because the Soviet fighters make a regular practice of opening fire on our crews when they have bailed out. After a few months with the squadron Plt./Off. Rehm has become a first-rate airman who is soon able to lead a section and often acts as flight leader. I have a fellow-feeling for those who are slow to learn.

Plt./Off. Schwirblat is not so lucky. He has already 700 operational sorties to his credit and has been decorated with the Knight's Cross of the Iron Cross. He has to make a forced landing after being hit in the target area just behind the front line and loses his left leg, as well as some fingers. We are to be together again in action in the final phase of the war.

We are given no respite in the air, not only in the area N. of Jassy, but also in the east where the Russians have established their bridgeheads over the Dniester. Three of us are out alone one afternoon in the loop of the Dniester between Koschnitza and Grigoriopol where large numbers of T 34s have penetrated our defences. Plt./Off. Fickel and a W.O. accompany me with bombers. Our own fighters are supposed to be waiting for us, and as I approach the loop of the river I can already

T 34

see fighters flying low in the target area. Being an optimist, I jump to the conclusion that they are ours. I fly on towards our objective, searching for tanks when I realise that the fighters are not my escort at all, but are all Ivans. Stupidly we have already broken our formation in quest of individual targets. The other two do not immediately close up and are slow in coming in behind me. Furthermore, as bad luck will have it, these Ivans are up to scratch; that does not happen too often. The W.O.'s aircraft very quickly bursts into flames and becomes a torch vanishing westward. Plt./ Off. Fickel calls out that he, too, has been hit and sheers off. A Lag 5 pilot who evidently knows his business is bang on my tail, with several others not quite so close behind him. Whatever I do I cannot shake off the Lag; he has partly lowered his flaps to check his speed. I fly into deep ravines so as to entice him far enough down to make the danger of touching the ground affect his aim. But he stays up and his tracer bullets streak closely past my cockpit. My gunner Gadermann yells excitedly that he will shoot us down. The ravine broadens somewhat S.W. of the river loop, and suddenly I bank round with the Lag still persistently on my tail. Behind me Gadermann's gun is jammed. The tracers shave the underside of my left wing. Gadermann shouts: "Higher." I reply: "Can't. I have the stick in my stomach as it is." It has been slowly puzzling me how the fellow behind me can follow my banking tactics in his fighter. Once again the sweat is running down my forehead. I pull and pull my stick; the tracers continue to zip under my wing. By turning my head I can look straight into the Ivan's tensely set face. The other Lags have given up, apparently waiting for their colleague to bring me down. This kind of flying is not their cup of tea: vertical banking at 30-45 feet level. Suddenly on the top of the escarpment, German soldiers. They wave like mad, but have seemingly failed entirely to grasp the situation. Now a loud whoop from Gadermann: "The Lag is down!"

Did Gadermann shoot her down with his rear M.G. or did she crash because the longerons cracked under the terrific pressure of these high speed turns? I couldn't care less. In my headphones I hear a mighty yelling from the Russians, a babel of noise. They have seen what has happened and it appears to be something out of the ordinary. I have lost sight of Plt./Off. Fickel and fly back alone. Below me a burning Ju. 87 lies in a field. The W.O. and his gunner are both standing safely near it, and German soldiers are coming towards them. So they will be back tomorrow. Shortly before landing I catch up with Plt./Off. Fickel. There will be ample reason for celebrating my Fickel's and Gadermann's birthdays. They, too, insist upon celebrating. The following morning the Flying Control Officer of this sector rings up and tells me how anxiously they watched yesterday's performance, and congratulates me heartily in the name of his division. A radio message picked up last night revealed that the fighter pilot was a quite

famous Soviet ace, several times "Hero of the U.S.S.R."
He was a good airman, that much I must give him.

Very shortly after this I have to report on two separate occasions to the Reichsmarschall. The first time
I land at Nuremberg and proceed to his ancestral
castle. As I enter the courtyard I am greatly surprised
to see Goering with his personal medical attendant
rigged out in a medieval German hunting costume and
shooting with a bow and arrow at a gaily coloured target. At first he pays no attention to me until he has
shot off all his arrows. I am amazed that not one of
them misses its mark. I only hope that he is not seized
with the ambition to show off his sporting prowess by
making me compete with him; in that case he is bound
to see that with my shoulder I cannot hold the bow, let
alone draw it. The fact that I am reporting to him in
fur boots anyhow gives some indication of my physical
infirmities. He tells me that he occupies much of his
leisure at this sport; it is his way of keeping fit and the
doctor, willy-nilly, has to join him in this pastime.
After a simple lunch in the family circle, at which
General Loerzer is the only other guest, I learn the
reason for my summons. He invests me with the Golden
Pilot's Medal with Diamonds and asks me to form a
squadron equipped with the new Messerschmitt 410
armed with 5 cm. cannon, and assume command of it.
He hopes with this type to achieve a decisive ascen-
dancy over the four-engined aircraft used by the enemy.
I draw my own conclusions: namely, that as I have
recently been decorated with the Diamonds his object
is to turn me into a fighter pilot. I feel sure that he is
thinking back to the First World War in which airmen
who had the "Pour le Mérite" were regularly fighter
pilots like himself. He has had a predilection for this
branch of the Luftwaffe and for those who belong to it
ever since, and would like to include me in this category. I tell him how much I would have liked to become a fighter pilot earlier on, and what accidents pre-
vented it. But since those days I have gained valuable

experience as a dive bomber pilot and am dead against a change. I therefore beg him to abandon the idea. He then tells me that he has the Führer's approval for this commission, though he admits he was not particularly pleased at the idea of my giving up dive bombing. Nevertheless the Führer agreed with him in wishing that I should on no account make another landing behind the Russian front to rescue crews. This was an order. If crews had to be picked up, then in future it should be done by someone else. This worries me. It is part of our code that "any one brought down will be picked up." —I am of the opinion that it is better that I do it because with my greater experience it must be easier for me than for any one else. If it has to be done at all, then I am the one who should do it. But to raise any objections now would be a waste of breath. At the critical moment one will act as necessity dictates. Two days later I am back again on operations at Husi.

During a lull of several days I decide to make a short trip to Berlin for a long deferred conference. On the return journey I land at Görlitz, stop off at my home and continue eastward via Vöslau near Vienna. Early in the morning I am rung up at the house of my friends: somebody has been ringing me up all night. A telephone message from the Reichsmarschall's H.Q. having been put through to Husi, they have been trying to contact me all along my itinerary, but have failed to reach me anywhere. I immediately put through a call, and Goering's adjutant tells me to proceed at once to Berchtesgaden. As I guess that this is another unwelcome attempt to have me seconded for staff or special duties, I ask him: "Is this good or bad from my point of view?" He knows me. "Certainly not bad."

Not altogether without misgivings I first fly low along the Danube. The weather is the worst imaginable. 120 feet cloud ceiling; no take-off or landing allowed at almost every aerodrome. The Vienna woods are continuously wreathed in the densest clouds. I fly up the valley from St. Pölten to Amstetten heading for Salzburg where I land. Here I am already expected and am

driven to the Reichsmarschall's country house not far
from the Berghof on the Obersalzberg. He is absent in
conference with the Führer and we are at table when
he returns. His daughter Edda is already a big and well
brought-up girl; she is allowed to sit down with us.
After a short constitutional in the garden the conversation takes an official turn, and I am all agog to know
what is in the wind this time. House and garden are in
really good taste; nothing vulgar or ostentatious. The
family leads a simple life. Now I am officially given
audience in his bright and many-windowed study, with
a glorious panorama of the mountains glittering in the
late spring sunshine. He evidently has a certain foible
for old customs and costumes. I am really at a loss to
describe the garment he is wearing: it is a kind of robe
or toga such as the ancient Romans wore, of a russet
colour and held together with a gold brooch. I cannot
precisely describe it. For me at all events it is a novel
rig out. He is smoking a long pipe reaching to the floor
with a prettily painted porcelain bowl. I can remember
my father having possessed a similar instrument; in
those days the pipe was taller than I. After eyeing me
in silence for a while he begins to speak. I am here
again for another decoration. He pins on my chest the
Golden Front Service Medal with Diamonds in recognition of my recently completed two thousand sorties.
It is an absolutely new kind of medal, never before
awarded to anyone, for no one but I had flown so many
sorties. It is made of solid gold with, in the centre, a
platinum wreath with crossed swords, beneath which is
the number 2000 in tiny diamonds. I am glad that
there are no unpleasant strings attached to this errand
on which I have come.

Then we discuss the situation, and he thinks I ought
to lose no time in returning to my base. I intended to do
so in any case. He tells me that a large scale offensive is
in preparation in my sector and that the balloon will go
up in the next few days. He has just returned from a
conference in which the whole situation has been dis-

cussed in minutest detail with the Führer. He expresses surprise that I have not noticed these preparations on the spot, as approximately three hundred tanks are to be employed in this operation. Now I prick my ears. The number three hundred flabbergasts me. This is an everyday occurrence on the Russian side, but on ours it is no longer credible. I reply that I find some difficulty in believing it. I ask if he is at liberty to divulge the names of the divisions with the number of tanks they each have at their disposal, because I am exactly informed about most units in my sector and their complement of serviceable tanks. On the eve of my departure from the front I had spoken with General Unrein, commanding the 14th armoured division. That was a fortnight ago, and he had complained bitterly to me that he had only one tank left, and even that was actually hors de combat because he had built into it all the flying control apparatus, and this was essentially more valuable to him than a serviceable tank, for with good intercommunications we Stukas were able to neutralise for him many objectives which his tanks could not put out of action. I therefore know the strength of the 14th armoured division exactly. The Reichsmarschall can hardly believe me as he thinks he has heard a different figure for this division. He says to me, half in earnest, half in jest: "If I didn't know you, for two pins I would have you put under arrest for saying such a thing. But we will soon find out." He goes to the telephone and is connected with the Chief of the General Staff.

"You have just given the Führer the figure of three hundred tanks for Operation X." The telephone is loud; I can overhear every word.

"Yes, I did."

"I want to know the names of the divisions concerned with their present strength in tanks. I have somebody with me who is well acquainted with the position."

"Who is he?" asks the Chief of the General Staff.

"He is one of my men who must know." Now the

Chief of the General Staff has the bad luck to begin with the 14th armoured division. He says it has sixty tanks. Goering can hardly contain himself.

"My man reports that the 14th has one!" A lengthy silence at the other end of the line.

"When did he leave the front?"

"Four days ago." Again silence. Then:

"Forty tanks are still on their way to the front. The rest are in repair shops on the line of communications, but will certainly reach their units by zero day, so that the figures are correct."

He has the same answer for the other divisions. The Reichsmarschall slams down the receiver in a rage.

"That's how it is! The Führer is given a totally false picture based on incorrect data and is surprised when operations do not have the success expected. Today, thanks to you, it is accidentally explained, but how often we may have built our hopes on such Utopias. The Southeastern zone with its network of communications is being incessantly blanketed by the enemy's bomber formations. Who knows how many of those forty tanks, for example, will ever reach the front or when? Who can say if the repair shops will get their spare parts in time and if they will be able to complete their repairs within the specified time? I shall at once report the matter to the Führer." He speaks angrily, then falls silent.

As I fly back to the front my mind is much concerned with what I have just heard. What is the purpose of these misleading and false reports? Is it due to slovenliness or is it intentional? In either case it helps the enemy. Who and what circles are committing these enormities?

I break my journey at Belgrade, and as I come in to land at Semlin, U.S. four-engined bomber formations appear heading towards the airfield. As I taxi in I see the whole personnel of the aerodrome running away. There are some hills to the west of the runway in which tunnels have apparently been cut to serve as shelters.

I see the formation straight ahead of me a short distance from the airfield. This does not look any too good. I sprint after the stream of people as fast as I can in my fur boots. I just enter the tunnel as the first stick of bombs explodes on the aerodrome, raising a gigantic mushroom of smoke. I cannot believe it possible that anything can remain intact. After a few minutes the smoke cloud thins a little and I walk back to the airfield. Almost everything is destroyed; beside the wreckage stands my faithful Ju. 87, riddled with splinters, but the engine is undamaged and so is the undercarriage. The essential parts of the control system still function. I look for a strip of ground off the actual runway suitable for take off, and am glad when I am airborne again. Loyally and gallantly my wounded kite carries me over the S.E. zone back to my wing at Husi.

During my absence a Rumanian Ju. 87 flight has been attached to us. The crews consist mainly of officers; some of them have a certain flying experience, but we soon discover that it is better if they only fly as a flight with us in close formation. Otherwise the number of casualties on every sortie is always high. The enemy fighters bother them especially, and it takes them some little time to realise through experience that with a slow aircraft in formation it is not absolutely necessary to be shot down. The Wing staff has gone over to Focke-Wulf 190s. Our 1 Squadron has been temporarily withdraw from operations for an eight weeks rest to an airfield in the rear at Sächsisch-Regen. Here old stager Ju. 87 pilots go back to school on the one-seater type. In the long run all our units may have to do the same, as the last production series of Ju. 87s has still to be completed after which no more aircraft of this type are to be built. Therefore while at Husi I personally practise flying between sorties in one of the Wing staff's new F.W. 190s so that there shall be no reason for my being withdrawn from operations. I finish up my self-training by going out straight away on one or two sorties in the frontal area with the new type and feel quite safe in it.

It is getting on for July; our sorties are much more frequent and the planned local offensive in the area N. of Jassy is under way. Not with the invented number of tanks and later than the date of the original plan, but nevertheless with fresher troops than we have recently been used to. It is necessary to capture the whole plateau between the Pruth and Targul Frumos. It is an easier line to hold and its capture will also deprive the enemy of a favourable springboard for an assault. The whole front line in this sector is on the move and we succeed in pushing the Soviets back a considerable distance. By stubborn resistance they manage to hang on to several key points. They are lucky because local attacks intended to mop up these nests of resistance are never carried out. Some of our assault units which are thrown in, like a fire brigade, wherever the fighting is hottest have to be withdrawn. I fly my 2100th operational sortie in the course of this offensive. My target is a familiar one: the bridge at Sculeni, of vital importance to the supply line of the hard-pressed Soviets. Every time we come in to attack it from N. of Jassy it is already hidden by a smoke screen and we can never be sure of not dropping our bombs too close to our own front line. Each time I see the smoke screen I have to laugh, imagining the faces of the Ivans down below gazing up at our approach. It does not require a linguist to distinguish the one always recurring word: "Stuka—Stuka—Stuka." Our days at Husi are numbered.

After a birthday party in my vineyard in the first half of July orders arrive for us to move to Zamosc in the central sector of the East Front. Here the Russians have launched a new large-scale offensive.

We arrive at this new operational base flying over the North Carpathians, over Stryj and by-passing Lemberg. Zamosc is a pretty little town, it makes a good impression. We are quartered in an old Polish barracks on the northern edge of the town. Our airfield itself lies rather far outside it and consists of stubble fields; the landing strip is narrow and at once causes a very regrettable accident. On his very first landing Warrant Officer W.'s aircraft pancakes and the pilot injures himself rather seriously. He is one of my best tank-snipers and it will be a long time before we have him with us again. Here again there is ample work for tankbusters, especially as the front lines are not stabilized but fluid. Break-throughs by tanks are the order of the day. We hold Kowel, but the Soviets have by-passed it and are endeavouring to cross the Bug. It is not long before their spearheads appear in the area N.W. of Lemberg—at Rawaruska and Towaszow, and at Cholm to the north. During this phase we have another move, this time to Mielec, a small Polish town sixty miles N.W. of Krakau. The aim of the Soviet advance is clear: they are trying to reach the Vistula on a comparatively wide front. Our targets are the oncoming masses of men and material now trying to cross the San to the north of Premysl. The fighter opposition is not to be underestimated as American fighters now more and more often put in an appearance after flying as escort to four-engined bomber formations. Originally they come from air bases on the Mediterranean. As we now have reasons to perceive, they do not return to base immediately on completion of the mission, but land on Russian territory to refuel. Then one day they come back on another mission and afterwards fly south to their starting base. On one sortie over the San I run into one such Mustang formation as I am already coming in to attack. There are nearly three hundred of them. I am flying with a formation of fifteen bombers without any fighter protection; we are still 23 miles from Jaroslaw, our target for today. In order not to endanger the squadron, and, above all, its several new crews, I give the order to jettison bombs so that we shall be better able to manoeuvre in the all too unequally matched air battle. I am reluctant to give this order; hitherto we have always attacked the target assigned to us, even in the face of great enemy superiority. This is the first time; it will also be the last until the end of the war. But today I have no choice.

So I bring my squadron home without loss and we are able to make up for our failure to carry out our mission the next day under more favourable conditions. Success justifies my action, for in the evening I hear that a neighbouring unit suffered heavy losses from this huge formation of Mustangs. At midday a few days later while we are refuelling we are again surprised by an American formation which immediately comes down to attack our aircraft. Our airfield defence is not strong and our A.A. gunners, at first taken by surprise, are slow in opening up on the attackers. The Americans had not reckoned with flak, and as it is certainly no part of their programme not to return today, they turn away without any material success in search of easier prey.

A telephone call from the Air Command: for the first time in this war the Russians have set foot on German soil and are pushing into East Prussia from the Willkowiscen area in the direction of Gumbinnen—Insterburg. I want to move to East Prussia at once; the transfer order arrives and the following day I am already at Insterburg with my flying personnel. In the heavenly peacefulness of East Prussia it is quite impossible to imagine that the war has already come so close, and that sorties with bombs and anti-tank aircraft have to be flown from this quiet spot. In the town of Insterburg itself the people have not yet adjusted themselves to the gravity of the situation. The aerodrome is still overcrowded with installations which are useless for such concentrated operational activity. Therefore it is better to move to Lötzen in the Mazurian lake district where we are alone on the tiny airfield.

Midsummer in the lovely East Prussian country. Is this land to become a battlefield? It is here that we realize that we are fighting for our homes and for our freedom. How much German blood has already drenched this soil in vain! It must not happen again! These are the thoughts which fill our minds as we fly towards our target—north of the Memel or at Schaulen, at Suwalki or Augustowo—and on the way home the same thoughts torment us. We are now back where we started from in 1941; it was from here that the invasion of the East began. Will the monument at Tannenberg acquire an even greater significance? The emblem of German chivalry is painted on our squadron aircraft; never has it meant so much to us as now.

Stiff fighting in the area round Wilkowiscen; the town itself changes hands time and again. A small German armoured unit stands its ground here, supported by us from the first to the last minute of daylight, resisting the incessant onslaught of the Russians for several days. Some of the T 34s take cover behind the corn stooks standing on the harvested fields. We set the stooks on fire with incendiaries so as to uncover the tanks, then we go for them. A broiling summer; we live quite close to the water and often bathe in a half hour break between sorties, a sheer enjoyment. The effects of the ceaseless activity on the ground and in the air are soon perceptible: the initial fury of the Russian assault has noticeably slackened. Counter-attacks are more and more frequent, and so the front can to some extent be stabilized again. But when fighting dies down in one place it is sure to flare up in another; so it is here. The Soviets are thrusting towards Lithuania, trying to outflank our armies in Estonia and Latvia. Consequently for us in the air there is always a job to be done. The Soviets are relatively well informed as to the strength of our defence on the ground and in the air.

One sortie again provides Flg./Off. Fickel with an occasion to celebrate his birthday. We are on our way to attack enemy concentrations and the Reds are up to their old trick of using our wave length. Personally I cannot at the moment understand what they are jabbering, but it evidently refers to us because the word "Stuka" keeps on recurring. My linguist colleague and a ground listening post which has an interpreter tell

me the story afterwards. This is, more or less, what
happened:

"Stukas approaching from the West—calling all Red
Falcons: you are to attack the Stukas immediately,
there are about twenty—in front a single Stuka with
two long bars—it is sure to be Squadron-Leader Rudel's squadron, the one that always knocks out our
tanks. Calling all Red Falcons and A.A. batteries:
you are to shoot down the Stuka with the long
bars."

Flg./Off. Markwardt gives me a rough translation
while we are in the air. Fickel says with a laugh:

"If they aim at No. 1 you can bet they'll hit No.
2."

He generally flies as my No. 2 and therefore speaks
from experience.

Ahead of us and below us Ivans with motor vehicles,
artillery and other stuff on a road between isolated
woods. The heavy flak is putting up a good show, the
Red Falcons are already there, Aircobras attack us; I
give the order to attack. A part of the formation dives
onto the trucks and lorries, a smaller section onto the
A.A. batteries, all manoeuvring frantically. The fighters now think their opportunity has come. Flak clouds
hang close to our aircraft. Shortly before he goes into a
dive Flg./Off. Fickel gets a direct hit in his wing; he
jettisons his bombs and flies off in the direction from
which we have come. His aircraft is on fire. We have
dropped our bombs and come out of our dive. I gain
height to see where Fickel has got to. He makes a landing in the middle of quite unsuitable country, fur-
rowed with ditches and full of potholes, tree stumps
and other obstacles. His aircraft skips over two ditches
like a rampagious he-goat; it is a miracle that he has
not pancaked long ago. Now he and his gunner clam-
ber out. The situation is bad: cavalry, followed by
tanks, are already converging on his aircraft from the
woods, naturally intent on capturing the crew. The
Aircobras are now attacking us furiously from above.
I call out:

"Someone must land at once. You know I am no longer allowed to."

I have a horrible feeling, because I have been expressly forbidden to land and it goes against the grain to consciously disobey orders. We are still banking low above the fallen aircraft; Fickel and Bartsch down there can surely not imagine that anyone can land safely under the circumstances. The Soviets are gradually closing in and still no one sets about landing; out-manoeuvring the fighters makes full demands on every crew's attention. The decision to land myself in spite of everything is a hard one to make, but as I see it, if I do not act now my comrades are lost. If it is at all possible for anyone to rescue them, I have the best chance of anybody. To disobey an order is, I know, unforgivable, but the determination to save my comrades is stronger than my sense of duty. I have forgotten everything else, the consequences of my action, everything. I must bring it off. I give my orders:

"7 Flight: you are to attack cavalry and infantry at low level. 8 Flight: you are to circle at moderate height to cover Fickel and me. 9 Flight: you are to stay up and divert fighters from this intended manoeuvre. If fighters dive, then 9 Flight is to attack them from above."

I fly very low over the scene of the forced landing and select a patch of ground which may serve, with a bit of luck, to land on. Slowly I open the throttle; now we are over the second ditch. Throttle back, a terrific jolt, for an instant my tail is in the air, then I come to a stop. Fickel and Bartsch run for their lives. They are quickly alongside. Ivan's bullets have so far not hit anything that matters. Both are in behind, I open the throttle. I am seething with excitement. Can I make it? Will my aircraft become airborne before it hits an obstacle on the ground and is smashed to pieces? Now comes a ditch. I snatch up the aircraft, clear it, and again my wheels lightly bump the ground. Then she stays up. Slowly the tension eases. The squadron closes up and we get home without loss.

Rudel's travelling circus has taken up a pitch on a stubble field near the town of Wenden, not far from the Latvian-Esthonian frontier. Field Marshal Schoerner has been trying his hardest all this time to get my squadron into his sector with the result that we are now up here on the Courland front. We are barely installed on our cornfield when the inevitable cake arrives with the Field Marshal's compliments; no matter where I turn up in his command one of these fabulous cakes always appears, usually with a T 34 in sugar icing and the number, whatever it is at the time, of tanks I am credited with. The cake is now piped with the figures 320.

The general situation up here is as follows: in the Tuckum area we have launched an attack to re-establish the broken communications with the rest of the East Front. It is delivered by the assault group under the Command of the distinguished Colonel Count Strachwitz, and is successful. The Soviets are, however, making a persistent effort to indent our front on the east of Courland. This sector has long been a thorn in their side. Hitherto they have been held by the unbounded gallantry of our German soldiers despite their immense numerical superiority. At this particular moment this sector is again being subjected to unusually violent pressure; it is to relieve this pressure that Field Marshal Schoerner has called for our support. On our very first sorties we observe that the front lines here are not too fluctuating; the Red positions everywhere are well fortified, their camouflage is excellent, their A.A. batteries well sited quite close to the front line and everywhere strong. Enemy activity in the air is constant and lively. Hordes of enemy fighters and very few of our own formations, if only because of the difficulties of bringing up supplies. Stores of petrol, bombs and equipment must always be immediately available when we require them and demand much transport space. The bread we eat here is bitterly earned, no matter in which direction we fly, whether to the east or the south of the pocket, on the Tuckum front or where the main thrust of the Russian offensive is aimed at Reval via Dorpat. In several sorties we are successful in destroying a big motorized convoy, including escorting tanks, which had reached the gates of Dorpat, so that this break-through was checked and could be finally sealed off by the army. Where do they get these endless masses of men and material from? It is positively uncanny. The lorries we have shot up are mostly of American origin. Only occasionally among the tanks have we come across small groups of Shermans. The Russians do not even need these American

**Sherman tank**

tanks, for their own are better adapted to the fighting conditions in Russia and their production is fabulous. These enormous quantities of material bewilder and often depress us.

We often encounter American types of aircraft, especially Aircobras, King Cobras and Bostons. The Americans are aiding their ally tremendously with motor vehicles, but also particularly in the air. Is it in their own interest to give the Russians so much help? We often argue this question.

One morning at half past two Flg./Off. Weisbach, my Int. Ops. officer, wakes me. Field Marshal Schoerner wishes to speak to me urgently. For a long time I have had my telephone disconnected during the night as I have to take off early and must have a good night's rest. So my Int. Ops. officer who has not to fly the next morning receives all night calls, but for the Field Marshal I am always there. He does not beat about the bush—that is not his way.

"Can you take off at once? Forty tanks with motorized infantry have broken through. Our units in the front line have let themselves be overrun and want to close the gap again this evening. But this Russian force has driven a deep wedge into our positions and must be attacked to stop them expanding the break-through area; if they can do that they may cause the greatest damage to our supply lines in the back army zone." It is the same old story. I have been in Schoerner's sector too often to be surprised. Our brothers-in-arms in the front line lie down and let the tanks walk over them, and expect us to pull the chestnuts out of the fire. They leave us to deal with the enemy forces in their rear, hoping to be able to seal up the gap the same evening or in a couple of days, thus rendering the encircled enemy harmless. Here in Courland this is especially important because any major penetration may lead to the collapse of the whole front.

After a quick consideration I tell the Field Marshal: "It is still pitch dark and a sortie now would have no chances of success, for I must have daylight for low level attacks on tanks and lorries. I promise to take off at dawn with my 3 squadron and the anti-tank flight for the map square you have given me. Then I will call you immediately and let you know how things look." According to what he has told me the Reds have infiltrated westward into a lake district and are at the moment, with their armoured spearhead, on a road running between two lakes. In the meantime I instruct Flg./Off. Weisbach to collect met. reports from every possible source by telephone and to have us wakened accordingly so that, taking off in the twilight, we can be over the target at break of day. A brief telephone call to the skippers of the flights and now everything goes automatically. What you have practised a hundred times you can do in your sleep. The cook knows exactly when to put on the coffee. The senior fitter knows to a second when to parade the ground staff to get the aircraft ready. All that is necessary is the short message to the flights:

"Take off for first sortie 05.30 hours."

In the early morning a high fog hangs over the airfield at about 150 feet. In view of the urgency of our mission and hoping that it will be better in the target area we take off. We head S.E. at low level. Fortunately the country is as flat as a board, otherwise flying would be impossible. Visibility is hardly more than about twelve hundred feet, especially as it is not yet fully light. We have flown for something like half an hour when the fog cover drops to about ground level because we are nearing the lake district. Now I give the order to change formation owing to the difficulty of flying at 150-200 feet. For safety we fly abreast in line. I can no longer make out the shapes of my outside aircraft, they are moving in the ground mist and are swallowed up from time to time in the fog bank higher up. There is no possibility of delivering a successful attack in these weather conditions. If we were to drop our bombs it would have to be from so low an altitude that the splinters would damage our aircraft with resultant losses, which could serve no useful purpose, so that is out. Merely to have been in the target area will not help anyone today. I am glad when the last of us has landed safely. I inform the Field Marshal, and he tells me that he has received the same met. reports from the front line.

At last, towards nine o'clock, the layer of fog above the airfield shreds out a little and lifts to 1200 feet. I take off with the anti-tank flight, accompanied by the 7th to deal with bombing targets. On the fringe of the fog bank we head S.E. again, but the further we fly in this direction, the lower the cloud base sinks again. Soon we are down once more to 150 feet, visibility is fantastically bad. There are hardly any landmarks and so I fly by compass. The lake district begins, the weather remains foul. I do not approach the point the Field Marshal has given me as the location of the spearhead directly from the N.E., but making a slight detour westward I fly past it, so that when I turn round to make the attack I shall be heading straight for home, a very necessary precaution in this weather. If the enemy is as strong as he has been described he is likely to have a corresponding A.A. strength. There is no question of coming in warily under cover of hills or trees because my approach is over water, consequently the ground defence must be a consideration in choosing my tactics. To keep out of sight by popping in and out of the clouds is not advisable for a whole formation because of the danger of collision so close to the ground, though it is possible for individual aircraft. Quite apart from this consideration, the pilots would then have to give their whole attention to their flying and would be unable to concentrate sufficiently on their objective.

We fly in low over the water from the south; it is dark and murky; I cannot distinguish anything more than 2000 to 2500 feet ahead. Now I see straight in the line of my flight a black moving mass: the road, tanks, vehicles, Russians. I at once yell: "Attack!" Already at almost point blank range the defence looses off a concentrated fire from in front of me, twin and quadruple flak, machine guns, revealing everything with a livid brightness in this foggy light. I am flying at 90 feet and have bumped right into the middle of this hornet's nest. Shall I get out of it? The others have fanned out on either side of me and are not so much the focus of the defence. I twist and turn in the craziest defensive manoeuvres to avoid being hit; I shoot without taking aim, for to balance my aircraft for a second in order to hit a definite target means being shot down for certain. Now I climb a little as I reach the vehicles

and tanks and soar over them, I feel I am sitting on
eggs and waiting for the smash. This is bound to end
badly; my head is as hot as the metal screaming past
me. A few seconds later a tell-tale hammering. Gadermann yells: "Engine on fire!" A hit in the engine. I
see that the engine is labouring with only a fraction of
its capacity. Flames lick the cockpit.

"Ernst, we are bailing out. I'll gain height a little
and fly on for as far as we can to get out of the way
of the Russians. I saw some of our own chaps not too
far from here." I try to climb—I have no idea of my
altitude. A dark patch of oil has spread over the inside
and the outside of the windows, I can no longer see a
thing and throw up the hood of the cockpit so as to be
able to see, but that is no good either, the flames outside screen my vision.

"Ernst, we must bail out now."

The engine stutters and rattles, stops, stutters again,
stops, stutters. . . . Our kite will be our crematorium on
this meadow. We must bail out!

"We can't," yells Gadermann, "we are only flying at
90 feet!" He can see from the back. He, too, has
thrown up the hood, it snaps the intercommunication
cord in two. Now we can no longer speak to each
other. His last words are: "We are over a forest!"—I
pull the stick for all I am worth, but the aircraft refuses
to climb. I know from Gadermann that we are flying
too low to bail out. Can we crash-land the Ju. 87?
Perhaps it is still possible, even if I can see nothing.
For that the engine must keep running, if only feebly.
It may come off provided the terrain is in any way
suitable.

I close the throttle slowly. As I feel the aircraft sink
I glance out sideways. I see the ground rushing by.
We can only be at 20 feet. I brace myself against the
shock. Suddenly we touch and I cut the ignition. We
crash. The motor stops. It must be the end of us. Then
comes a grinding crash and I know no more.

I am aware of the stillness round me—therefore I
am still alive. I try to reconstruct: I am lying on the

ground, I want to get up, but I cannot, I am pinned down, my leg and my head hurt me. Then it occurs to me that Gadermann must be somewhere. I call out:

"Where are you? I can't get out."

"Wait a second—perhaps we can manage it—are you badly hurt?" It takes some time before he hobbles up and tries to get to me through the wreckage. Now I understand what is causing me so much pain: a long piece of metal from the tail of the aircraft is skewering the lower part of my thigh and the whole of the tail is on top of me so that I cannot move. I can thank my stars that nothing is burning near me. Where can the burning parts have got to? First, Gadermann pulls the piece of metal out of my leg, then he extricates me from the other parts of the aircraft which are crushing me. It requires all his strength to heave them off. I ask:

"Do you think the Russians are already here?"

"It's hard to say."

We are surrounded by scrub and forest. Once I am up on my feet I take stock of the scene of wreckage: about a hundred yards away lies the engine, burning; fifty or sixty yards to one side the wings, one of them also smouldering. Straight in front of me, a good distance away, lies a part of the fuselage with the R/T operator's seat in which Gadermann was stuck. That is why his voice came from in front of me when I called out; normally it should have come from the other side because he sits behind me. We bandage our wounds and try to explain our luck in being still alive and relatively safe, for without a proper dressing I cannot contemplate escape as I am losing a lot of blood. Our ninety foot fall seems to have happened in the following stages: the main force of our impact was broken by the trees on the edge of the forest, then the aircraft was flung onto a patch of sandy soil where it smashed up and the different parts flew asunder as already described. We had both unstrapped our safety belts and were ready to bail out. I still cannot understand why I did not hit my head against the instrument panel. I was lying a long way behind the remains of my pilot's seat; I must therefore have been flung there with the tail. Yes—one must be born lucky.

There is a sudden rustling in the bushes; somebody is pushing his way through the undergrowth. We look in the direction of the sound with bated breath . . . then we heave a sigh of relief. We recognise German soldiers. They have heard the crash from the road, after hearing the noise of gunfire in the distance and shortly afterwards seeing a German aircraft on fire. They urge us to hurry.

"There are no more of our chaps behind us . . . only masses of Ivans. . ." One of them adds with a grin: "But I guess you noticed the Ivans yourselves," and throws a significant glance at the smouldering wreckage of our aircraft. We climb into the truck they have with them and off we go, hell for leather, heading northwest.

We are back with the squadron early that afternoon. No one had seen us crash as everybody had his hands full at the time. The first four hours of my absence have not occasioned much concern as I often have to bring down a gallant Ju. 87 onto its belly somewhere near the front line as a result of enemy action and then report my whereabouts by telephone. If more than four hours elapse, however, faces darken and faith in my proverbial and infallible guardian angel sinks. I ring up the Field Marshal; he, more than anyone, rejoices with me that I have got back again and, needless to say, gives notice that yet another "birthday" cake will be on its way over tonight.

The sky is now a brilliant blue, the last vestiges of the blanket of fog are dissipating. I report to the Field Marshal that we are about to take off again, I myself being particularly incensed against our Soviet friends. They or I: that is a rule of war. It wasn't me this time, logically therefore it must now be them. The wing has sent over their M.O. in a Fieseler Storch; he puts a fresh dressing on my wounds and declares that I have concussion. Gadermann has broken three ribs. I cannot say that I feel exactly in the pink, but my deter-

mination to fly outweighs every other consideration. I
brief the crews, assigning them their targets. We shall
attack the flak with all our bomber aircraft and when it
has been neutralised destroy tanks and vehicles in low
level attacks.

Quickly my squadron is airborne and heading S.E.
The lake district comes into view. We are flying at 6,600
feet. We make our approach from the S.W. so that we
can appear out of the sun; the A.A. gunners will have
difficulty in distinguishing us and we shall be better able
to pick out their guns if they are glittering in the sunshine. There they are, too, still on the same spot as before! Apparently they do not intend to make any further advance until reinforcements have arrived. We
bank round our objective, baiting the flak to open up
on us. The A.A. guns are partly mounted on lorries,
the rest have made themselves emplacements in a circle
round the vehicles. As soon as the fireworks have started
I briefly recapitulate the targets and then follows the
order to attack, beginning with the flak. I find this a
satisfaction because I owe it to them that a few hours
ago my life once again hung by a silken thread. We
anti-tank aircraft fly through the bomb smoke and
spurting clouds of dust and attack the T 34s. One has
to keep a sharp look-out not to fly into the exploding
bombs. The flak is soon silenced. One tank after another blows up, trucks catch fire. They will never reach
Germany. This spearhead has certainly lost its impetus.

We return home with the feeling that we have done
all that lies within our power. In the night the Field
Marshal rings up again to tell me that our comrades
on the ground have counter-attacked successfully, the
break-through has been sealed off and the encircled
enemy mopped up. He thanks us in the names of
his command for our support. I shall pass on his message to the squadron first thing tomorrow. It is always
our highest reward to hear from our brothers-in-arms
on the ground that our co-operation was indispensable
and made their own success a possibility.

Alarming reports reach us in Latvia that the Soviets
are driving into Rumania. We are transferred overnight
to Buzau, a town N. of Bucharest, our route being East
Prussia—Krakau—Debrecen: a wonderful flight
across Eastern Europe in brilliant Indian summer sunshine. The flight is made by the III Squadron with the
Wing staff, the II is in the Warsaw zone and the I
already in Rumania. At Debrecen a lot of time is wasted
refuelling so it becomes too late to take off for Rumania before dark. We have to cross the Carpathians
and I have no intention of losing a crew on a transfer
flight. So we stay the night at Debrecen, and at
my suggestion go for an evening bathe. There are
marvellous baths in the town, supplied by natural warm,
medicinal springs. We find women of all ages sitting
stolidly in the baths with handbags, books, needlework
or their lapdogs, to the delight and amazement of my
companions; this squatting in the baths with the interminable female gossip which is part of the routine is
their daily occupation. It is a strange spectacle for old
Russian campaigners to see such a collection of scant-
ily clad femininity.

The next morning we take off for Klausenburg, a
lovely old town where the Transylvanian Germans set-
tled centuries ago; that is why the natives here speak
German. We make only a short stop here to refuel, for
we are in a hurry. At the same time an American reconnaissance plane appears at about 20,000 feet which
means that a visit from American bomber formations
may be expected before very long. The flight over the
Carpathians to Buzau is grand, as is every flight above
beautiful mountain scenery in perfect weather. The
town now comes into view ahead of us; it used to be
an unimportant landing stage on the way up to the front
which ran a long way to the north of it, it is now an operational base. What has happened to the stable front
line Jassy—Targul—Frumos, and to Husi?

The aerodrome lies in the open country and offers no
possibilities of camouflage for our aircraft, and Ploesti,

the oil centre of Rumania, which is quite close, is being attacked incessantly by American bombers with very strong fighter protection; the fighters can afterwards turn their attention to us, in as far as we may be thought worth a plastering. The number of American fighters sent up to escort a bomber formation on every sortie here is greater than the total German fighter strength on the whole front.

As I come in to land I see the roads leading to the aerodrome are packed with endless streams of Rumanian military trekking southward; in places convoys are halted by traffic jams. Heavy artillery of all calibres are among them. But there are no German units there. I am witnessing the last act of a tragedy. Whole sectors were held by Rumanian units which have ceased to offer any resistance whatever and are now in full retreat. The Soviets are at their heels. Where the front line ran the German soldier fights and stands his ground, and will therefore be cut off and taken prisoner. He does not think it possible that our Rumanian allies will let the Russians invade Rumania without a fight and expose their people to this gruesome fate; he just does not believe it.

After landing our aircraft are immediately got ready for operations while I report to my old wing. They are glad to have us back with them. They think we are going to have our hands full. The Russian tanks are already up to Foscari, their objective being the quick capture of Bucharest and Ploesti. Further north, German units are still putting up a fight in the Southern Army Group.

In the meantime our aircraft have been got ready and we take off at once, flying high and following the main road north to Foscari. Six miles south of this town we observe gigantic clouds of dust: if that is not already the tanks—it is! We attack; they leave the road and scatter in the fields. But that does not save them. We shoot up some of them, then go back for fresh ammunition and continue our engagement with the same

column. Wherever you look, masses of men and material, all Russian, mostly Mongolians. Are their reserves
of manpower so inexhaustible? We get fresh practical
evidence that the productive capacity of the U.S.S.R.
has been greatly underestimated by everybody and that
no one knows the true facts. The masses of tanks,
time and again unimaginable in their number, are the
most convincing proof of this. Many motor vehicles are
also of American origin. One sortie follows hard upon
another, from dawn till dusk, as during all these years.

It is one of the last days of August. I take off early in
the morning to fly into the area where the Reds have
broken through in the north and have climbed to 150
feet above my own aerodrome. Suddenly the flak opens
fire; it is manned by Rumanians who are supposed to
defend our airfield against attacks by Russian and
American aircraft. I look in the direction of the bursting
shells and search the sky for enemy bombers. Have the
Americans got up so early this morning? I bank over
the runway with my formation so as to wait for further
developments under the protection of our own A.A.
defence. Curiously, the puffs of the bursting shells have
shifted lower down and some of them are unpleasantly
close to my aircraft. I look down at the firing batteries
and see that the guns are swiveling round to follow our
manoeuvres; one burst just misses me. There is not an
enemy plane in sight. Now there is no longer any
doubt, the flak is firing at us. It is quite inexplicable to
me, but it must be so. We fly north on our mission
against the Soviet offensive which is pushing on in force
from the area Husi—Barlad—Foscari.

On our return to the aerodrome I am prepared for
any further flak antics on the part of the Rumanians;
my ground control has already told me as we fly back
that the guns were aimed at me. From now on, Rumania is at war with us. We at once come in at low
level, landing singly. Individual A.A. guns again open
fire on us, but with no more success than before. I im-

mediately go to the telephone and get put through to the Rumanian Air Commodore Jonescu. He is in command of Rumanian air force units, including flak, and I know him well personally from Husi, he wears German decorations. I tell him I have to assume that the unfriendly attentions of this morning were meant for me and my squadron, and ask him if this is so? He does not deny it; he says that his A.A. gunners have seen a German fighter shoot down a Rumanian courier plane and that consequently, even here, they are greatly incensed and are firing at all German aircraft. He does not yet make any mention of the state of war existing between Germany and Rumania. I reply to his complaint that I have not the least intention of standing for this nonsense and that I was going out on another sortie against the Russians N. of Ramnicul Sarrat. Now, however, I propose first to bomb and machine gun the flak on our aerodrome with my Stuka squadron in order to eliminate the possibility of any interference with our start. With the other squadron we shall attack his staff headquarters; I know exactly where they are.

"For God's sake don't do that. We have always been the best of friends and we cannot be held responsible for the actions of our governments. I made you a proposition: we will neither of us do anything and, as far as we are concerned, the declaration of war does not exist. I give you my personal guarantee that not another shot will be fired in my command against your Stukas."

He reasseverates his old friendship for me and his friendly feelings towards us Germans in general. With this a separate peace enters into force for both of us, nor have I any further grounds for complaint. A curious situation: I am here alone with my flying personnel on this aerodrome in a country at war with us. Two Rumanian divisions with all their equipment, including heavy artillery, surround our airfield. Who is to stop them liquidating us overnight? In the hours of darkness this is a very uncomfortable predicament, in the daylight we are strong again. Even two divisions are not likely to show themselves too aggressive against my Stukas when they are so concentrated and exposed in this open country.

Our store of bombs and petrol on the aerodrome are running low, and no supplies are reaching us as Rumania can no longer be held. Our only chance is to move to the other side of the Carpathians and to attempt there to form a new front out of the remnants of our armies which are able to fight their way out of Rumania, and such other troops as can be scraped together anywhere as reserves. It is perfectly clear that our heavy artillery will never get across the Carpathians, but will be left behind in Rumania. If only a large part of our gallant army could extricate itself from this witches' cauldron of treachery for which the Rumanian government is to blame! Weapons can be replaced, however difficult it may be, but men never! Our ground staff gets ready to take the road over the Bazau pass; we use up the last drop of petrol attacking the Russian spearhead which has thrust closer and closer to Buzau. Partly, our missions take us far behind the Russian lines to relieve German units which are still engaged in bitter fighting here. It is a pitiful spectacle, enough to drive one to desperation, the way these veterans of the Russian campaign, surrounded by the enemy, still butt their heads against an oncoming wall of vastly superior numbers until gradually they have nothing left to resist with save their small arms. The artillery have long since used up all their ammunition, soon they will not have even a rifle or revolver cartridge. To attack and attack again is the only way to endure it. A little Stalingrad.

Now our stores on the aerodrome are finally exhausted and we fly west over the Carpathians to our new operational base at Sächsisch-Regen in Hungary. In this little town almost everyone speaks German; it is a citadel of the Transylvanian Germans. Here there is a German church and German schools; as one walks through the town one never has the feeling that one is

not in Germany. It nestles picturesquely between
chains of hills and little mountains, with large tracts of
woodland in the vicinity. Our airfield is on a kind of
plateau with woods on either side; we are billeted in
the town and in neighbouring purely German villages
N. and N.E. of it. Our operations at the moment are
directed against the enemy pushing across the Carpathian passes from the east. The country offers excellent
defensive positions, but we have not the strength to hold
it, having lost the essential heavy artillery in Rumania.
Even the most favourable terrain cannot be defended
against the most modern weapons by heroism alone.
We make low level attacks on the Oitoz Pass and the
Gymnoz Pass and the mountain roads to the north of
them. I have had experience of mountain flying in the
Caucasus, but the valleys here are extremely narrow,
particularly at the bottom, and it is necessary to gain
considerable height before one can turn round in them.
The roads over the passes are tortuous and for long
stretches are engulfed in cuttings hewn out of the craggy
mountain slopes. As the vehicles and tanks generally
keep under the lee of the cliffs one has to be devilishly
careful not to bump into them here or there. If another
formation is out in the same area at the same time, perhaps approaching its target from the other side of the
valley and not so quickly recognized through the haze,
then for a fraction of a second "Death lays a bony finger on the joy-stick" when the one formation meets the
other flying in the opposite direction. That is a greater
danger than the flak, through this is by no means negli-
gible. It is partly sited on the mountain sides, to right
and to left of the roads over the passes, because the enemy flak has realised its relative ineffectiveness if it
remains with the convoys on the road while we, for instance, attack a unit lower down from behind another
group of rocks. There is for the time being not much
fighter opposition. Are the Russians so slow in getting
the Rumanian airfields in operation? I doubt it, because
they have plenty of supply lines and the available airfields, at Buzau, Roman, Tecuci, Bakau and Silistea,

are perfectly situated and amply sufficient for this battle. Presumably the Ivans do not take any too kindly to mountain flying; they seem especially shy of low level flying in the valleys because of the possibility of suddenly running into a cul de sac blocked by a sharply rising mountain. I gained the same impression two years ago in the passes and valleys of the Caucasus.

I receive orders at this time to take over the command of the Wing and to relinguish my 3rd Squadron. As my successor as commander of the old squadron I put up the name of Flt./Lt. Lau; he served with it in Greece in the battle with the English fleet and distinguished himself there. After the first phase of the Russian campaign he was seconded for staff duties and is now back at the front. As far as operational flying is concerned the change hardly affects me; I have all types of utilisable aircraft put on the Wing staff strength so that I may be able to fly with one or other of my units at any time.

One day at the beginning of September I am out early with my 3rd Squadron, the 2nd accompanying us as escort; I myself am tank-hunting in the Oitoz Pass with an anti-tank aircraft. The situation up there does not look too pretty. I decide, therefore, to take off again as soon as we return in my FW 190. In the meantime the others can have their aircraft serviced for the next sortie. Plt./Off. Hofmeister has one ready to take off and accompanies me as scout.

We fly back to Oitoz, make low level attacks and reconnoitre the state of affairs in all the Carpathian passes and on the heights, from which we gain an overall picture of the general situation in our sector. I return, literally without a drop of petrol or a round of ammunition, to our airfield, where I see forty silvery shining aircraft flying towards me at the same altitude. We race close past each other. No deception is any longer admissible. They are all American Mustangs. I call to Hofmeister: "You are to land at once." I lower my undercarriage, my landing flaps, and am down before the Mustang formation has time to turn round and attack.

The gliding in to land was nervous work, for this is the moment when your aircraft is absolutely defenceless and there is nothing you can do but wait patiently until you come to a stop. Hofmeister has evidently not come down as quickly as I have; I have lost sight of him. I am still taxying in at speed when looking out I see the Mustangs coming in for the attack and one of

**P 51 Mustang**

them heading straight for my aircraft. I hurriedly throw up the cockpit hood—I must still be moving at about 30 m.p.h.—climb out onto the wing and drop off onto the ground, and lie there flat, a few seconds before the Mustang's cannon begin to bark. My aircraft which has taxied on by herself for quite a distance catches fire in the first attack. I am glad I am no longer in her.

We have no flak on the airfield, because no one had anticipated or been prepared for our withdrawal to the Hungarian airfields. Our material is unfortunately so reduced that "all the airfields of Europe" cannot be provided with A.A. defence at the drop of a hat. Our enemies who have unlimited material at their disposal can site flak batteries at every street corner, we unhappily cannot. The Mustangs have dispersed over the whole airfield and are having some peacetime target practice. My squadron which should have refuelled and reloaded during my absence is still on the ground. A

number of transport planes which have brought up ammunition, petrol and bombs stand exposed in the open.
Serviceable aircraft are in improvised hangers in the
forest and are difficult to hit. But aircraft under repair
and transport planes with bombs and petrol fly up into
the air; the forty Mustangs' cannon keeps up an unbroken tattoo as they shoot everything they see in
flames. A helpless fury takes possession of me at having
to look on without being able to hit back; all round
the airfield, mushrooms of black smoke where isolated
aircraft are on fire. In this pandemonium one might
think the end of the world has come. Absurd as it must
sound, I try to snatch a wink of sleep; by the time I
wake up it will all be over. If the chap who keeps on
coming at me happens to hit me, it will be easier to
take if I am asleep.

After the Mustang pilot set fire to my aircraft in the
first attack he must have spotted me lying to the side of
her path. Perhaps he actually saw me drop off as he
flew in; at any rate he comes back at me again and
again with his cannon and machine guns. Apparently
he cannot see clearly through the window behind which
his sights are and through which he must aim; he probably cannot believe after every fly-in that he has not hit
me, for after coming in once or twice he roars over
me obliquely, dipping his aircraft, at 12-15 feet and
takes a look at me. I lie flat on my stomach all the time
hugging the pock-marked grass; I have not budged except to turn my head slightly to one side so as to squint
at him through my lowered eyelids. Every time he
comes in at me from in front earth and sand from his
bullets bespatter me right and left. Will he hit me the
next time? To run for it is out of the question, for everything moving is instantly fired on. So it goes on for
what seems to me an eternity. Now I feel sure that he
has run out of ammunition, for after skimming once
more obliquely over me he flies off. His colleagues
have also used up their ammunition; very profitably, it
must be admitted. They reassemble above the airfield
and fly away.

Our airfield looks a terrible mess, especially at first
sight. The first thing I do is to look for Plt./Off. Hofmeister. His aircraft is lying on the perimeter of the
field; he must have been slower in landing and was
caught on the way down. He is wounded; one foot has
to be amputated. Fifty aircraft are burning and exploding on the airfield, luckily only a few of my serviceable
planes which, well covered as they were, were not an
easy target. Now I am told when visiting each unit in
the forest that during the attack the ground personnel
kept up an uninterrupted small arms fire, as ordered,
with MP-40s, rifles, machine guns and revolvers. Four
Mustangs lie near the airfield. Seeing that we had no
flak this is a gratifying achievement. The Mustangs
have not had their safe target practice so gratuitously
after all. A few days later A.A. batteries arrive for my
airfield and raids as successful as this one are not likely
to be repeated.

German aircraft types often appear in our area flown
by Rumanians whom we have equipped with them.
They now bear the Rumanian markings and are flying
on the Russian side. The Rumanian operational base is
not very far from us. We therefore spend two days
making low level attacks on their airfields in the area
Karlsburg, Kronstadt and Hermannstadt. Malicious
tongues among us suggest that we are trying to emulate
the Mustangs; they would have done it before. We destroy more than 150 aircraft on the ground, some of
them in the air; in any case they are mostly training
and courier planes, but even so are of use for training
the Rumanian air force. Success in attacks of this kind
is to a very great extent dependent on the strength of
the enemy defence.

The fighting in Rumania is at an end. The Soviet
floods pour in over the whole country to try to force a
passage into Hungary at every possible point. Tightly
packed convoys are at this moment streaming through
the Roter-Turm Pass in the direction of Hermannstadt.

Sorties against this invading spearhead are particularly difficult because this army is very strongly defended against air attack. On one flight over the northern end of the pass 4 cm. flak rips off the cockpit hood of my FW 190 and I find myself suddenly sitting in the open. Luckily none of the splinters wounds me.

The same evening my intelligence officer tells me that he listens almost every day to the radio propaganda broadcasts in German, atrocity-stories about German soldiers and incitement of the guerillas. The broadcaster always begins: Kronstadt calling. After communicating with the group the first attack on this radio station is fixed for tomorrow; it must be possible to deal with these provocateurs. At day-break we set course for Kronstadt, an old settlement of the Transylvanian Saxons. The town shimmers straight ahead in the morning mist under the first rays of the sun. We do not need to fly over it; the transmitting station with its two tall masts stands on a main road about five miles northeast. Between the high masts is a little building, the nerve centre of the whole transmitting organism. As I fly in, preparatory to going into a dive, I see a motor car drive out of the courtyard of the building. If I could be sure its passengers were the men who are instigating the partisans to stab us in the back it would be worth a little extra effort to catch them. The car disappears into a wood and sees our attack on the transmitting station from afar. One has to be careful not to dive too low in this attack because the masts are connected by many cables and it is easy to fly into them. The little building is centered in my sights, I press the button, pull out and circle round the masts, waiting to see the result and for my squadron to reform. By chance one of my little 35 lb. bombs has hit the tip of one of the masts; it snapped and bent at a right angle. There is nothing more to be seen of the building down below as the bombs have done their work. They will not be broadcasting their vicious propaganda from here for quite a while. With this comforting thought we return to base.

The increasing pressure on the Carpathian passes shows more and more clearly the extent of the damage to our strength caused by the Rumanian débâcle. The Soviets have advanced a long way beyond Hermannstadt; they are nearly at Thorenburg and are trying to capture Klausenburg. Most of the units in this sector are Hungarian, chiefly the first and second Hungarian armoured divisions. There are practically no German reserves available to form a backbone of resistance in this important sector. This Soviet advance will imperil the German units holding the Carpathians far to the north. They will have to abandon their positions in the passes with serious consequences because the Carpathians, being a natural fortress, are the key to the Hungarian plains and it will be extremely difficult to hold them with our diminished strength. For the most part the Soviets have had a soft job the last few weeks, for they are advancing through an "allied" Rumania where a coherent German resistance has been impossible. Our motto has been: "Get out of Rumania; next stop the Carpathians." But Rumania has an elongated frontier and this means an extension of our already too thinly defended front.

We move back for a few days to an airfield west of Sächsisch Regen from where we make almost daily sorties over the Thorenburg area. For the first time since goodness knows how long the Iron Gustavs again participate in the fighting on the ground. On every sortie we stay in the target area as long as our petrol lasts, always hoping for an encounter with our competition from the other side. The 3rd Squadron does the bombing, escorted by the 2nd with the Wing staff and myself in FW 190s. During this phase we are successful in shooting down a large number of Russian attack planes and fighters. The skipper of my 2nd Squadron, Flight Lieutenant Kennel, who has the Oak Leaves, has particularly good hunting. It is not actually our business as dive bombers and attack aircraft to shoot down enemy aircraft, but in the present crisis it seems to me very important for our comrades on the ground that

we should master the enemy's air force. So our expert
tank marksmen also engage aircraft, and with excellent
results. These operations show us old Ju 87 fliers very
clearly that the hounds have a better time of it than
the hare. None the less we still swear by our old
kites.

In September 1944 the battle for the Hungarian
plains becomes an actuality. As this moment the news
of my promotion to Wing Commander reaches me. The
Wing staff with ground personnel is stationed for a short
time at Tasnad, South of Tokay. The 1st and 2nd Squadrons with their operational elements and myself S.E. of
Tasnad, the 3rd Squadron moves into the Miskolcz
area where they are seriously hampered by airfield conditions: the whole surrounding country, including the
roads leading to the airfield, have been turned into a
swamp by torrential rain.

Our stay is only a short one here, where we are able
to put up a fight in the area Grosswardein—Cegled—
Debrecen. The Russian hordes move fast, almost exclusively by night. They remain stationary during the day
well camouflaged in the woodland near the roads or in
maize fields, or keeping under cover in the villages.
Bombing and aerial attack becomes of secondary importance to reconnaissance, for targets must be recognized before it is possible to do any vital damage.
There is at present no cohesion on the German front;
there are merely isolated battle groups hastily improvised by welding together units which have either
fought their way back from Rumania or have previously formed part of the lines of communication
troops in Hungary. These units are a medley of all
branches of the army. At special focal points the names
of crack formations appear: infantry regiments with
great traditions, armoured divisions, S.S. formations, all
old acquaintances of ours and friends with whom we
have shared the hardships of the arduous years in
Russia. They love and esteem their Stukas and we feel
the same. If we know that one of these units is below

us we can be sure there will be no untoward surprises. We know most of their flying control officers personally, or at any rate their voices. They indicate to us every nest of resistance however small, and we then attack them with everything we have got. The ground units follow up our attack with lightning speed and sweep everything before them. But the enemy's numerical superiority is so immense that the biggest local successes are merely a drop in the bucket. The Russians are established to right and left of these engagements and we have not soldiers enough to hold them there, and another break-through follows with the result that even those units who are standing firm are compelled to retire lest their line of retreat be cut.

This happens here time and again until we are back on the Theiss which is to be held as a new defence line. This river is narrow, and in a war with modern technical resources does not represent much of an obstacle. At Szeged the Russians have very soon gained a strong bridgehead which we are unable to dent, and from which they make a swift thrust N.W. towards Kecskemet. My Wing has moved back once again and we are now at Farmos, W. of Szolnok, on the railway line from Szolnok to Budapest. Our airfield is frequently visited by four-engined American bombers which have hitherto concentrated their attentions on the railway bridge at Szolnok.

We have no complaints about our rations here because Niermann has obtained permission to shoot game and one can almost speak of a plague of hares. Every day he returns with a big bag; Fridolin is sick of the very sight of a hare. Sometimes now there is a real nip in the air, the year is making giant strides towards the winter. When taking my evening cross country run in the neighbourhood of Farmos I succumb to the fascination of the plains in a way I would not have thought possible for a mountaineer like myself.

We are out mostly in the vicinity of the Theiss beyond the river, but also on our side of it as the Soviets have succeeded in forming bridgeheads on the west bank at several places. Our targets, as in the case of all previous river crossings, are concentrations of material on the river bank and on the approach roads, in addition to the constantly newly built bridges and the traffic across the river which is partly carried out with very primitive methods. Rafts, old sailing craft, fishing boats and private pleasure boats all ply across the narrow Theiss. Ivan has lost no time in collecting together this heterogenous ferry service. It is chiefly active at first in the area between Szeged and Szolnok, later also further north. The creation of many bridgeheads is always a warning that the Soviets are piling up material preparatory to a fresh advance. A minor offensive of our own is being successfully conducted in the area Szolnok —Mezotuer—Kisujzalas—Turkewe with the object of upsetting these preparations. We fly incessantly in support of it. The new Russian assault on the Theiss is considerably delayed and weakened by this interruption of their lines of communication, at least in this northern sector, but they are able to keep expanding the big bridgehead at Szeged and joining it up with a smaller one further north.

At the end of October the offensive is launched from the whole of this area; it begins with a thrust N.W. and N. from E. and S.E. against Kecskemet. Its objective is clear: to achieve the collapse of our defence line on the Theiss and to push forward across the plain as far as the Hungarian capital and the Danube. Ivan is extremely active in the air. He appears to have occupied the whole batch of airfields round Debrecen, and we are again in action against far superior numbers thereabouts. We are further handicapped by the loss of a number of aircraft shot down by flak, and supplies and replacements leave much to be desired. The Soviets cannot claim the credit for our predicament; they can thank their Western allies who have seriously imperilled our communications by their four-engined attacks on railway stations and towns. The patrolling of railway lines and roads by American Jabos does the rest.

We lack the indispensable means of protecting our traffic routes owing to shortage of man-power and material. With the few aircraft left to my wing, including the anti-tank flight, I often take off on a sortie in the area S.E. of Kecskemet. Our aircraft strength, for the reasons set forth above, has been so greatly reduced that one day I go out alone, escorted by four FW 190s to attack the enemy's armour in this area. As I approach my objective I can hardly believe my eyes; a long distance north of Kecskemet tanks are moving along the road; they are Russians. Above them, like a bunch of grapes, hangs a dense umbrella of Soviet fighters protecting this spearhead. One of the officers escorting me knows Russian and promptly translates for me everything he understands. The Soviets are again using almost the same wave length as ourselves. They are yelling at one another and making such an appalling din that it is a wonder anyone understands a word the other is saying. My interpreter in the 190 makes out this much:

"Calling all Red Falcons—a single Stuka with two long bars is coming in to attack our tanks—we are sure it is the Nazi swine who shoots up our tanks—there are some Fockes with him (my escort). You are all to attack the Stuka, not the Fockes—he must be shot down today!"

During this pandemonium I have long since come down and made an attack. One tank is on fire. Two FW 190s are weaving above me trying to draw off a few Lag 5s. The two others stick to me, manoeuvring as I do; they have no intention of leaving me alone which is bound to happen if they engage in aerial combat with any Ivans. Twenty or thirty Lag 5s and Yak 9s now turn their attention to us; apparently the control officer on the ground directing the fighters is near the tanks, for he yells like a stuck pig: "Go on, go on and shoot the Nazi swine down. Don't you see one tank is already on fire?" For me this is the surest confirmation of my success. Every time one of them attacks I make a sharp turn just as he is bearing down on me; his speed

prevents him from following my manoeuvre and he
loses his firing position because he is carried out of
range. I then bank round again and come in behind
him, even if at some distance away. Although I am
sorry to waste my anti-tank ammunition I fire two 3.7
cm. shells after him; of course I shall want them later
for other tanks. Even if they now miss their mark the
chap they were intended for cannot have failed to observe their trail and he gets a shock at seeing these fire
balls streak close by him. Now again one of those I have
fired at yells: "Look out—be careful—didn't you see?
The Nazi swine is firing back. Look out." He bellows
as if he had already been shot down. Another, certainly
the leader of the formation:

"We must attack him from different angles simultaneously. Rendezvous over the village for which I am
now heading. We will discuss what is to be done."

Meanwhile I attack another tank. So far they have not
run for cover, doubtless believing that they are sufficiently protected by their fighters. Again one bursts
into flame. The Red Falcons are circling over the village
and making the craziest hullabaloo; they all want to
give advice on the best way to shoot down my Ju. 87.
The control officer on the ground rages, threatens,
asks whether they have not seen that four tanks are already burning. Now they come back again, from different angles in fact, and I am glad that my fifth tank
has used up my last round of ammunition, for if we
keep up this game much longer one cannot count on a
happy ending. The sweat has been pouring off me all
the time though it is very cold outside; excitement is
more warming than any fur jacket. The same is true
of my escort. Flying Officers Biermann and Kinader
are less afraid of being shot down themselves than of
failing in their duty to protect me, yet it is more than
likely that one or other of the Ivans may say to himself: if I cannot bring down the Stuka with the bars
as ordered, I can at least have a go at the Fockes. We
set course for home; the Ivans do not stay with us very
long before turning back. For quite a while we still hear

the reproachful bellowing of the control officer on the ground and the Red Falcons making their excuses.

Often nothing stands in the way of the Russian advance apart from local units thrown together in some critical emergency and frequently composed of airfield and flak personnel and army service corps troops. We lack men and material: the old story, all over again. Individual gallantry and isolated actions may delay but cannot entirely check the advance of colossal numbers of men and material. The few crack units we still have left cannot be everywhere at the same time. Nevertheless our comrades on the ground are putting up an inconceivably gallant fight. The Theiss front is no longer tenable; the next defence line has to be the Danube. I am disturbed by signs of a Soviet thrust in the extreme South through Fünfkirchen in the direction of Kaposvar; if it succeeds, then this new position is again in danger. It is only a very short time before my fears are confirmed.

# 15

## BATTLE FOR HUNGARY

It is one of our last days at Farmos. A message has just been received that Ivan had infiltrated with a strong armoured spearhead in the direction of the Matra Mountains and has reached the outskirts of Goengjes. Our troops, which have been outflanked, are anxious if possible to restore the situation and close the gap. The weather is bad, and we find this particularly trying because this part of the country is very hilly and the cloud cover is even lower than elsewhere. We leave Budapest to port and soon see the Matra Mountains ahead, and shortly afterwards the town of Goengjes. Fires are burning some miles to the south; it is apparent that something is going on there. Sure enough, tanks are travelling along the road, and they are certainly not German. As I make a wide sweep in that direction to obtain a general picture of the enemy's strength I am met by intense light and medium flak fire. We circle round the advance guard at low level. Right out in front of the T 34s and Stalins is a type of tank I have never seen before; nor have I yet come across it as an American model. I deal with this stranger first, and then turn my attention to the others. When five tanks are in flames I have used up all my ammunition. The anti-tank flight has also done an excellent job and it has been a bad morning for Ivan. We reform and head for home, being engaged for part of the way by Soviet Yak 9 fighters which have appeared on the scene but do us no harm.

We are within ten minutes of our base and well behind our own lines when it suddenly strikes me: how am I to describe the first tank I shot up when making out my report? Will my automatic camera have taken a good enough photograph for me to be able to say for certain what type of tank it was? It is very important that the general staff should be informed whether and

**Stalin tank**

what new types are appearing on any sector of the front; such information is an indication that new weapons are being put into production, or delivered from other countries. I must know what model that first tank was. So I tell the 3rd Squadron leader to take the formation home while I turn round and fly back to the tanks.

I throttle back a little and circle four or five times at 12-15 feet in a narrow radius round the mysterious steel monster and give it a leisurely examination from the closest proximity. To one side of it stands a Stalin, which has apparently just driven up from the rear of the party to see what has happened here. The strange tank is still burning. As I circle round it for the last time I see some Ivans crouching under the projecting chain guard of the Stalin behind a 13 mm. A.A. machine gun mounted on a tripod. Squeezed close against the tank with their heads down they look up at me and, seeing smoke come out of the muzzle of their machine gun, I perceive that they are busy firing at me. I am within about fifty, at the very most sixty yards range, but the variations caused by the wide arc I am describing are too great for them to make sure of hitting me, unless they are experienced gunners and have learnt just the right thing to do. I am still speculating in this fashion when two hammer blows strike my aircraft and I feel a searing pain in my left thigh. I struggle hard to overcome the blackness in front of my eyes and become aware that a wet, warm flow of blood is running down my leg. Gadermann sits behind me; I tell him, but he cannot do anything for me because it is impossible for him to get forward. I have no bandages with me. The country we are flying over is only thinly inhabited, the terrain not specially suitable for a forced landing. If we come down here goodness knows how long it will take to get proper medical aid, and I shall bleed to death. So I must try to reach Budapest twenty-five minutes away.

I can see that my strength is failing fast. The blood is still flowing freely . . . I have a queer feeling in my head . . . a sort of trance . . . but I keep on flying and feel that I still have control of my senses. I switch on the intercom, and ask Gadermann:

"Do you think I will pass out suddenly . . . or will my strength go on ebbing gradually?"

"You'll never reach Budapest . . . in all probability . . . but you won't faint suddenly."

The last words are a quick addition, presumably so as not to upset me.

"Then I'll go on flying . . . and chance it."

The throttle is forward as far as it will go . . . minutes of anxious tension. . . . I won't give in . . . I won't . . . there is the fighter airfield, Budapest . . . flaps down . . . throttle back . . . I am down . . . it's all over! . . .

I come to on an operating table in a private hospital. The nurses gathered round me are watching me with a peculiar look on their faces. Behind the surgeon, Professor Fick, stands Gadermann; he is wagging his head. He tells me afterwards that while I was under the anaesthetic I had just said some very curious things which did not seem to have exactly delighted the nurses. What can one do in a situation like that? Professor Fick explains that he has extracted a 13 mm. machine gun bullet which had entered my leg at an angle, another having passed clean through the flesh. He tells me I have lost a great deal of blood and that as soon as he has set my leg in plaster of Paris I must go into a nursing home on Lake Balaton to recuperate as quickly as possible under the best medical care and to give my wounds a chance to heal in peace and quiet. Fridolin has meanwhile arrived as well and curses me for having let my curiosity land me in this mess, but although he does not admit it he is glad it was no worse. He reports that we are to move back into the Stuhlweissenburg area, we ourselves will be at Boergoend. Now they hoist me onto a Storch ambulance plane and fly me to Hevis on Lake Balaton where I am admitted to Dr. Peter's sanatorium. I have already asked Professor Fick how long it will be before I am able to walk, or at least fly. His answer was ambiguous, presumably because he had been tipped off by Gadermann who has sufficient reason to know my impatient nature. I insist on Dr. Peter immediately taking off my bandage and telling me how long he thinks I shall have to remain here. He refuses to disturb the dressing, then after a good deal of argument he examines the wound and says:

"If there are no complications you will be on your back for six weeks."

Up till this moment I had not been depressed because of my wound, but now I feel that I am again out of everything, condemned to inactivity at a time when every able bodied man is needed. I could play merry hell I am so mad. That's a good one when my leg is in plaster of Paris and I can hardly move. But one thing I am sure off: I shall never stand it that long. No matter how good the nursing and the bodily rest may be for me, I shall never have any rest until I am back with the Wing and able to fly with it. Fridolin comes over from Boergoend and visits me every other day with a briefcase full of papers for me to sign and keeps me posted about the unit's operations, its worries and requirements. Between Farmos and our present airfield the Wing was temporarily stationed, for a few days only, one the aerodrome at Veces, a suburb of Budapest. Latterly bad November weather conditions have often prevailed, and despite the critical situation only very few sorties could be carried out. On the eighth day he visits me again with the news that the Soviets are attacking Budapest with strong forces, and have already established bridgeheads on this side of the Danube; worse still, a fresh offensive from the South towards Lake Balaton is aimed at thrusting a wedge between our lines. He is not a little astonished when I tell him that I have had enough of lying in bed and am going to get up and drive back with him to the wing.

"But . . ." He does not finish his sentence. He knows my obstinacy. The sister hears Fridolin packing my things and cannot believe her eyes when she puts her head in at the door to see what is going on. By the time Dr. Peter has been fetched he finds me ready to leave. I am well aware that he cannot accept the responsibility, I do not ask him to. He shakes his head as he watches the departure of our car which will bring us to our station in an hour.

We are billeted in the village, as at Farmos. The people are more than friendly, which is only to be expected seeing that they look to us to halt the Russians and to liberate their already partly occupied country. Dahlmann, my batman, has already prepared and heated a room in a tiny cottage, doubtless believing that it will at first be needed as a sickroom. A few days, and then the spell of bad weather ends. From the first day I am back in harness after my plaster of Paris bandage has been given some extra support. Locomotion is not exactly easy, but I manage. In the middle of December our airfield becomes more and more of a bog owing to heavy rain and snow, and we move again to Varpalota. This airfield is well situated on high ground and we are able to take off at any time.

My 3rd Squadron is eventually to be re-equipped with Focke Wulf 190s; in view of the situation I should not like to have it withdrawn from operations for any time because of this change of aircraft. Therefore one or two pilots in rotation are temporarily attached to the Wing staff, and between sorties I introduce them to the new type and teach them how to handle it. Each of them flies a number of circuits, varying according to his airmanship, and then I take him with me as No. 2 on operations. After fifteen to twenty sorties their initiation to the unfamiliar aircraft may be considered satisfactorily concluded, and other crews have their turn. In this way the 3rd Squadron is able to remain in action without interruption.

On their first operational flights the crews generally have to learn the hard way, for the defence is everywhere strong and, besides, they are still a bit scared of the new type, especially as they have no rear gunner to insure them against enemy fighter interference from behind. One his first sortie in a FW 190 Flg./Off. Stähler is hit in the engine by flak so that he has to come down at once. He succeeds in making a neat forced landing within our lines. Everything goes wrong on that day. I am just about to take off on a sortie with Flt./Lt. M., who is also having a course of instruction with me, when a strong formation of IL IIs with fighter escort flies past on the horizon at 1800 feet. It is a cold December day and it would take me some time to warm up the engine so as to get it running properly, but meanwhile Ivan is sure to have disappeared. Then it occurs to me that during the last few really cold days the mechanics have again been making use of the warming up apparatus which enables us to take off at once without having to let the engine run for a longer time than is usual. This apparatus depends on a special fuel preparation. I make a sign to M. to waste no time in filling up and to take off with me. Our bomb load is under our aircraft for the mission which has been planned, I do not want to leave the bombs behind for we have a mission to fulfil. Perhaps even with this load we can still overtake the IL II formation. M. is apparently flying a slow aircraft and lags behind, I gradually gain on the Iron Gustavs which cross their own lines when I am still eight hundred yards away. But I am pigheaded and determined to have a go at them, even though I am alone. With my FW 190 I am not afraid of the skill of the fighter pilots flying Lag 5s and Yak 9s. There is a sudden noise in my engine, a spurt of oil gums up everything so that I can no longer see out; in a twinkling all the cockpit windows are opaque. In the first instant I think that my engine has been hit by flak or a Russian fighter, but then I realise that it is a defect in the engine, causing a piston seizure. The engine is puttering and rumbling horribly, it may cut out altogether at any moment. The second I heard the noise I had put my nose down by a kind of reflex action and headed for our own lines. Now I must be over them. To bail out is out of the question with my plaster of Paris splint, quite apart from the fact that I am flying much too low. This aircraft will never be able to climb another foot. I throw off the hood in order at least to be able to see out at the side and to the rear. I am flying at 150 feet; there is still no terrain below me suitable for a forced landing; besides which I am anxious to come as near as possible to the airfield so as not to lose time in getting back to my unit. A church steeple whizzes past me very close; lucky it was not in my path. Obliquely ahead I see a road embankment; any second now I can expect the propeller to stop. I can only hope the aircraft will clear the embankment. I pull the stick and wait. Will she make it or not? She makes it! Now I touch down on the ground. Skidding and crunching over the hard-frozen earth the aircraft slides parallel with a broad ditch and comes to a standstill. Nothing has happened to my leg, my chief anxiety. I look out

over a silent, peaceful winter landscape, only the distant rumble of artillery reminds me that it is not yet
peace although Christmas is on the doorstep. I hoist
myself out of my seat with a glance at the smoking engine, and sit down on the fuselage. A car with two
soldiers is coming along the road. They first look me
over carefully to make sure I am not a Russian, for they
come down more often than we do on our side of the
line, and mostly shot down at that. The men lay a small
plank across the ditch and carry me to their car. An
hour later I am back on the airfield and ready for another sortie.

Our billets are in a barracks a few miles below the
airfield on the outskirts of Varpalota. The next day between sorties I am lying on my bed for a little rest
when I hear a roar of aircraft: those are no German
planes. At an angle through the open window I catch
sight of a Russian Boston formation flying at 1200 feet.
They are coming straight towards us. Now they are already screaming down, the bombs. Even with sound
legs I could not have been more quickly on the floor. A
heavy bomb bursts fifteen yards in front of my window
and blows to bits my B.M.W. car, which was waiting there for me. Dahlmann, who comes in at the door
opposite the window at that very moment to warn me
of the alert, suddenly finds the window frame round
his neck. He gets off with a shock but no further damage. Ever since he has taken to crawling about with
bent shoulders and a crab-apple face like a little old
man. Evidently he no longer thinks much of war and
we laugh every time we see this youngster in his new
role.

Presently, with our support from the air, there is a
lull in the Lake Balaton area, but to the East the Soviets have bypassed Budapest and reached the Gran
River north of the Danube. South of Budapest they have
pushed out of their bridgeheads, and co-operating
with forces thrusting N.W. from the south have gone
over to the offensive. The spearheads of their advance

are on the eastern edge of the Vecec mountains north of Stuhlweissenburg, so that Budapest is encircled. Some of our sorties are flown in this area or even further eastward. We try to disrupt their communications far behind the front in the Hadvan area, where Soviet supply trains are already running. In this rush of events we soon become maids of all work: we are dive bombers, attack planes, fighters, and reconnaissance aircraft.

# 16
## CHRISTMAS, 1944

The battle for the relief of Budapest is in full swing. We are now stationed at Kememed St. Peter in the Papa area. We, the flying personnel, have just got in from the airfield at Varpalota, and before we have even had time to settle down Fridolin pops his head in and asks: "Don't you chaps know it's only two days to Christmas?" He is right; according to the calendar it must be so. Take-off—sortie—land—take-off—sortie —land, that has been our rhythm; day in, day out—for years. Everything else is absorbed into this rhythm: cold and heat, winter and summer, weekdays and Sundays. Our lives are condensed into a few ideas and phrases which fill our minds and refuse to be dismissed, especially now that the war has indeed become a struggle for survival. One day follows another, the breath of today the same as that of yesterday. "Sortie!" "Where to?" "Against whom?" "Met." "Flak." These words and thoughts preoccupy the very youngest pilot just as they do the Wing Commander. Will it go on like this forever?

So the day after tomorrow will be Christmas. Fridolin with one of the administrative staff drives over to Group Headquarters to fetch our Christmas mail. Meanwhile greetings to the "Immelman Circus" come in even from army units. We return from our last sortie on Christmas Eve at five o'clock. The place looks really Christmassy, gay and festive, almost like home. As there is no large hall available, each flight has its own celebrations in the biggest room in their headquarters. I drop in on them all. Every unit observes the occasion in its own fashion, reflecting the personality of its skipper. It is jolly everywhere. I myself spend the greater part of Christmas Eve with the Wing staff company. Here, too, the room is festively decorated with mistletoe and holly, and cheerful in the light of many candles. Two large Christmas trees with a table covered with presents set up in front of them remind us of our childhood. My soldiers' eyes are bright pools of nostalgic dreams, their thoughts are with wife and child at home, with parents and families, in the past and in the future. Only subconsciously do we perceive among the green the German flag of war. It jerks us back to reality: we are celebrating Christmas in the field. We sing "Stille Nacht, Heilige Nacht" and all the other Christmas songs. The raucous military voices blend in a softer euphony. Then the great miracle happens in our hearts: the thoughts of bombs and targets, shells and flak and death are softened by an extraordinary sense of peace, of serene and soothing peace. And we are able to think of sublime and beautiful things with the same ease as we think of walnuts, punch and *pfefferkuchen*. The final echo of the lovely German Christmas carols has died away. I say a few words about our German Christmas, I want my men to see me today, above all, as their comrade, not their commanding officer. We sit together happily for another hour or two; then Christmas Eve is over.

St. Peter is kind to us on the first day of the holidays: there is a dense fog. From conversations over the telephone during Christmas I know that Ivan is attacking and that we are urgently needed, but flying is absolutely impossible. The next morning I play a short game of ice hockey with my men, which this time means standing in goal in my fur boots as with my five weeks old wounds I can do no more than hobble clumsily about. Skating is out of the question. In the afternoon I am invited with a few colleagues by the people on

which I am billeted to a shoot. I know very little about
this "common or garden" shooting on terra firma.
Our party consists of a large number of guns, but only a
very few beaters. The hares know that the odds are on
their side and invariably dart through the wide gaps in
our "pocket" in the nick of time. Wading through the
deep snow does not admit of any very rapid progress
either. My driver, L.A.C. Böhme, is on my flank. All of
a sudden I see a magnificent specimen of a hare break
out of cover in his direction. Pointing my gun, I swivel
round like a born hunter, close one eye, and . . .
bang! I pull the trigger. A body rolls over, not the hare,
but Böhme whom in my novice enthusiasm I have entirely overlooked. He is still mistrustful of my intentions, for he looks at me out of the snow with an expression of dismay and says reproachfully: "Really, sir!"
He had noticed my aim in time and thrown himself flat
in a flash. The buckshot missed him, but also the hare.
Afterwards I am more scared by what happened than
either of them. That would have been a Christmas surprise indeed. Another confirmation of the truth of our
old Stuka maxim: "Nothing comes off—except what
you have practised."

The following morning we have at last good flying
weather. Ivan is early abroad; he raids our airfield.
Again their bombing is pitifully bad, it is a disgrace.
Their low level attacks stop at 1200 feet; we suffer
practically no damage. We are out the whole of the
second holiday to relieve the ground forces up in the
N.E. on the River Gran and on the rest of the Budapest
front. Our peaceful Christmas mood has been dispelled.
The rigours of war envelope us again, the quiet cheer-
fulness of the peace of Christmas Eve has passed into
the limbo of yesterday.

Fierce battles are raging in the air and on the ground.
On our side fresh reinforcements have been thrown in,
all old acquaintances of mine—friends from the Eastern Front, tank-men who, like ourselves, are the High
Command's "fire brigade." Their task and ours will be
to "punch a way out" for those parts of our divisions

which are trapped in Budapest, to open a lane for them to rejoin the rest of the army. Together we should be able to pull the chestnuts out of the fire. Year in, year out, almost day by day, I have fought in every sector of the Eastern Front; I fancy that I have gained a fair knowledge of military tactics. Experience teaches that practice makes perfect; practical knowledge is the sole criterion of what is possible or impossible, good or bad. Through our daily flying we have learnt to know every ditch, every stretch of country thoroughly, we are constantly low above them. It is quite impossible to approve of the conduct of the battle here. Some of our armoured units have been broken up and the grenadiers which are part of them are being thrown in separately. The tanks, who have always worked with them as a team, feel at sea and uncertain of themselves without them; the troops which have been assigned to them have no practical experience of co-operating with tanks, and this may result in dangerous surprises. I fail to understand how such an order can have been given; moreover one could hardly imagine a worse choice than the sector selected for the offensive, because of marshes and other difficulties of terrain, when there are so many other favourable alternatives. The infantry, on the other hand, have to advance across flat, open country which is ideal for tanks, but no place for infantry. The enemy takes full advantage of all this and so our infantry is opposed to the Soviet steel monsters without tank support. Why these unnecessary losses? This is courting failure. Who issues these orders? We sit together of an evening brooding over these questions.

On 30th December a wireless signal is received ordering me to come to Berlin immediately and to report to the Reischsmarschall. I fume because I feel that now especially my presence here is indispensable during these difficult operations. I take off for Berlin the same day, going via Vienna and determined to be back with my comrades in two or three days. Orders are orders. The only luggage I take with me is a large despatch case

with a change of linen and toilet articles. In view of
the seriousness of the situation at the front I dismiss
the possibility of being kept in Berlin for longer.

On the way I already have an uncomfortable hunch
that I have not been sent for for anything pleasant.
When I was wounded the last time, in November, I
received another order grounding me in spite of which
I went up again as soon as I got out of hospital. Up till
now no one has taken the matter up and I had gradually
interpreted this silence as tacit acquiescence; but now, I
guess, the question has come to a head and I am going
to be put on the mat. I am flying to Berlin very reluctantly, knowing as I do that I shall never obey this order. I cannot bear to be merely looking on, giving advice or issuing orders at a time when my country is in
direct need, especially as my wide practical experience
gives me an advantage over others who lack this training. Success is the fruit of experience and commensurate
with it. In spite of having been wounded five times,
some of them seriously, I have always had the luck to
make a quick recovery and to be able soon afterwards
to pilot my aircraft again day after day, year in, year
out, up and down the Eastern Front—from the White
Sea to South of Moscow, from near Astrachan to the
Caucasus. I know the Russian front inside out. Therefore I feel an unremitting obligation to go on flying and
fighting until the guns are silent and our country's liberty is assured. Physically, I can do this because I have
a healthy constitution and a body trained by sport; my
fitness is one of the most valuable sources of my
strength.

After a short stay with friends in Vienna I land in
Berlin three hours later and immediately report by telephone to Karinhall. I would prefer to drive straight out
there, so as to be able to fly back without any loss
of time. To my bewilderment I am told to remain at
the Fürstenhof and to apply in the morning at the
Air Ministry for a pass to travel on the Reischsmarschall's special train which is leaving for the West. My
trip is going to be longer than I expected—so much is

clear. It does not seem to have anything to do with a reprimand.

We leave for the West the following evening from Grünewald station. This means I shall see the New Year in on board the train. I dare not let my thoughts dwell on my unit; if I do I shall see red. What does the year 1945 hold in store for us?

We are in the Frankfurt area early on 1st January. I hear the roar of aircraft and look out into the greying morning. An armada of fighter planes, flying low, roars past the carriage window. My first thought is: Americans! It is an age since I have seen so many of our aircraft in the sky at the same time. But this is unbelievable: they are all marked with the German swastika and are Me 109s and FW 190s. They are heading

**FW 190**

westward. Later I am to learn the nature of their mission. Now the train pulls up; it seems we are somewhere near Nauheim-Friedberg. I am met by a car and driven through a tract of forest to a building which resembles an ancient castle. Here I am greeted by the Reichsmarschall's adjutant. He tells me that the Chief has not arrived yet, I shall have to wait. He does not know what I am here for. I have no choice but to kick my heels here at Western G.H.Q.

I go for a walk for a couple of hours. What wonderful air in these German woods and hills! I fill my lungs with relish. Why have I been ordered here?—I have been instructed to be back at three o'clock, at which time the Reichsmarschall is expected. I hope I shall not be kept waiting before he receives me. He is not there when I return. Besides myself, a general has arrived, an old friend of mine from my Stuka training days at Graz. He tells me about today's operations, for the planning and conduct of which he is very largely responsible. Reports continually come in of large-scale attacks on airfields in Belgium and Northern France.

"The aircraft you saw this morning were part of one of the formations we have sent out to make low level attacks on the allied air bases. We hope to be able to destroy so many aircraft that the enemy's air superiority above their offensive, which has been halted in the Ardennes, will be neutralised."

I tell the general that such a thing would be impossible on the Eastern Front because the distances which would have to be flown over enemy territory are too great, and to fly at low level is merely inviting heavy losses from the very strong ground defence. Could it be different in the West? It seems improbable. If the Americans are successful with similar attacks over Germany this is only because we have not sufficient protection for our airfields and their approaches, for the simple reason that we cannot divert enough men and material for this purpose. He tells me that today all formations have clearly mapped low level approach routes. In the East we have long since ceased to develop practice from theory; we do just the opposite. One can do no more than give the formation leader his assignment; how he performs it is his affair, for it is he who has to carry it out. At the present time the war in the air has become so variable that one can no longer rely on theories; only formation leaders have the necessary experience at the critical moment and are likely to make the proper decisions. It is a good thing we realised this in the East in time, otherwise it is a sure thing that none of us would be flying any more. Besides, have they not yet grasped the fact that we are helpless against the enemy's masses of men and material?

For the enemy five hundred aircraft more or less on the ground is not decisive, as long as their crews remain in action. It would be infinitely better to use the fighters which have been saved up for so long over our own front to clear the air space above it. If we could remove for a while the nightmare of the allies' immense air superiority we could give our comrades on the ground a chance to get their second wind. And movements of troops and supplies behind the lines could be carried out unmolested. Any enemy aircraft we might destroy would in most cases be a genuine loss, because the crews would be lost with them.

All these reflections pass through my mind. A few hours later the final result of the operation confirms my misgivings. Five hundred allied aircraft have been destroyed on the ground; over two hundred and twenty of ours with their crews have failed to return. Among those lost today are veteran formation leaders, old timers of which so few are left. It saddens me. Tonight the operation will be reported to the Reichsmarschall and to the Supreme Commander as a great victory. Is this intentional deception, or exaggerated personal ambition?

The adjutant comes in and says to me:

"Wing Commander von Below has just rung up. He would like you to go over for a cup of coffee."

"But can I not report direct to the Reichsmarschall?"

"The Reichsmarschall is not here yet, and there is no reason why you should not pay this short visit to Wing Commander von Below."

I consider whether I ought to change, but decide against it because I would like to keep my last clean shirt for my interview with the Reichsmarschall.

A fairly long drive through the forest brings us into a town of huts and chalets, the Führer's Western H.Q. Over coffee I tell Wing Commander von Below about the latest happenings on the Russian front; after twenty minutes he leaves me, comes back at once and briefly asks me to follow him. Quite unsuspectingly I follow him through several rooms, then he opens a door, stands aside for me to pass and I am face to face with the Führer. All I can think of is that I have not put on a

clean shirt; otherwise my mind is a blank. I recognise
the other persons standing round him: the Reichsmarschall, beaming—very unusual of late—Admiral Dönitz, Field Marshal Keitel, the Chief of the General
Staff, Lieutenant General Jodl and a number of other
military notabilities including Generals from the Eastern
Front. They are all grouped round an enormous table
spread with a map showing the present situation in the
field. They look at me and this scrutiny makes me nervous. The Führer has noticed my embarrassment and
regards me for a while in silence. Then he offers me his
hand and praises my last operation. He says that in
recognition of it he is awarding me the highest decoration for bravery, the Gold Oak Leaves with Swords
and Diamonds to the Knight's Cross of the Iron Cross,
and is promoting me to the rank of Group Captain. I
have been listening to his words in a semi-daze, but
when he says with marked emphasis: "Now you have
done enough flying. Your life must be preserved for
the sake of our German youth and your experience,"
I am on the alert in a twinkling. This means I am to be
grounded. Goodbye to my comrades!

"My Führer, I cannot accept the decoration and
promotion if I am not allowed to go on flying with my
wing."

My right hand is still clasped in his, he is still looking
me in the eyes. With his left hand he gives me a black,
velvet lined case containing the new decoration. The
many lights in the room make the diamonds sparkle in a
blaze of prismatic colours. He looks at me very gravely,
then his expression changes, and he says: "All right,
you may go on flying," and smiles.

At this a warm wave of joy wells up in my heart and
I am happy. Afterwards von Below tells me that he
and the generals nearly had a stroke when I made my
proviso; he assures me that the sheet lightning in the
Führer's face does not always resolve into a smile.
Everyone offers his congratulations, the Commander in
Chief of the Luftwaffe with especial cordiality; he gives
me a hefty pinch in the arm from sheer delight. Admiral

Dönitz's congratulations are rather qualified, for he adds a trifle snappishly:

"I consider your persuading the Führer to allow you to go on flying unsoldierly. I have also had good U-boat captains, but sooner or later they have had to give up."

It is a good thing he is not my C.-in-C.!

The Führer takes me over to the map table and tells me that the conference they have just had concerned the situation at Budapest; I have come from that sector, have I not? He recapitulates the reasons given him for the not exactly satisfactory operation now in progress in the Budapest area, which has so far failed to affect a link-up with the encircled city. I gather that weather, transport and other difficulties have been offered as an excuse, but no mention has been made of the blunders which we see every day on our sorties: the splitting up of the armoured divisions and the choice of unsuitable terrain for both the tank and infantry assaults. I express my opinion, based on long experience of the Eastern Front and the fact that during this engagement I have flown as much as eight hours daily over this sector, mostly at low altitudes. They all listen to me in silence. After a short pause the Führer remarks, with a glance at the circle of his advisers:

"You see, this is how I have been misled—who knows for how long?"

He reproaches nobody although he knows the true circumstances, but it is evident that he resents the deception practised on him. With reference to the map he shows his willingness to regroup our forces for a fresh attempt to relieve Budapest. He asks me where I think would be the most favourable terrain for the armoured units to attack. I give my opinion. Later this operation is successful, and the assault group reaches the outposts of the defenders of Budapest who are able to break out.

When the conference is ended he takes me into his private study in an adjoining room, furnished in good taste and with utilitarian simplicity. I wished my comrades could be there and live through these hours with me, for it is because of their achievement that I am here. The Führer gives me a drink, and we talk of many things. He asks after my wife, our boy, my parents and my sisters. Having made the most detailed enquiries about my personal affairs, he begins to speak of his ideas of rearmament. Not unnaturally he starts with the Luftwaffe, dwelling particularly on the proposed modification of the aircraft we are using. He asks me if I still think it practicable to continue flying with the slow Ju. 87 now that the enemy's fighters are as much as 250 m.p.h. faster than they are. Referring to some blue prints and calculations he points out to me that a retractable undercarriage might increase the speed of the Ju. 87 by 37 m.p.h. at the very most; on the other hand, its diving performance would be disadvantageously affected. He solicits my opinion on every point. He discusses the minutest details in the field of ballistics, physics and chemistry with an ease which impresses me who am a critical observer in this department. He also tells me of his wish to have experiments carried out to test the feasibility of installing four 3 cm. cannon in the wings instead of the present two 3.7 cannon. He thinks that the aerodynamic qualities of our anti-tank aircraft would be very greatly improved by this change; the ammunition would have the same *Wolframkern* with the result that the total effectiveness of the aircraft as a weapon would certainly be enhanced.

After explaining to me far-reaching improvements in other departments, such as artillery, infantry weapons and U-boats—all with the same astonishing knowledge—he tells me that he has personally drafted the wording of the citation for my latest decoration.

We have probably been chatting for an hour and a half when an orderly reports that "the film is ready for showing." Every new weekly newsreel is immediately shown to him and given his sanction for release. It so happens—we have gone down only one flight of stairs and are seated in the film theatre—that the first pictures actually show a scene taken at my dispersal at Stuhlweissenburg, followed by our Stukas taking off and ending with a picture of tanks being shot up by me in the area west of Budapest. After the film has been shown I take my leave of the Supreme Commander. Wing Commander von Below hands me the citation for the Knight's Cross, the Oak Leaves, the Swords and the Diamonds, which have lain in the Reichs Chancery. Each of them weighs several pounds, especially the last two which are framed in gold and, apart from their great sentimental value, must be worth quite a lot. I drive to Goering's H.Q. The Reichsmarschall expresses his pleasure which is all the greater because recent events have made his position very difficult. The enemy's air superiority has aggravated almost all our troubles and even made things impossible, but who could prevent it? He is overjoyed and proud that at this moment one of his men should have been instrumental in making the Führer create a new German decoration for bravery. Drawing me a little aside he says to me roguishly:

"You see how envious the others are of me and the awkwardness of my position? At a conference the Führer said that he was creating a new and unique decoration for you because your achievement is unique. Whereupon the representatives of the other services objected that the recipient is a soldier of the Luftwaffe whose problems are the cause of so many headaches. They wanted to know whether it was not at least theoretically possible for a soldier belonging to one of the other services to earn this distinction? So you see what I am up against."

He goes on to say that he would never have believed I could induce the Führer to change his mind about letting me go on flying. Now that I have his authorization he could not himself renew his prohibition. He begs me, as he has done repeatedly before, to accept the appointment offered me to command the attack units. But seeing that I have got round the Führer I do not think he seriously believes he will win me over today.

In the late afternoon I am on board the special train

for Berlin where my aircraft is waiting to carry me
back to my comrades at the front. I am in Berlin for
only a few hours, but that is long enough to attract a
whole mob of "Gold Oak Leaves rubbernecks" as the
story has already been given out in the press and on the
radio. In the evening I meet Ritter von Halt, at this time
Leader of German Sport. He tells me that after prolonged endeavour he has succeeded in convincing
Hitler that I ought to assume the leadership of the
Reich sport movement at the end of the war. When
my war experiences have been written and I have initiated my successor in my present field of activity I am
to be offered the post.

I fly by way of Görlitz, stopping to see my family
and taking off again for Budapest on the same day as
reports from this sector of the front are very grave. The
Wing has been paraded when I land, so that the senior
squadron leader may congratulate me in the name of
the unit on my new honour and promotion. Then into
the air again on a sortie in the Budapest area.

"If the Russian flak only knew how much gold and
diamonds was flying overhead," said one of the ground
staff with a grin, "you can bet they would shoot better
and exert themselves more."

Some days later I receive a message from the Hungarian Leader, Szalaszy, inviting me to his H.Q. South of
Sopron. General Fütterer, commanding the Hungarian
air force, and Fridolin accompany me. In recognition of
our operations against Bolshevism in Hungary he invests
me with the highest Hungarian military decoration, the
Medal for Bravery. This has hitherto been awarded to
only seven Hungarians. I am the eighth to receive it and
the only foreigner. The grant of an estate which goes
with the award does not interest me much. It is to be
presented after the war and doubtless it will become a
holiday resort for the unit.

Shortly before the middle of January we get alarming reports that the Soviets have launched an offensive
from the bridgehead at Baranov and have already made

a deep penetration thrusting towards Silesia. Silesia is my home. I request an immediate transfer of my Wing to this sector of the front. No definite orders come through until 15th January when I am instructed to move the unit, with the exception of One Squadron, to Udetfeld in Upper Silesia. Being short of transport aircraft, we take the first shift and the armourer personnel with us on board our Ju. 87s so as to be ready for operations the moment we arrive, landing en route at Olmütz to refuel. When we are over Vienna the skipper of the anti-tank flight comes through over the R/T:

"I shall have to land . . . engine trouble."

I am very annoyed at this, not so much because I can make a shrewd guess that the fact that his fiancée lives in Vienna has contributed to the misbehaviour of his engine, as because my operations officer, Pilot Officer Weisbach, is travelling in his aircraft. This means that Weisbach will not be with me when we land on our new airfield and I shall again have to be bothered with that confounded telephone!

We approach our destination above the familiar, snow clad slopes of the Sudeten. Who would ever have thought I should one day be flying on operations over this region? When we were over the endless steppes of Russia—1250 miles from home—and the first retreat became necessary we used to say jokingly: "If this goes on we shall soon be based on Krakau."

We regarded this town as a typical L. of C. supply base with all the amenities associated with such a town and possessing a certain attraction for some—at least for a few days. Now our jest has actually come true, even worse. Krakau now lies a long way behind the Russian lines.

We land at Udetfeld. I learn very little from the air division stationed here. The situation is confused, communications with our forward units being mostly cut. They tell me that Russian tanks are already 25 miles east of Tschenstochau, but nothing is yet known for certain as is always the case when things have got out of hand. The Panzer "fire brigade" in this sector, the

16th and 17th Armoured Divisions, is at the moment isolated and fighting desperately for its existence, unable to come to the aid of the other Divisions. The Russian drive seems again to have been mounted on a massive scale; overnight they have penetrated the defence positions of the 16th and 17th Panzer Divisions and consequently our air attacks will have to be carried out with the greatest caution, for the fact that a unit is far behind the apex of the Russian drive does not guarantee its being an enemy.

They may well be units of ours trying to fight their way back. So I order all pilots to make certain by low level flying before attacking that they are really Soviet troops. We munitioned before leaving Hungary, but there is as yet no sign of our tanker lorries. I glance at my petrol gauge: we shall just have enough petrol for a short sortie. Twenty minutes after landing at Udetfeld we take off on our first sortie in this area. We are now in sight of Tschenstochau. I am searching the roads running eastward, where the Russian tanks have been reported. We fly low over the houses of the town. But what on earth is going on there? There is a tank moving along the main street, it is followed by a second and then a third. They look very like T 34s, but surely that is not possible. They must belong to the 16th and 17th Panzer Divisions. I circle round once more. Now no mistake is admissible; they are T 34s sure enough with infantry perched on top of them. There is no doubt that they are Ivans. They cannot be captured enemy tanks which we are using to supplement our own, for if this were so they would identify themselves by firing Vereys or showing the swastika. My last hesitation is dispelled when I see that the snipers mounted on them are opening fire at us. I give the order to attack. We must not drop bombs inside the town; there is always the chance that the population is still there, that the people have been taken by surprise and have not been able to evacuate the town. The high trolley cables and the tall houses with wireless aerials and other obstructions make low level attack with our cannon-carrying aircraft extremely difficult. Some of the T 34s career in circles round the blocks of houses so that one is apt to lose sight of them when coming in to dive. I shoot up three of them in the centre of the town. These tanks must have come from somewhere; the first of them certainly did not enter the town alone. We fly on eastward following a railway line and a road. Only a few miles beyond the town the next party of tanks are rolling forward in front of a convoy of lorries with infantry, supplies and A.A. guns. Here in the open country we are in our element and give the tanks an unwelcome surprise. Gradually the light begins to fail and we return to base. Eight tanks are burning. We have run out of ammunition.

We have never taken our task lightly, but we may perhaps have been inclined to regard these tank-hunts as a kind of sport; now I feel it has ceased to be a game. If ever I see another tank after I have used up all my ammunition, for two pins I would ram the thing with my aircraft. I am seized with an uncontrolled fury at the thought that this horde from the Steppes is driving into the very heart of Europe. Will anyone ever be able to drive them out again? Today they have powerful allies supporting them with material and the creation of a second front. Will not poetic justice one day bring a terrible retribution?

We are out from dawn till dusk irrespective of losses, regardless of opposition and bad weather. We are involved in a crusade. We have become very taciturn between sorties and in the evenings. Every one carries out his duty in tight-lipped silence, ready if need be to lay down his life. Officers and men are conscious of a vital current uniting them in the spirit of comradeship without distinction of rank and class. It has been that way with us always.

On one of these days a wireless priority message from the Reichsmarschall summons me immediately to Karinhall; I am absolutely forbidden to fly, this is an

order from the Führer. I am feverishly agitated. To
have to miss a day's flying and go to Berlin with the
situation what it is! Impossible. I just won't do it! At
this moment I feel answerable only to myself. I ring
up Berlin between two sorties with the intention of asking the Reichsmarschall to grant me a reprieve until the
present crisis is past. Relying on the Führer's latest con-
cession I must obtain leave to continue flying; I cannot
look on, it is unthinkable. The Reichsmarschall is not
there. I try to contact the Chief of the General Staff.
They are all in conference with the Führer and so un-
reachable. The matter is urgent; I am anxious to leave
no stone unturned before wittingly disobeying the orders. As a last resort I ring up the Führer. The switch-
board operator at the Führer's headquarters does not
seem to understand me and presumably jumps to the
conclusion that I wish to be connected with some general or other. When I repeat that I want my call put
through to the Führer the voice enquires: "What is your
rank?"

"Corporal," I reply. Somebody at the other end of
the line laughs as if he understood the joke and puts me
through. Wing Commander von Below answers.

"I know what you want, but I beg you not to exas-
perate the Führer. Hasn't the Reichsmarschall told
you?"

I reply that this is the reason for my ringing up and
describe the seriousness of the present situation. It is no
use. He advises me at all events to come to Berlin and
talk to the Reichsmarschall; he believes he has a new
assignment for me. Furious because for the moment I
am baffled I hang up. A hush descends upon the conversation in the mess. Everyone knows that when I am
boiling over it is best to let me simmer down in silence.

Tomorrow we are to move to Klein-Eiche. I know the
district well; our "tank acquaintance," Count Strachwitz lives near by. The best way to forget my distress at this new move is to fly to Berlin to see the
Reichsmarschall. He receives me at Karinhall; I am

struck by his irritability and lack of geniality. We have
our talk during a short walk in his forest. He opens up at
once with his heaviest guns:

"I went to see the Führer about you a week ago and
this is what he said: when Rudel is there I have not the
heart to tell him that he must stop flying, I just cannot
do it. But what are you the C.-in-C. of the Luftwaffe
for? You can tell him, I cannot. Glad as I am to see
Rudel, I do not want to see him again until he has
reconciled himself to my wishes. I am quoting the Führer's words and now I am telling you. Nor do I want to
discuss the matter any further. I know all your arguments and objections!"

This is a stunning blow. I take my leave and fly back
to Klein-Eiche. On the journey my mind is full of the
last hours. I know now that I shall have to defy the
order. I feel it my duty to Germany, to my native land,
to throw into the scales my experience and my continued personal effort. Otherwise I should seem a trait-
or to myself. I shall go on flying whatever the consequences may be.

The Wing flies a sortie in my absence. Pilot Officer
Weisbach, whom I have grounded because I need
him as operations officer, goes out on a tank hunt with
W.O. Ludwig, a first rate gunner and holder of the
Knight's Cross of the Iron Cross. They fail to return, a
loss to us of two invaluable comrades. These days we
must give everything we have, we cannot spare ourselves. To me these operations are a greater strain
than ever before because my disobedience to an order
of the Supreme Commander preys on my mind. If anything should happen to me I should be refused military
honours and be disgraced; the thought often worries
me. But I cannot help it, I am in the air from morning
till night. All my officers have been tipped off that if I
am wanted I am not flying, but "have just gone out."
Individual claims of tanks destroyed have always to be
entered on the daily returns, sent every evening to
the Group and the Air Command naming the gunner
in every case. Since the new order grounding me has

been in force my claims are no longer included, but
are credited to the unit as a whole. Hitherto claims
have been entered in this category only when two separate gunners have attacked the same tank when, in
order to avoid duplication, the claim was reported under the heading: "Name of gunner doubtful; success attributed to unit." Latterly we have constant queries
from higher levels pointing out that we have previously
always been able to give the gunner's name, why this
sudden large entry under "joint account?" At first we
get out of it by saying that now whenever one of us
spots a tank we all dive onto it simultaneously as everyone wants to be in at the kill. One day during my
absence on a sortie a spy in the person of an officer of
the Luftwaffe turns up to investigate and pumps my operations officer who after exacting a promise that he will
keep it under his hat lets the cat out of the bag. On top
of this a general catches me once at Grottkau airfield to
which we have recently been moved just as I return
from a sortie. He does not believe my assurances that
it was only "a short test flight," but it does not matter,
for he tells me "he has seen nothing." I was soon to
discover, however, that the truth had filtered through
to the High Command. One day soon after the general's
visit I am again credited in the war communiqué with
eleven tanks destroyed and simultaneously another distance call summons me to Karinhall. I fly there and
meet with a very disagreeable reception. The Reichsmarschall's first words are:

"The Führer knows that you are still flying. I pre-
sume you have realised that the news has reached him
from yesterday's communiqué. He has told me to warn
you to give it up once and for all. You are not to em-
barrass him by forcing him to take disciplinary action
for disobedience to an order. Furthermore he is at a
loss to reconcile such conduct with a man who wears
the highest German decoration for gallantry. It is not
necessary for me to add any comments of my own."

I have heard him out in silence. After briefly asking
me about the situation in Silesia he dismisses me and I

fly back the same day. Obviously I have now reached the end of my tether. I am clear in my own mind that I must go on flying if I am to keep my mental balance in my country's present predicament. Regardless of the consequences, I still feel that I am answerable only to myself. I shall continue to fly.

We hunt for tanks in the industrial and woodland region of Upper Silesia, where it is comparatively easy for the enemy to camouflage himself and difficult for us to spot him. Our attacking Ju. 87s dodge in between the chimney stacks of the Upper Silesian industrial towns. At Kiefernstädtel we meet some of our own shock artillery whom we have not seen for a long time, and help them liquidate the numerically greatly superior Soviets and their T 34s. Gradually a new line is being established on the Oder. To build up a new front out of nothing, that is something only Field Marshal Schoerner can do! We often see him now when he visits our base to confer with me on the momentary situation and to discuss possible operations. The results of our reconnaissance, especially, are of the greatest value to him. At this time Squadron Leader Lau is reported missing with his crew; he is hit by flak and has to force-land in the Gross-Wartenberg area and is captured by the Russians. He comes down right in the midst of a Soviet force after an attempt to land near-by has proved impossible.

Slowly the Oder front is established a little. I receive an order by telephone to move the Wing immediately to Märkisch Friedland in Pommerania and the 2nd Squadron to Frankfurt, the situation there being more dangerous than it is in Silesia. Thick driving snow prevents our moving in close formation, so we take off at intervals in threes heading for Märkisch Friedland over Frankfurt. Some of our aircraft come down at the intermediate airfields at Sagan and Sorau. The weather is abominable. At Frankfurt they are already waiting for me to land; I am to ring up my old base at Grottkau without delay. When my call has been put through

I learn that soon after my departure Field Marshal
Schoerner had been over to see me and had raised
Cain. Banging his fist on the table he had asked who
had given the order for me to leave his sector. Flight
Lieutenant Niermann, my operations officer, had told
him that the order came from the Group and the Air
Command.

"Group and Air Command indeed! All window dressing! I want to know who took Rudel away from here.
Ring him up at Frankfurt and tell him to wait there.
I am taking the matter up with the Führer himself. I
insist on his staying here. Am I supposed to hold the
front with nothing but rifles?"

I learn all this over the telephone. If I am to reach
Märkisch Friedland before dark I have no time to
waste. I ring up the Führer's H.Q. to ask whether I am
now to continue or return to Silesia. In the first case,
Field Marshal Schoerner must release my personnel at
present detained by him at Grottkau so that I may
have my full complement of staff and material when I
arrive. I am informed that a decision has just been
reached: my wing has definitely been transferred to the
north as the situation in that sector which has recently
been put under the command of S.S. Reichsführer
Himmler is indeed more serious. I land at Märkisch
Friedland with the first few aircraft in a dense snow
storm and complete darkness; the rest of the unit is due
to arrive tomorrow, the 2nd Squadron will remain at
Frankfurt and operate from there. When we have
found makeshift quarters for the night I ring up
Himmler at Ordensburg Krössinsee to report my arrival
in his sector. He is pleased that I am here and that he
has won the duel with Field Marshal Schoerner. He
asks me what I would like to do now. The time is 11
P.M., so I reply: "Go to sleep"—for I want to be out
early to get a general picture of the situation. He thinks
differently.

"I can't sleep," he says.

I tell him that he has not got to fly tomorrow morning, and that when one is flying without intermission

sleep is indispensable. After much palaver he tells me that he is sending over a car to fetch me as soon as possible. As in any case I am short of fuel and ammunition an introduction to the new sector by its commander may at least simplify a number of organisation problems. On the drive to Ordensburg we are stuck in a snow drift. When I get there at last it is 2 A.M. I first see his Chief of Staff with whom I have a long talk about the situation and general matters. I am particularly curious to hear from him how Himmler is squaring up to his new task seeing that he lacks the necessary training and experience. The Chief of Staff is an army officer, not a member of any S.S. unit. He tells me that it is a pleasure to work with Himmler because he is not opinionated and does not seek to impose his authority. Instead of thinking that he knows better than the experts on his staff, he readily falls in with their suggestions and then lends the full weight of his authority to implement them in every way. And so everything goes smoothly.

"Only one thing will strike you. You will always have the feeling that Himmler never says what he really thinks."

A few minutes later I am discussing the situation and my task in this sector with Himmler. I notice at once that he looks worried. The Soviet have by-passed Schneidemühl on both sides, pushing on into East Pommerania towards the Oder, partly along the Netze valley and partly to the north and south of it. There are very few of our formations in the area which can be described as effective. A battle group is being formed in the neighbourhood of Märkisch Friedland to hold up the enemy forces which have broken through and to prevent their further advance to the Oder. No one can yet foresee to what extent our units in the Posen-Graudenz area will be able to fight their way back; in any case they would not immediately recover their full fighting strength. The present reconnaissance leaves much to be desired so that it is not possible to take stock of the position comprehensively. This will there-

fore be one of our tasks, besides attacking the enemy at points which he is known to have reached,
chiefly his mechanised and armoured forces.

I detail my requirements in bombs, petrol and ammunition. If they are not satisfied it is a matter of days
before I shall cease to be able to operate. In his own interest he promises to see that the matter receives priority
attention. I explain to him what possibilities I see for
the use of my formation, basing my views on the picture he has given me of the position here.

I leave Ordensburg Krössinsee at 4.30 A.M. knowing that in two hours time I shall already be flying
above this sector. From now on the Stukas are out
without a pause the whole day long. Our aircraft are
painted with the emblem of the German Order of Chivalry, for now, as six centuries ago, we are engaged in
a battle with the East. Intensely cold weather has set
in, a powdery snow lies on the airfield an inch and a
half deep in places; when we take off this snow dust
is blown into the mechanism of the cannon of our anti-
tank aircraft and ices up as soon as we are airborne.
After firing one or two rounds the cannon jam when
we are on the target. I feel an agony of frustration.
There are the Russian armoured columns advancing
into Germany and when we come in to the attack in
the face, at times, of a very strong defence what happens? Nothing comes out of our cannon. One has half
a mind to crash the aircraft onto the tank in sheer desperation. We come in again and again for another try
—it is hopeless. This happens to us at Scharnikau, at
Filehne, at many places. The T 34s race on westward.
Sometimes a single shot is enough to blow up a tank,
but more often not. Most valuable days are lost before I finally get enough labour to have the runway
more or less cleared of snow. The enormous numbers
of tanks make one's hair stand on end. We fly to all
points of the compass; if the day were three times as
long it would be too short. The co-operation of our
fighter squadron in this area is excellent; they react
to every fresh reconnaissance report from us—"The

enemy's advance guard is at this point or that." In a joint operation east of Deutsch Krone we are able to inflict considerable losses on the Soviets, also at Schloppe in the forest regions lying south of it. When the tanks are in a village they generally drive into the houses and try to conceal themselves there. Then one can only spot them by a long pole projecting from the front of the house; this pole is the barrel of their gun. Behind them the house is open and as it is unlikely that any Germans are still living in these houses we come in from behind and fire into the engine. No other method of attack is feasible. The tanks catch fire and blow up into the air with the ruins of the houses. If the crew is still alive they sometimes attempt to drive the blazing tank out into fresh cover, but in that case it is indeed lost because the tanks are then assailable in every vulnerable place. I never drop bombs on villages even if it is militarily expedient, for I shudder at the thought of hitting the German inhabitants with our own bombs when they are already exposed to the Russian terror.

It is a dreadful thing to be flying and fighting above our homes, the more so when one sees what masses of men and material are pouring into our country like a flood. We are no more than a boulder, a small obstruction but unable to stem the tide. The devil is now gambling for Germany, for all Europe. Invaluable forces are bleeding to death, the last bastion of the world is crumbling under the assault of Red Asia. Of an evening we are more exhausted by this realisation than by the incessant operations of the day. Stubborn refusal to accept this fate and the determination that "this must not happen" keep us going. I would not like to have to reproach myself for having failed to do everything within my power till the eleventh hour to stave off the appalling, menacing spectre of defeat. I know that every decent young German thinks as I do.

South of our sector the situation looks very grim. Frankfurt-on-the-Oder is threatened. So overnight we

get the order to move to Fürstenwalde which brings us
nearer to the critical sector. A few hours later we are
flying in the operation area Frankfurt—Küstrin. The
spearheads of the Soviet advance have reached the
Oder on the outskirts of Frankfurt. Further north
Küstrin is encircled and the enemy is wasting no time
in his efforts to establish a bridgehead at Göritz-Reit-
wein on the west bank across the frozen river.

One day, like the Prussian cavalry general Ziethen
three hundred years ago, we are in battle east of Frankfurt above historic soil. Here a small German force has
been surrounded by Soviet tanks. We attack them and
those tanks which have not immediately caught fire try
to escape across the open country. We come in at them
time and again. Our comrades on the ground who had already given themselves up as lost leap for joy, throwing
their rifles and steel helmets into the air and heedless of
cover pursue the fleeing tanks. Our fire put every one
of them out of action. We in the air have for once
the exhilaration of witnessing our success. After all the
tanks have been captured I prepare a container and
scribble a message of congratulations to our comrades
from the Wing and me. I circle round very low and drop
the container with some chocolate at their feet. The
sight of their grateful, happy faces will steel us for the
difficult operations ahead of us and spur us on to fresh,
unremitting efforts to relieve our brothers-in-arms.

Unluckily the first days of February are very cold;
at many places the Oder is frozen so hard that the
Russians are able to cross the river. For stability they
lay planks on the ice and I often see vehicles driving
over them. The ice does not seem to be strong enough
yet to bear the weight of tanks. As the Oder front is still
in flux and there are gaps in the line where there is not
one German soldier to oppose them, the Soviets are
successful in establishing several bridgeheads, one, for
example, at Reitwein. Our Panzer forces which are
brought up too late arrive to find a strong enemy already lodged with heavy artillery on the west bank of

the Oder. His crossing places are powerfully protected by flak from the first day. Ivan is accurately informed of our presence in this sector. My orders are to destroy all bridges day after day so as to delay the enemy and to give us time to bring up reinforcements and material from the rear. I report that at the moment this is more or less pointless, because it is possible to cross the Oder almost anywhere. The bombs crash through the ice, leaving relatively small holes, and this is the sum total of our achievement. I am for attacking only recognized enemy targets on both sides of the river or the traffic crossing it, but not the so-called bridges of which in point of fact there are none. What look like bridges on aerial photographs are really the tracks of feet and vehicles on the ice; these and the planks laid between them to simulate bridges. If we bomb these tracks Ivan simply crosses the ice to the side of them. This is clear to me from the very first day because I have flown over them at low level countless times and, besides, this trick is nothing new to me, I know it from the Don, the Donetz, the Dniester and other Russian rivers.

So disregarding the order I concentrate my attacks on genuine targets on either bank: tanks, vehicles and artillery. One day a general sent from Berlin turns up and tells me that reconnaissance photographs always show new bridges.

"But," he says, "you do not report that these bridges have been destroyed. You must keep on attacking them."

"By and large," I explain to him, "they are not bridges at all," and when I see him contort his face into a question mark an idea occurs to me. I tell him that I am just about to take off, I invite him to sit behind me and promise to give him practical proof of this. He hesitates for a moment, then observing the curious glances of my junior officers who have heard my proposition with some glee, he agrees. I have given the unit a standing order to attack the bridgehead, I myself approach the objective at the same low level and fly from Schwedt to Frankfurt-on-the-Oder. At some points we encounter quite respectable flak and the general soon admits that he has now seen for himself that the bridges are in fact tracks. He has seen enough. After landing he is as pleased as Punch that he has been able to convince himself and can make his report accordingly. We are quit of our daily bridge chore. One night Minister Speer brings me a new assignment from the Führer. I am to formulate a plan for its execution. Briefly, he tells me:

"The Führer is planning attacks on the dams of the armament industry in the Urals. He expects to disrupt the enemy's arms production, especially of tanks, for a year. This year will then give us the chance of exploiting the respite decisively. You are to organize the operation, but you are not to fly yourself, the Führer repeated this expressly."

I point out to the minister that there must surely be some one better qualified for this task, namely in Long Distance Bomber Command, who will be far more conversant with such things as astronomical navigation, etc. than I am who have been trained in dive-bombing and therefore have quite a different kind of knowledge and experience. Furthermore, I must be allowed to fly myself if I am to have an untroubled mind when briefing my crews.

"The Führer wishes you to do it," objects Speer.

I raise some fundamental technical questions regarding the type of aircraft and the kind of bombs with which this operation is to be carried out. If it is to be done soon only the Heinkel 177 comes into consideration, though it is not absolutely certain that it will prove suitable for this purpose. The only possible bomb for such a target is, in my opinion, a sort of torpedo, but that too has yet to be tested. I flatly refuse to listen to his suggestion to use 2000 lb. bombs; I am positive that no success can be achieved with them. I show the Minister photographs taken in the Northern sector of the Eastern Front where I dropped two thousand pounders on the concrete pillars of the Newa bridge and it did not collapse. This problem must therefore be resolved and also the question of my being allowed to accompany the mission. These are my stipulations should the Führer insist on my undertaking the task. He already knows my objections that my practical experience is confined to a totally different field.

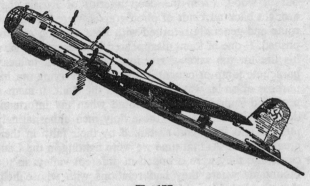

**He. 177**

Now I take up the file of photographs of the factories in question and study them with interest. I see that a high percentage of them are already underground and are therefore partly unassailable from the air. The photographs show the dam and the power station and some of the factory buildings; they have been taken during the war. How can this have been done? I think back to my time in the Crimea and put two and two together. When I was stationed at Sarabus and keeping myself fit by a little putting the weight and discus throwing after operations a black-painted aircraft often used to land on the airfield, and very mysteriously passengers alighted. One day one of the crew told me under the seal of secrecy what was going on. This aircraft carried Russian priests from the freedom-loving states of the Caucasus who volunteered for important missions for the German command. With flowing beards and dressed in clerical garb each of them carried a little packet on his chest, either a camera or explosives according to the nature of his mission. These priests regarded a German victory as the only chance of regaining their independence and with it their religious liberty. They were fanatical enemies of world Bolshevism and consequently our allies. I can still see them: often men with snow white hair and noble features as if chiseled out of wood. From the deep interior of Russia they brought back all kinds of photographs, were months en route and generally returned with their mission accomplished. If one of them disappeared he presumably gave his life for the sake of freedom, either in an unlucky parachute jump or caught in the act of carrying out his purpose or on his way back through the front. It made a profound impression on my mind when my informant described to me the way these holy men unhesitatingly jumped into the night, sustained by their faith in their great mission. At that time we were fighting in the Caucasus and they were dropped in different valleys in the mountains where they had relations with whose help they proceeded to organise resistance and sabotage.

It all comes back to me as I puzzle over the origin of the photographs of these industrial plants.

After some general remarks on the present state of the war, in which Speer expresses his complete confidence in the Führer, he leaves in the small hours of the morning, promising to send me further details about the Urals plan. It never got as far as that, for a few days later the ninth of February made everything impossible.

So the task of working out this plan devolved upon somebody else. But then in the rush of events to the end of the war its execution was to be no longer practical.

## 17

# THE DEATH STRUGGLE OF
# THE LAST MONTHS

Early on the morning of the 9th February a telephone call from H.Q.: Frankfurt has just reported that last night the Russians bridged the Oder at Lebus, slightly north of Frankfurt and with some tanks have already gained a footing on the west bank. The situation is more than critical; at this point there is no opposition on the ground and there is no possibility of bringing up heavy artillery there in time to stop them. So there is nothing to prevent the Soviet tanks from rolling on towards the capital, or at least straddling the railway and the autobahn from Frankfurt to Berlin, both vital supply lines for the establishment of the Oder front.

We fly there to find out what truth there is in this report. From afar I can already make out the pontoon bridge, we encounter intense flak a long way before we reach it. The Russians certainly have a rod in pickle for us! One of my squadrons attacks the bridge across the ice. We have no great illusions about the results we shall achieve, knowing as we do that Ivan has such quantities of bridge-building material that he can repair the damage in less than no time. I myself fly lower with the anti-tank flight on the look-out for tanks on the west bank of the river. I can discern their tracks but not the monsters themselves. Or are these the tracks of A.A. tractors? I come down lower to make sure and see, well camouflaged in the folds of the river valley, some tanks on the northern edge of the village of Lebus.

There are perhaps a dozen or fifteen of them. Then something smacks against my wing, a hit by light flak. I keep low, guns are flashing all over the place, at a guess six or eight batteries are protecting the river crossing. The flak gunners appear to be old hands at the game with long Stuka experience behind them. They are not using tracers, one sees no string of beads snaking up at one, but one only realises that they have opened up when the aircraft shudders harshly under the impact of a hit. They stop firing as soon as we climb and so our bombers cannot attack them. Only when one is flying very low above our objective can one see the spurt of flame from the muzzle of a gun like the flash of a pocket torch. I consider what to do; there is no chance of coming in cunningly behind cover as the flat river valley offers no opportunities for such tactics. There are no tall trees or buildings. Sober reflection tells me that experience and tactical skill go by the board if one breaks all the fundamental rules derived from them. The answer: a stubborn attack and trust to luck. If I had always been so foolhardy I should have been in my grave a dozen times. There are no troops here on the ground and we are fifty miles from the capital of the Reich, a perilously short distance when the enemy's armour is already pushing towards it. There is no time for ripe consideration. This time you will have to trust to luck, I tell myself, and in I go. I tell the other pilots to stay up; there are several new crews among them and while they cannot be expected to do much damage with this defence we are likely to suffer heavier losses than the game is worth. When I come in low and as soon as they see the flash of the A.A. guns they are to concentrate their cannon fire on the flak. There is always the chance that this will get Ivan rattled and affect his accuracy. There are several Stalin tanks there, the rest are T 34s. After four have been set on fire and I have run out of ammunition we fly back. I report my observations and stress the fact that I have only attacked because we are fighting fifty miles from Berlin, otherwise it would be inexcusable. If we were holding a line further east I should have waited for a more favourable situation, or at least until the tanks had driven out of range of their flak screen round the bridge. I change aircraft after two sorties because they have been hit by flak. Back a fourth time and a total of twelve tanks are ablaze. I am buzzing a Stalin tank which is emitting smoke but refuses to catch fire.

Each time before coming in to the attack I climb to 2400 feet as the flak cannot follow me to this altitude. From 2400 feet I scream down in a steep dive, weaving violently. When I am close to the tank I straighten up for an instant to fire, and then streak away low above the tank with the same evasive tactics until I reach a point where I can begin to climb again—out of range of the flak. I really ought to come in slowly and with my aircraft better controlled, but this would be suicide. I am only able to straighten up for the fraction of a second and hit the tank accurately in its vulnerable parts thanks to my manifold experience and somnambulistic assurance. Such attacks are, of course, out of the question for my colleagues for the simple reason that they have not the experience.

The pulses throb in my temples. I know that I am playing cat and mouse with fate, but this Stalin tank has got to be set alight. Up to 2400 feet once more and on to the sixty ton leviathan. It still refuses to burn! Rage seizes me; it must and shall catch fire!

The red light indicator on my cannon winks. That too! On one side the breech has jammed, the other cannon has therefore only one round left. I climb again. Is it not madness to risk everything again for the sake of a single shot? Don't argue; how often have you put paid to a tank with a single shot?

It takes a long time to gain 2400 feet with a Ju. 87; far too long, for now I begin to weigh the pros and cons. My one ego says: if the thirteenth tank has not yet caught fire you needn't imagine you can do the trick with one more shot. Fly home and remunition, you will find it again all right. To this my other ego heatedly replies:

"Perhaps it requires just this one shot to stop the tank from rolling on through Germany."

"Rolling on through Germany sounds much too melodramatic! A lot more Russian tanks are going to roll on through Germany if you bungle it now, and you will bungle it, you may depend upon that. It is madness to go down again to that level for the sake of a single shot. Sheer lunacy!"

"You will say next that I shall bungle it because it is the thirteenth. Superstitious nonsense! You have one round left, so stop shilly-shallying and get cracking!"

And already I zoom down from 2400 feet. Keep your mind on your flying, twist and turn; again a score of guns spit fire at me. Now I straighten up . . . fire . . . the tank bursts into a blaze! With jubilation in my heart, I streak away low above the burning tank. I go into a climbing spiral . . . a crack in the engine and something sears through my leg like a strip of red hot steel. Everything goes black before my eyes, I gasp for breath. But I must keep flying . . . flying . . . I must not pass out. Grit your teeth, you have to master your weakness. A spasm of pain shoots through my whole body.

"Ernst, my right leg is gone."

"No, your leg won't be gone. If it were you wouldn't be able to speak. But the left wing is on fire. You'll have to come down, we've been hit twice by 4 cm. flak."

An appalling darkness veils my eyes, I can no longer make out anything.

"Tell me where I can crash-land. Then get me out quickly so that I am not burnt alive."

I cannot see a thing any more, I pilot by instinct. I remember vaguely that I came in to each attack from south to north and banked left as I flew out. I must therefore be headed west and in the right direction for home. So I fly on for several minutes. Why the wing is not already gone I do not know. Actually I am moving north north west almost parallel to the Russian front.

"Pull!" shouts Gadermann through the intercom, and

now I feel that I am slowly dozing off into a kind of fog . . . a pleasant coma.

"Pull!" yells Gadermann again—were those trees or telephone wires? I have lost all sensation in my mind and pull the stick only when Gadermann yells at me. If this searing pain in my leg would only stop . . . and this flying . . . if I could let myself sink at last into this queer, grey peace and remoteness which invites me . . .

"Pull!" Once again I wrench automatically at the joy-stick, but now for an instant Gadermann has "shouted me awake." In a flash I realise that I must do something here.

"What's the terrain like?" I ask into the microphone.

"Bad—hummocky."

But I have to come down, otherwise the dangerous apathy brought on from my wounded body will again steal over me. I kick the rudder-bar with my left foot and howl with agony. But surely it was my right leg that was hit? Pull to the right, I bring the nose of the aircraft up and slide her gently onto her belly, in this way perhaps the release gear of the undercarriage will not function and I can make it after all. If not we shall pancake. The aircraft is on fire . . . she bumps and skids for a second.

Now I can rest, now I can slip away into the grey distance . . . wonderful! Maddening pains jerk me back into consciousness. Is someone pulling me about? . . . Are we jolting over rough ground? Now it is over. . . At last I sink utterly into the arms of silence . . .

I wake up, everything around me is white . . . intent faces . . . a pungent smell . . . I am lying on an operating table. A sudden, violent panic convulses me: where is my leg?

"Is it gone?"

The surgeon nods. Spinning downhill on brand new skis . . . diving . . . athletics . . . pole jumping . . . what do these things matter? How many comrades have been far more seriously wounded? Do you remember . . . that one in the hospital at Dnjepropetrovsk whose whole face and both hands had been torn off by a mine? The loss of a leg, an arm, a head are all of no importance if only the sacrifice could save the fatherland from its mortal peril . . . this is no catastrophe, the only catastrophe is that I cannot fly for weeks . . . and in the present crisis! These thoughts flash through my brain in a second, and now the surgeon says to me gently:

"I couldn't do anything else. Except for a few scraps of flesh and some fibrous tissue there was nothing there, so I had to amputate."

If there was nothing there, I think to myself with a wry humour, how could he amputate? Well, of course, it is all in the day's work for him.

"But why is your other leg in plaster of Paris?" he asks in astonishment.

"Since last November—where am I here?"

"At the Waffen S.S. main dressing station at Selow."

"Oh, at Selow!" That is less than five miles behind the front. So I evidently flew north-north-west, not west.

"Waffen S.S. soldiers brought you in and one of our M.O.s performed the operation. You have another wounded man on your conscience," he adds with a smile.

"Did I by any chance bite the surgeon?"

"You didn't go as far as that," he says shaking his head. "No, you didn't bite him, but a Pilot Officer Koral tried to land with a Fieseler Storch on the spot where you crashed. But it must have been difficult, for he pancaked . . . and now he, too, has his head swathed in bandages!"

Good old Koral! It seems as if when I was flying subconsciously I had more than one guardian angel!

Meanwhile the Reichsmarschall has sent his personal doctor with instructions to bring me back at once to the bomb-proof hospital in the Zoo bunker, but the surgeon who operated will not hear of it because I have lost too much blood. It will be all right tomorrow.

The Reichsmarschall's doctor tells me that Goering immediately reported the incident to the Führer.

Hitler, he says, was very glad that I had got off so lightly.

"Of course, if the chickens want to be wiser than the hen," he is reported to have said among other things. I am relieved that no mention has been made of his veto on my flying. I also believe that in view of the desperate struggle in which the whole situation has been involved in the last few weeks my continuance in action is accepted as a matter of course.

The next day I am moved into the Zoo bunker, sited below the heaviest A.A. guns aiding in the defence of the capital against the allied attacks on the civil population. On the second day there is a telephone on my bedside table; I must be able to communicate with my wing about operations, the situation, etc. I know that I shall not be on my back for long and I do not want to lose my command and therefore I am anxious to be kept informed of everything in detail and participate in my unit's every activity even if I can only be kept informed and participate by telephone. The doctors and the nurses whose care of me is touching are, in this respect at least, not overpleased with their new patient. They keep on saying something about "rest."

Almost every day I am visited by colleagues from the unit or by other friends, some of them people who call themselves my friends in order to force a way into my sickroom. When those who "crash" my sickroom are pretty girls they open their eyes wide and raise their eyebrows interrogatively when they see my wife sitting at my bedside. "Did you ever?" as the Berliner would say.

I have already had a professional discussion about an artificial limb; if only I had made that much recovery. I am impatient and fidgeting to get up. A little later I wangle a visit from a maker of artificial limbs. I ask him to make me a provisional artificial leg with which I can fly even if the stump is not yet healed. Several first class firms refuse on the grounds that it is too soon.

One accepts the order if only as an experiment. At all events he sets about it so energetically that he almost makes me dizzy. He sets the whole of my thigh up to the groin in plaster of Paris without first greasing it or fitting a protective cap. After letting it dry he remarks laconically:

"Think of something nice!"

At the same moment he wrenches with all his strength at the hard plaster of Paris cap in which the hairs of my body are embedded and tears it off. I think the world is falling in. The fellow has missed his vocation, he would have made an excellent blacksmith.

My 3rd Squadron and the Wing staff have meanwhile moved to Görlitz where I went to school. My parents' home is just nearby. The Russians are at this moment fighting their way into the village; Soviet tanks are driving across the playgrounds of my youth. I could go mad to think of it. My family, like many millions, must long since have become refugees, able to save nothing but their bare lives. I lie condemned to inactivity. What have I done to deserve this? I must not think of it.

Flowers and presents of every kind are proof of the people's affection for their soldiers; every day they are delivered to my room. Besides the Reichsmarschall, Minister Goebbels whom I did not before know visits me twice. A conversation with him is very interesting. He asks my opinion of the purely strategic situation in the east.

"The Oder front," I tell him, "is our last chance of holding the Soviets; beyond that I see none, for with it the capital falls too."

But he compares Berlin with Leningrad. He points out that it did not fall because all its citizens made every house a fortress. And what Leningrad could do the population of Berlin could surely help him to do. His idea is to achieve the highest degree of organisation for a house to house defence by installing wireless sets in every building. He is convinced that "his Berliners" would prefer death to falling victims to the Red hordes.

How seriously he meant this his end was afterwards to prove.

"From a military point of view I see it differently," I reply. "Once the battle for Berlin is joined after the Oder front is broken I think it is absolutely impossible that Berlin can be held. I would remind you that the comparison between the two cities is not admissible. Leningrad has the advantage of being protected on the west by the Gulf of Finland and on the east by Lake Ladoga. There was only a weak and narrow Finnish front to the north of it. The only real chance of capturing it was from the south, but on that side Leningrad was strongly fortified and could make use of an excellent system of prepared positions; also it was never entirely cut off from its supply line. Lighters could cross Lake Ladoga in the summer and in winter they laid railway lines over the ice and so were able to feed the city from the north." My arguments fail to convince him.

In a fortnight I am up for a short while for the first time and am able to enjoy a little fresh air. During the allied air attacks I am up on the platform with the A.A. guns and see from below what is probably very unpleasant up above. I am never bored; Fridolin brings me papers which require my signature or other additional problems, sometimes accompanied by one or other of my colleagues. Field Marshal Greim, Skorzeny or Hanna Reitsch look in for an hour's chat; something is always doing, only my inner restlessness at being out of it torments me. When I came into the Zoo bunker I "solemnly" declared that I would walk again in six week's time, and fly. The doctors know that their veto is anyhow useless and would only anger me. At the beginning of March I go out for a walk in the fresh air for the first time—on crutches.

During my convalescence I am invited by one of my nurses to her home, and so am the guest of the Minister for Foreign Affairs. A real soldier is seldom likely to make a good diplomat, and this meeting with von Ribbentrop is rather intriguing. It is an opportunity for conversations which shed light on the other side of the war which is being conducted without weapons. He is greatly interested in my opinion of the strength of the east front and our military potential at this particular moment. I make it clear to him that we at the front hope he is doing something through diplomatic channels to loosen the strangle-hold in which we are caught on every side.

"Cannot the Western Powers be made to see that Bolshevism is their greatest enemy and that after an eventual victory over Germany it will be the same menace to them as to us, and that alone they will no longer be able to get rid of it?"

He takes my remarks as a gentle personal reproof; no doubt I am only playing over a record he has had to listen to many times. He at once explains to me that he has already made a number of attempts which have failed, because every time the necessity for a fresh military retirement on one or other sector of the front shortly after he had opened negotiations has encouraged the enemy to continue the war in any case and to leave the conference table. He cites instances and says somewhat reproachfully that the treaties which he had brought off before the war, among other things those with England and Russia, were surely no mean achievement if not a triumph. But nobody mentions them any longer; today people see only the negative aspects, the responsibility for which is not his. Naturally even now negotiations were still going on, but whether with the general situation such as it was the success he wished for would still be possible was problematical. This peep behind the scenes of diplomacy sates my curiosity and I am not anxious to learn more.

In the middle of March I take my first walk in the spring sunshine with a nurse in the Zoo and on my very first excursion I have a slight accident. We, like so many, are fascinated by the monkey cage. I am attracted by a particularly big ape sitting quite unconcernedly and lazily on a bough with his long tail hanging down. Of course I cannot resist doing just what one should not do and I push both my crutches through the bars with the intention of tickling his tail. I have hardly touched it when he suddenly grabs hold of my crutches and tries with all his monkey strength to pull me into the cage. I stumble on my one leg as far as the bars; of course the beast will not get me through them. Sister Edelgarde hangs on to me and we both pull on our end of the crutches in a tug of war with the monkey. Man versus Ape! His paws have begun to slip a little along his end, and meet the rubber caps at the bottom which are supposed to prevent the crutches from sinking into the ground or skidding when one is walking. The rubber caps excite his curiosity, he sniffs at them, tears them off and swallows them with a broad grin. At the same moment I am able to pull the bare sticks out of the cage and so have at least wrested part of his victory from the ape. A few seconds later the wailing of sirens gives warning of an air raid. The exertion of walking over the sandy paths of the Zoo makes me sweat because the crutches sink deep into the ground and meet with hardly any resistance. Everyone round about me is hurrying and scurrying and so I can hardly use them to support me and hobble on clumsily. It is slow work. We just reach the bunker in time as the first bombs come down.

Gradually Easter approaches. I want to be back with my colleagues on Easter Sunday. My Wing is now stationed in the Grossenhain area in Saxony, my First Squadron has again moved from Hungary into the Vienna area and still remains on the Southeastern front. Gadermann is in Brunswick, for as long as I am away, so that during this time he can exercise his profession as a doctor. I ring him up to tell him that I have ordered a Ju 87 to fetch me at Tempelhof at the end of the week and intend to fly to the unit. As shortly before he has spoken to the professor in charge of my case he does not really believe it. Besides he is feeling ill himself. I shall not see him again in this war, for the last operations now has come.

His place as my gunner is taken by Flight Lt. Niermann who has no lack of operational experience and wears the Knight's Cross of the Iron Cross.

After first obeying the order to report to the Führer before I leave I say goodbye to the bunker. He reiterates his pleasure that everything has gone relatively smoothly. He makes no allusion to my flying, for presumably the idea of my doing so does not enter his head. I am sitting in my aircraft again for the first time in six weeks, my course is set for my comrades. It is Easter Eve and I am happy. Shortly before I take off Fridolin rings up and tells me to fly straight to the Sudetenland; he is just on the point of moving the unit to Kummeram-See near Niemes. In the aircraft at first I feel very strange, but I am soon back in my element. Steering is complicated by the fact that I can use only one foot on the rudder-bar. I can exert no pressure on the right because I have not yet got an artificial limb, and have to use my left foot to lift the left rubber-bar, thus depressing the right one which gives the desired result. My stump is wadded into a plaster of Paris sheath and projects under the instrument panel without knocking against anything. So an hour and a half later I land on my new airfield at Kummer. The Wing flying personnel have arrived here an hour before me.

Our airfield lies amid magnificent scenery between two spurs of the Sudeten mountains surrounded by forest with good-sized lakes near by and at Kummer itself a lovely forest-girt tarn. Pending the solution of the billeting problem we foregather of an evening in the room of an inn. Here in the Sudetenland everything still gives an impression of utter peace and tranquillity. The enemy is behind the mountains and this front is defended by Field Marshal Schoerner; consequently this unruffled calm is not unreasonable. Towards eleven o'clock we hear the treble voices of a children's choir singing: "Gott grüsse dich." The local school with its mistress is treating us to a serenade of welcome. This is something new to us hard-boiled soldiers, it touches us in a place which now in this phase of the war we would as soon forget. We listen meditatively, each of us sunk

in his own thoughts; we feel that these children have
faith in our power to ward off the impending danger
with all its accompanying horrors. Here on the threshold
of their home we shall not fail them for lack of determination. At the end of their song I thank them for
their charming welcome and invite them to visit our
airfield in the morning to have a peep at our "birds."
They are keen as mustard. They turn up next day
and I start the proceedings by taking up my anti-tank
aircraft and firing at a three foot square target. The
children stand round in a semi-circle and can now imagine an attack on an enemy tank; it is a good try-out for
me to manage with one leg. On the other side of the
Sudeten mountains it is still foggy and as we cannot go
out on a sortie I have a little time to waste, so I take up a
FW 190 D 9 and give an exhibition of low and high
flying acrobatics. That genius, Flight Lt. Klatzschner, my
engineer officer, has already readjusted the foot brakes,
which are indispensable for this fast aircraft, so that
they can be operated by hand.

As I come down to land all the men are gesticulating
violently and pointing up into the sky. I look up and
through the gaps in the ragged cloud cover I can see
American fighters and Jabos, Mustangs and Thunderbolts circling above. They are flying at 4800 to 5400

**P 47 Thunderbolt**

feet above a layer of mist. They have not yet caught
sight of me alone up there, otherwise I should have ob-
served them while in the air. The Thunderbolts carry
bombs and seem to be searching for a target, so our
airfield is presumably their objective. Quickly, as far as
one can use the word of a one-legged man in plaster, I
hop over to where the others are standing by. They
must all be got under cover. I hustle the children into
the cellar where they will at least be safe from splinters
but no more, for the house which we use as our operations room being the only one on the airfield is pretty
certain to tempt one of those chaps up there. I enter
last to pacify the children just as the first bombs drop,
one of them close to the building; the blast smashes the
window panes and sweeps away the roof. Our aircraft defence is too feeble to drive the bombers off,
but enough to prevent low level attack. Fortunately we
have no casualties among the children. I am sorry that
their innocent, romantic ideas of aviation should have
thus been brutally converted into grim reality. They
soon quiet down again and the school-teacher marshals
her little flock into a crocodile and shepherds them towards the village. Flight Lt. Niermann is radiant, he
hopes he has got a film of the whole attack. Throughout the performance he has been standing in a foxhole,
filming the falling bombs from the moment of their release to their impact with the ground and the fountains
of earth they spout into the air. This is a tid-bit for the
expert photographer from Spitzbergen, where he has
also succeeded in taking some unique pictures.

Fresh met. reports from the Görlitz-Bautzen area
forecast a gradual clearing-up of the weather, so we
take off. The Soviets have by-passed Görlitz and pushed
on beyond Bautzen, which is encircled with its German
garrison, in the hope of reaching Dresden by way of
Bischofswerda. Continual counter-attacks are launched
against these spearheads trying to effect the collapse of
Field Marshal Schoerner's front, and with our support
Bautzen is relieved and we destroy a large number of
vehicles and tanks. This flying takes a lot out of me, I

must have lost much blood and my apparently inexhaustible stamina has its limitations after all. Our successes are shared by battle and fighter formations placed under my command and stationed on our airfield and in the vicinity.

In the first fortnight of April a wireless signal summons me to the Reichskanzlei. The Führer tells me that I am to take over the command of all jet units and with them clear the air space above General Wenk's new army now being assembled in the region of Hamburg. This army's first objective will be to strike from the neighbourhood of this city into the Harz, in order to cut the supply lines of the allied armies already established further east. The success of the operation at this critical juncture depends on the preliminary clearance of the air space above our own lines, otherwise it is doomed to failure; the Führer is convinced of this and General Wenk who is to conduct the operation agrees with him. I beg the Führer to relieve me of this assignment because I feel that I am at the moment indispensable in Field Marshal Schoerner's sector, his army being engaged in a most arduous defensive battle. I recommend him to choose for the task someone from jet command who will not be so out of his depth as I should. I point out to him that my experience is limited to dive-bombing and tank combat, and that I have always made a point of never giving an order which I could not assist in carrying out myself. With jet aircraft I could not do this, and should therefore feel ill at ease with the formation leaders and crews. I must always be able to show my subordinates the way.

"You have not got to fly at all, you have only to organize. If any one questions your bravery because you are on the ground I will have him hanged."

A trifle drastic, I reflect, but probably he only wishes to dispel my scruples.

"There are plenty of people with experience, that alone is not enough. I must have somebody who can organize and carry out the operation energetically."

A final decision is not reached that day. I fly back,

only to be recalled a few days later to the Reichsmarschall who passes on to me the order to undertake
this task. Meanwhile the situation at the front has so
far deteriorated that Germany threatens to be divided
into two pockets, and the conduct of the operation
would hardly be possible. For this reason and those
already mentioned I refuse. As the Reichsmarschall lets
me guess, this is no surprise to him as since my flat
refusal to accept the combat bomber command he
knows my attitude exactly. This time, however, the prin-
cipal motive of my refusal is that I cannot accept the
responsibility for something which I am no longer convinced in my own mind is feasible. I very soon perceive
how gravely the Reichsmarschall views the situation. As
we are discussing the position at the front, bending over
a table spread with maps, he mutters to himself:

"I wonder when we shall have to set fire to this
shack"—he means Karinhall. He advises me to go to
the Führer's headquarters and personally inform him of
my refusal. As, however, I have received no orders
to this effect I fly back immediately to my Wing where
I am urgently awaited. But this is not to be my last
flight to Berlin.

A wireless signal on the 19th April summons me
once again to the Reichskanzlei. To reach Berlin from
Czechslovakia in an unescorted aircraft is at this time
no longer a simple matter; at more than one place the
Russian and the American fronts are very close to one
another. The air space is alive with aircraft, but none
of them are German. I arrive at the Reichskanzlei and
am admitted to the anteroom of the Führer's bunker.
There is an atmosphere of calm and confidence, those
present are mainly army officers taking part in present or
contemplated operations. From outside one can hear
the thump of the two thousand pounders which Mos-
quitos are dropping in the centre of the city.

It is nearly 11 P.M. when I stand in the presence of
the Supreme Commander. I have foreseen the object of
this interview: the definite acceptance of the assignment
previously discussed. It is an idiosyncrasy of the Führer

to beat about the bush and never to come directly to the point. So on this evening he begins with a half-hour lecture explaining the decisiveness in the course of the centuries of technical developments in which we have always led the field, an advantage which we must also now exploit to the limit and so positively turn the tide of victory in our favour. He tells me that the whole world is afraid of German science and technology, and shows me some intelligence reports which indicate the steps the Allies are already taking to rob us of our technical achievements and our scientists. Every time I listen to him I am astounded at his memory for figures and his specialised knowledge of all things technical. At this time I have about six thousand flying hours behind me and with my extensive practical experience there is very little I do not know about the various types of aircraft he refers to, but there is nothing on which he cannot expatiate with an incomparable ease and on which he does not make apt suggestions for modifications. His physical condition is not as good as it was perhaps three or four months ago. There is a perceptible glitter in his eyes. Wing Commander von Below tells me that for the last eight weeks Hitler has had virtually no sleep; one conference after another. His hand trembles, this dates from the attempt on his life on the 20th July. During the long discussion that evening I notice moreover that he is apt to repeat certain trains of thought, which he never used to, though his words are clearly thought out, and full of determination.

When the long preamble is finished the Führer comes to the main theme I have listened to so often. He recapitulates the reasons communicated to me a few days ago and concludes:

"It is my wish that this hard task should be undertaken by you, the only man who wears the highest German decoration for bravery."

With the same and similar arguments as on the last occasion I once again refuse, especially as the situation at the front has still further deteriorated, and I emphasise that it is only a matter of time before the East and West fronts will meet in the middle of the Reich and when that happens two pockets will have to operate separately. Only the northern pocket would then come under consideration for the execution of his plan, and it would be necessary to concentrate all our jet aircraft inside it. It interests me that the number of serviceable jet aircraft, including bombers and fighters, on the returns for the day is given as 180. At the front we have long felt that the enemy has a numerical superiority of almost twenty to one. Seeing that the jet aircraft require particularly large airfields it is obvious to start with that only a limited number of airfields within the northern pocket come into question. I point out that as soon as we have assembled our aircraft at these bases they will be pounded day and night by enemy bombers and from a merely technical aspect their operational effectiveness will be nil in a couple of days, in which case it will no longer be possible to keep the air space above General Wenk's army free of the enemy and the catastrophe will then be inevitable because the army will be strategically immobilised. I know from my personal contact with General Wenk that the army includes my guarantee of a free air space as a reliable factor in all its calculations as we have so often done successfully together in Russia.

This time I cannot take upon myself the responsibility, and I stick to my refusal. And once again I discover that anyone of whom Hitler has reason to believe that he only desires to serve the best interests of the whole is free to express his opinion, and that he is willing to revise his own ideas, while understandably he has ceased to have any confidence in people who have repeatedly deceived and disappointed him.

He declines to accept my "two pocket theory" as an accurate prediction. He bases his opinion on a firm and unqualified promise given to him by the respective army commanders of each sector that they will not retreat from the present fronts which are, broadly speaking, the line of the Elbe in the West and in the East the line of the Oder, the Neisse and the Sudeten mountains. I remark that I trust the German soldier to acquit himself with especial gallantry now that he is fighting on German soil, but that if the Russians mass their forces for a concentrated blow at one key point they are bound to batter a gap in our defences and then the two fronts will link up. I quote instances from the Eastern Front in recent years when the Russians hurled tank after tank into the battle and if three armoured divisions failed to reach their objective they simply threw in ten, gaining ground on our depleted Russian front at the cost of enormous losses in men and material. Nothing could have stopped them. The question then was whether or not they would exhaust this immense reserve of man-power before Germany was beaten to her knees. They did not, because the help they received from the West was too great. From a purely military standpoint every time we gave ground at that time in Russia and the Soviets suffered heavier losses in men and material it was a victory for the defence. Even though the enemy ridiculed these victories we know that it was so. But this time a victorious retirement was useless, for then the Russians would be only a few miles behind the Western Front. The Western Powers have accepted a grave responsibility—perhaps for centuries to come—by weakening Germany only to give additional strength to Russia. At the end of our talk I say to the Führer these words:

"In my opinion at this moment the war can no longer be ended victoriously on both fronts, but it is possible on one front if we can succeed in getting an armistice with the other."

A rather tired smile flits across his face as he replies:

"It is easy for you to talk. Ever since 1943 I have tried incessantly to conclude a peace, but the Allies won't; from the outset they have demanded unconditional surrender. My personal fate is naturally of no consequence, but every man in his right mind must see that I could not accept unconditional surrender for the German people. Even now negotiations are pending, but I have given up all hope of their success. Therefore we must do everything to surmount this crisis, so that decisive weapons may yet bring us victory."

After some further talk about the position of Schoerner's army he tells me he intends to wait a few days to see whether the general situation develops as he anticipates or my fears are justified. In the first case he will recall me to Berlin for a final acceptance of the assignment. It is nearly one o'clock in the morning when I leave the Führer's bunker. The first visitors are waiting in the anteroom to offer their congratulations on his birthday.

I return to Kummer early, flying low to avoid the Americans, Mustangs, four-engined bombers and Thunderbolts, which soon infest the upper air and are above me almost all the way back. Having to fly like this alone below these enemies and constantly on the *qui vive* —"have they spotted you or not?"—is a greater strain than many an operational flight. If Niermann and I occasionally get rather hot under the collar with the suspense it is not to be wondered at. We are glad to set foot again on our home base.

The slight relaxation of the pressure exerted by the Russians west of Görlitz is partly due to our daily operations which have inflicted heavy losses. One evening after the last sortie of the day I drive into Görlitz, my home town, now in the battle zone. Here I meet many acquaintances of my youth. They are all in some job or other, not the least of their activities being their home defence duties with the Volkssturm. It is a strange reunion; we are shy of uttering the thoughts that fill our minds. Each has his load of trouble, sorrow and bereavement, but at this moment our eyes are focussed only on the danger from the East. Women are doing men's work, digging tank traps, and only lay down their spades for a brief pause to suckle their hungry babies; greybeards forget the infirmities of age and labour till their brows are damp with sweat. Grim resolution is written on the faces of the girls;

they know what is in store for them if the Red hordes break through. A people in a struggle for survival! If the nations of the West could see with their own eyes the happenings of these days pregnant with destiny and realise their significance they would very soon abandon their frivolous attitude towards Bolshevism.

Only the 2nd Squadron is billeted in Kummer; the wing staff has its headquarters in the schoolhouse at Niemes, some of us live in the homes of the local inhabitants who are 95 per cent German, and do everything possible to meet our every wish. The business of getting to and from the airfield is not altogether plain sailing, one man always squats on the mudguard of every car as look-out for enemy aircraft. American and Russian low-flying planes scour the country at every minute of the day, actually criss-crossing one another in this region. The more unpleasant visitors come from the West, the others from the East.

When we take off on a sortie we often find the "Amis" lying in wait for us in one direction and the "Ruskis" in another. Our old Ju. 87 crawls like a snail in comparison with the enemy aircraft, and when we approach the objective of our mission the constant aerial combat strains our nerves to snapping point. If we attack the air is instantly alive with swarming foes; if we are on our homeward course we have again to force a passage through a ring of hostile aircraft before we can land. Our flak on the airfield usually has to "shoot us a free path."

American fighters do not attack us if they see that we are headed for the front and already engaged in aerial combat with the Ivans.

We generally take off from the Kummer airfield in the morning with four or five anti-tank aircraft, accompanied by twelve to fourteen FW 190s carrying bombs and at the same time acting as our escort. The enemy then waits for our appearance in overwhelming superiority. Rarely, if we have sufficient petrol, we are able to carry out a combined operation with all the formations attached to my command, and then the ene-

my in the air outnumbers us by only five to one! Yes
indeed, our daily bread is earned with sweat and tears.

On the 25th April another wireless signal from the
Führer's headquarters reaches me, completely jum-
bled. Practically nothing is intelligible, but I assume I
am again being summoned to Berlin. I ring up the air
command and report that I have been presumably ordered to Berlin and request permission to fly there. The
commodore refuses, according to the army bulletin
fighting is going on round the Templehof aerodrome
and he does not know if there is any airfield free of
the enemy. He says:

"If you come down in the Russian lines they will
chop my head off for having allowed you to start."

He says he will try to contact Wing Commander von
Below immediately by wireless to ask for the correct text
of the message and where I can land if at all. For some
days I hear nothing, then at 11 P.M. on the 27th April
he rings me up to inform me that he has at last made
contact with Berlin and that I am to fly there tonight in
a Heinkel 111 and land on the wide east-to-west arterial road through Berlin at the point where the Bran-
denburg Gate and the Victory monuments stand. Niermann will accompany me.

The take off with a Heinkel 111 at night is not altogether easy as our airfield has neither flares round the
perimeter nor any other lighting; it is, besides, small
and has good-sized hills on one side of it. In order to
be able to take off at all we have to partly empty the
petrol tank so as to reduce the weight of the aircraft.
Naturally this cuts the time we can stay in the air, a serious handicap.

We make a start at 1 A.M.—a pitch dark night. We
fly over the Sudeten mountains into the battle zone on a
north north westerly course. The country below us is
illumined eerily by fires, many villages and towns are
burning, Germany is in flames. We realise our helpless-
ness to prevent it—but one must not think about it. On
the outskirts of Berlin the Soviet searchlights and flak

already reach up at us; it is almost impossible to make out the plan of the city as it is enveloped in thick smoke and a dense pall of vapour hangs above it. In some places the incandescence of the fires is so blinding that one cannot pick out the landmarks on the ground, and I just have to stare into the darkness for a while before

He. 111

I can see again, but even so I cannot recognise the east-to-west arterial road. One conflagration next to another, the flash of guns, a nightmare spectacle. My radio operator has made contact with the ground; our first instructions are to wait. That puts the lid on it, especially as we have only so much petrol. After about fifteen minutes a message comes through from Wing Commander von Below that a landing is impossible as the road is under heavy shell fire and the Soviets have already captured the Potsdamer Platz. My instructions are to fly on to Rechlin and to telephone to Berlin from there for further orders.

My radio operator has the wave length of this station; we fly on and call Rechlin, not a minute too soon, for our petrol tank is nearly empty. Below us a sea of flame, which can only mean that even on the other side of Berlin the Reds have broken through in the Neuruppin area and at the best only a narrow escape corridor to the west can still be free. On my request for landing lights the Rechlin airfield refuses; they are afraid of instantly attracting a night attack from enemy aircraft. I read them in clear the text of my instructions to land there, adding a few not exactly polite remarks. It is gradually becoming uncomfortable because our petrol may give out at any moment. Suddenly below us to port a niggardly show of lights outlines an airfield. We land. Where are we? At Wittstock, nineteen miles from Rechlin. Wittstock has listened in to our conversation with Rechlin and decided to show its airfield. An hour later, getting on for 3 A.M., I arrive at Rechlin where the V.H.F. is in the commodore's room. With it I am able to get in touch with Berlin by telephone. Wing Commander von Below tells me that I am not now to come into Berlin as, unlike me, Field Marshal Greim has been reached in time by wireless and has taken over my assignment; moreover, he says, it is momentarily impossible to make a landing in Berlin. I reply:

"I suggest that I should land this morning by daylight on the east-west arterial road with a Stuka. I think it can still be done if I use a Stuka. Besides it is essential to get the government out of this danger point so that they do not lose touch with the situation as a whole."

Von Below asks me to hold the line while he goes to make enquiries. He comes back to the telephone and says:

"The Führer has made up his mind. He is absolutely decided to hold Berlin, and cannot therefore leave the capital where the situation looks critical. He argues that if he left himself the troops which are fighting to hold it would say that he was abandoning Berlin and would draw the conclusion that all resistance was useless. Therefore the Führer intends to stay in the city. You are no longer to come in, but are to fly back immediately to the Sudetenland to lend the support of your formations to Field Marshal Schoerner's army which is also to launch a thrust in the direction of Berlin."

I ask von Below what the feeling is about the situation because he tells me all this so calmly and matter-of-factly.

"Our position is not good, but it must be possible for a thrust by General Wenk or Schoerner to relieve Berlin."

I admire his calmness. To me everything is clear, and I fly back to my unit forthwith to carry on operations.

The shock of the news that the Head of State and Supreme Commander of the armed forces of the Reich is dead has a stunning effect upon the troops. But the Red hordes are devastating our country and therefore we must fight on. We shall only lay down our arms when our leaders give the order. This is our plain duty according to our military oath, it is our plain duty in view of the terrible fate which threatens us if we surrender unconditionally as the enemy insists. It is our plain duty also to the destiny which has placed us geographically in the heart of Europe and which we have obeyed for centuries: to be the bulwark of Europe against the East. Whether or not Europe understands or likes the rôle which fate has thrust upon us, or whether her attitude is one of fatal indifference or even of hostility, does not alter by one iota our European duty. We are determined to be able to hold our heads high when the history of our continent, and particularly of the dangerous times ahead, is written.

The East and West fronts are edging closer and closer to each other, our operations are of increasing difficulty. The discipline of my men is admirable, no different from on the first day of the war. I am proud of them. The severest punishment for my officers is, as it has always been, not to be allowed to fly with the rest on operations. I myself have some trouble with my stump. My mechanics have constructed for me an ingenious contrivance like a devil's hoof and with it I fly. It is attached below the knee joint and with every pressure upon it, that is to say when I have to kick the right rudder-bar, the skin at the bottom of the stump which was doing its best to heal is rubbed sore. The wound is reopened again with violent bleeding. Especially in aerial combat when I have to bank extremely to the right I am hampered by the wound and sometimes my mechanic has to wipe the blood-spattered cockpit clean.

I am very lucky again in the first days of May. I have an appointment with Field Marshal Schoerner, and before keeping it want to look in on my way at Air Command H.Q. in a castle at Hermannstädtel, about fifty miles east of us. I fly there in a Fieseler Storch and see that the castle is surrounded by tall trees. There is a park in the middle on which I think I can land. My faithful Fridolin is behind me in the plane. The landing comes off all right; after a short stay to pick up some maps we take off again towards the tall trees on a gentle rise. The Storch is slow in gathering speed; to help her start I lower the flaps a short distance before the edge of the forest. But this only brings me just below the tops of the trees. I give the stick a pull, but we have not sufficient impetus. To pull any more is useless, the aircraft becomes nose-heavy. I already hear a crash and clatter. Now I have finally smashed my stump, if nothing worse. Then everything is quiet as a mouse. Am I down on the ground? No, I am sitting in my cockpit, and there, too, is Fridolin. We are jammed in a forking branch at the top of a lofty tree, merrily rocking to and fro. The whole tree sways back and forth with us several times, our impact was evidently a bit too violent. I am afraid the Storch will now play us another trick and finish by tipping the cockpit over backwards. Fridolin has come forward and asks in some alarm: "What is happening?"

I call out to him: "Don't budge or else you will topple what remains of the Storch off the tree into a thirty foot drop."

The tail is broke off as well as large pieces of the wing planes; they are all lying on the ground. I still have the stick in my hand, my stump is uninjured, I have not knocked it against anything. One must have luck on one's side! We cannot get down from the tree, it is very high and has a thick, smooth trunk. We wait, and after a time the General arrives on the scene; he has heard the crash and now sees us perched up aloft on the tree. He is mightily glad we got off so lightly. As there is no other possible way of getting us down he sends for the local fire brigade. They help us down with a long, extending ladder.

The Russians have by-passed Dresden, and are trying to cross the Erzgebirge from the north so as to reach the protectorate and thus outflank Field Marshal Schoerner's army. The main Soviet forces are in the Freiberg area and southeast of it. On one of our last sorties we see south of Diepoldiswalde a long column of refugees with Soviet tanks going through it like steam rollers, crushing everything under them.

We immediately attack the tanks and destroy them; the column continues its trek towards the south. Apparently the refugees hope to get behind the protecting screen of the Sudeten mountains where they think they will be safe. In the same area we attack some more enemy tanks in a veritable tornado of flak. I have just fired at a Stalin tank and am climbing to 600 feet when, looking round, I notice a drizzle of bits and pieces behind me. They are falling from above. I ask:

"Niermann, which of us has just been shot down?"

That seems to me the only explanation and Niermann thinks the same. He hurriedly counts our aircraft, all of them are there. So none of them was shot down. I look down at my Stalin and see only a black spot. Could the explanation be that the tank exploded and the explosion flung up its wreckage to this height?

After the operation the crews which were flying behind me confirm that this tank blew up with a terrific explosion into the air behind me; the bits and pieces which I saw raining down from above were from the Stalin. Presumably it was packed with high explosive, and its mission was to clear tank barriers and other obstacles out of the way of the other tanks. I do not envy Niermann on these operations, for now flying is certainly no life insurance; if I am forced to land anywhere there is no longer any chance of making an escape. He flies with an incomparable placidity; his nerve amazes me.

# 18

# THE END

On the 7th May there is a conference of all Luftwaffe commanders in Schoerner's army zone at Group H.Q. to discuss the plan which has just been released by the Supreme Command. It is proposed gradually to retire the entire Eastern front, sector by sector, until it is parallel with the Western front. We perceive that very grave decisions are about to be taken. Will the West even now recognize its opportunity against the East or will it fail to grasp the situation? Opinions among us are divided.

On the 8th May we search for tanks north of Bruex and near Oberleutensdorf. For the first time in the war I am unable to concentrate my mind on my mission; an indefinable feeling of frustration suffocates me. I do not destroy a single tank; they are still in the mountains and unassailable there.

Wrapped in my thoughts I head for home. We land and go into the flying control building. Fridolin is not there; they tell me he has been summoned to Group H.Q. Does that mean . . . ? I jerk myself sharply out of my depression.

"Niermann, ring up the squadron at Reichenberg and brief them for a fresh attack and fix the next rendezvous with our fighter escort." I study the map of the situation . . . what is the use? Where is Fridolin all this time? I see a Storch land outside, that will be he. Shall I dash out? No, better wait in here . . . it seems to be very warm for this time of the year . . . and the day before yesterday two of my men were ambushed and shot dead by Czechs in civilian clothes . . . Why is Fridolin away so long? I hear the door open and somebody comes in; I force myself not to turn round. Someone coughs softly. Niermann is still speaking on the telephone . . . so that was not Fridolin. Niermann is having trouble getting through . . . it is a funny thing . . . I notice that today my brain is registering every detail very sharply . . . silly little things without the least significance.

I turn round, the door opens . . . Fridolin. His face is haggard, we exchange glances and suddenly my throat is parched. All I can say is: "Well?"

"It's all over . . . unconditional surrender!" Fridolin's voice is scarcely more than a whisper.

The end . . . I feel as though I were falling into a bottomless abyss, and then in blurred confusion they all pass before my eyes: the many comrades I have lost, the millions of soldiers who have perished on the sea and in the air and on the battlefield . . . the millions of victims slaughtered in their homes in Germany . . . the oriental hordes which will now inundate our country . . . Fridolin suddenly snaps out:

"Hang up that blasted telephone, Niermann. The war is over!"

"We shall decide when we stop fighting," says Niermann.

Someone guffaws. His laughter is too loud, it is not genuine. I must do something . . . say something . . . ask a question . . .

"Niermann, tell the squadron at Reichenberg that a Storch is landing in an hour from now with important orders."

Fridolin notices my helpless embarassment and goes into details in an agitated voice.

"A retirement westward is definitely out . . . the English and the Americans have insisted on an unconditional surrender by the 8th of May . . . that is today. We are ordered to hand over everything to the Russians unconditionally by 11 to-night. But as Czechoslovakia is to be occupied by the Soviets it has been decided that all German formations shall retire as fast as possible to the West so as not to fall into Russian hands. Flying personnel are to fly home or anywhere . . ."

"Fridolin," I interrupt him, "parade the wing." I cannot sit still and listen to any more of this. But will not what you have now to do be an even greater ordeal? . . . What can you tell your men? . . . They have never yet seen you despondent, but now you are in the depths—Fridolin breaks in upon my thoughts:

"All present and correct." I go out. My artificial limb makes it impossible for me to walk properly. The sun is shining in its full spring glory . . . here and there a slight haze shimmers silvery in the distance . . . I come to a stop in front of my men.

"Comrades!" . . .

I cannot go on. Here stands my 2nd Squadron, the 1st is stationed down in Austria . . . shall I ever set eyes on it again? And the 3rd at Prague . . . Where are they now, now when I want so much to see them round me . . . all . . . our dead comrades as well as the survivors of the unit . . .

There is an uncanny hush, the eyes of all my men are riveted upon me. I *must* say something.

". . . after we have lost so many comrades . . . after so much blood has flowed at home and on the fronts . . . an incomprehensible fate . . . has denied us victory . . . the gallantry of our soldiers . . . of our whole people . . . has been unparalleled . . . the war is lost . . . I thank you for the loyalty with which you . . . in this unit . . . have served our country . . ."

I shake hands with every man in turn. None of them utters a word. The silent hand-grip shows me that they understand me. As I walk away for the last time I hear Fridolin snap the order:

"Eyes—right!"

"Eyes—right!" for the many, many comrades who sacrificed their young lives. "Eyes—right!" for the conduct of our people, for their heroism, the most splendid ever shown by a civilian population. "Eyes—

right!" for the finest legacy that Germany's dead have ever bequeathed to posterity . . ."Eyes—right!" for the countries of the West which they have striven to defend and which are now caught in the fatal embrace of Bolshevism. . .

What are we to do now? Is the war over for the "Immelmann" Wing? Could we not give the youth of Germany a reason to hold up their heads in pride again one day by some final gesture, such as crashing the whole Wing onto some G.H.Q. or other important enemy target and by such a death bringing our battle record to a significant climax? The Wing would be with me to a man, I am sure of that. I put the question to the group. The answer is no . . . perhaps it is the right one . . . there are enough dead . . . and perhaps we have still another mission to fulfill.

I have decided to lead the column which is going back by road. It will be a very long column because all formations under my command including the flak are to march with the ground personnel. Everything will be ready by 6 o'clock and then we shall make a start. The squadron leader of the 2nd Squadron has instructions to fly all his aircraft west. When the commodore hears of my intention to lead the ground column he orders me because of my wound to fly while Fridolin is to lead the march. There is a formation under my command on the airfield at Reichenberg. I can no longer reach it by telephone, so I fly there with Niermann to inform it of the new situation. On the way the cockpit hood of my Storch flies off, its climbing performance is bad; I need it, however, because Reichenberg lies on the other side of the mountains. I approach the airfield cautiously through a valley; it already presents an appearance of desolation. At first I see nobody and taxi the aircraft into a hangar with the intention of using the telephone in the flying control room. I am just in the act of getting out of the Storch when there is a terrific explosion and a hangar goes up in the air before my eyes. Instinctively we fall flat on our stomachs and wait for the hail of stones which tear a few holes in our aerofoil, but we are unscathed. Next to the flying control hut a lorry loaded with flares has caught fire and the flares explode all around up in a harlequinade of colours. A symbol of the debâcle. My heart bleeds—only to think of it. Here at all events no one has waited for my news that the end has come; seemingly it has arrived considerably earlier from another quarter.

We climb back into the crippled Storch and with an interminably long take-off she lifts herself wearily from the airfield. Following the same valley route by which we came we get back to Kummer. Everybody is busily packing his things; the order of march is arranged in a way that seems tactically most convenient. The A.A. guns are parcelled up through the length of the column so that they may be able to put up a defence against attack, should the need arise, if anyone tries to hinder our westward march. Our destination is the American-occupied southern part of Germany.

After the column has started all the rest, except those who want to wait until I take off, will fly away; many of them will have a chance to escape capture if they can land somewhere near their homes. This being out of the question for me, I intend to land on an airfield occupied by the Americans as I need immediate medical attention for my leg; therefore the idea of my going into hiding is not to be considered. Besides, too many people would recognise me. I see no reason either why I should not land on a normal aerodrome, believing that the allied soldiers will treat me with the chivalry due even to a defeated enemy. The war is over, and so I do not expect to be detained or held prisoner for long; I think that in a very short time everyone will be allowed to go home.

I am standing by, watching the column loading up when I hear a droning high above; there are fifty or sixty Russian bombers, Bostons. I have barely time to give warning before the bombs come whistling down. I lie flat on the road with my crutches and think that if those beggars' aim is good there will be appalling casual-

ties with us all so close together. Already the crash of
the bombs as they make impact with the earth, a little
carpet of bombs in the middle of the town, a thousand
yards from the road where we were drawn up. The
poor people of Niemes!

The Russians come in twice to drop their bombs.
Even at the second attempt they do no damage to our
column. Now we are in column of route and make a
start. I take a last comprehensive look at my unit which
has been for seven years my world and all that means
anything to me. How much blood shed in a common
cause cements our fellowship! For the last time I salute
them.

Northwest of Prague, near Kladno, the column runs
into Russian tanks and a very strong enemy force. According to the terms of the armistice arms must be sur-
rendered and laid down. A free passage is guaranteed
to unarmed soldiers. It is not long after this that armed
Czechs fall upon our now defenceless men. Bestially,
with outrageous brutality, they butcher German soldiers. Only a few are able to fight their way through to
the West, among them my young intelligence officer,
Pilot Officer Haufe. The rest fall into the hands of the
Czechs and the Russians. One of those who fall victim
to the Czech terrorism is my best friend, Fridolin.
It is infinitely tragic that he should meet with such an
end after the war is over. Like their comrades who have
laid down their lives in this war, they too are martyrs
for German liberty.

The column has set off and I return to the Kummer
airfield. Katschner and Fridolin are still at my side;
then they drive away after the column to meet their
fate. Six other pilots have insisted on flying West with
me; we are three Ju. 87s and four FW 190s. Among
them are the 2nd Squadron leader and Pilot Officer
Schwirblatt who, like myself, has lost a leg and has
nevertheless in recent weeks done grand work knock-

ing out enemy tanks. He always says: "It is all the same to the tanks whether we knock them out with one leg or two!"

After bidding a difficult farewell to Fridolin and Flight Lt. Katschner—a dark premonition tells me that we shall never see each other again—we take off on our last flight. A singular and indescribable feeling. We are saying goodbye to our world. We decide to fly to Kitzingen because we know it to be a large aerodrome, and therefore assume that it will now be occupied by the American Air Force. In the Saaz area we have a skirmish with the Russians who appear suddenly out of the haze and hope, in the intoxication of victory, to make mincemeat of us. What they have failed to do in five years they do not succeed in doing today, our last encounter.

After close on two hours we approach the aerodrome, tensely wondering if, even now, the American A.A. guns will open up at us. The large airfield already lies ahead. I instruct my pilots over the R/T that they may only crash-land their aircraft; we do not mean to hand over any serviceable planes. My orders are to unlock the undercarriage and then rip it off in a high speed taxi in. The best way to achieve our object will be to brake violently on one side and to kick the rudder-bar on the same side. I can see a crowd of soldiers on the aerodrome; they are paraded—probably a sort of victory roll-call—under the American flag. At first we fly low above the aerodrome in order to make certain that the flak will not attack us as we land. Some of the parade now recognise us and suddenly perceive the German swastika on our wing planes above their heads. Part of the ceremonial muster falls flat. We land as ordered; only one of our aircraft makes a smooth landing and taxis to a stop. A flight sergeant of the 2nd Squadron has a girl on board lying in the tail of his aircraft and is scared that if he makes a so-called belly-landing the damage will extend to his precious feminine stowaway. "Of course" he does not know her; she just happened to be standing so forlornly on the perimeter of the airfield and did not want to be left behind with the Russians. But his colleagues know better.

As the first to come down, I now lie flopped at the end of the runway; already a soldier is standing beside my cockpit pointing a revolver at me. I open the canopy and instantly his hand is outstretched to grab my golden oak-leaves. I shove him back and shut down the hood again. Presumably this first encounter would have ended badly had not a jeep driven up with some officers who dress this fellow down and send him about his business. They come closer and see that I have a blood-drenched bandage: the result of the skirmish above Saaz. They take me first to their dressing station where I am given a fresh bandage. Niermann does not let me out of his sight and follows me like a shadow. Then I am taken to a large partitioned-off room in an upstairs hall which has been fitted out as a kind of officers' mess.

Here I meet the rest of my colleagues who have been brought straight there: they spring to attention and greet me with the salute prescribed by the Führer. On the far side of the room stands a small group of U.S.A. officers; this spontaneous salute displeases them and they mutter to themselves. They evidently belong to a mixed fighter wing which is stationed here with Thunderbolts and Mustangs. An interpreter comes up to me and asks if I speak English. He tells me that their commanding officer objects, above all things, to this salute.

"Even if I can speak English," I reply, "we are in Germany here and speak only German. As far as the salute is concerned, we are ordered to salute in this way and being soldiers we carry out our orders. Besides, we do not care whether you object to it or not. Tell your C.O. that we are the 'Immelmann' Wing and as the war is now over and no one has defeated us in the air we do not consider ourselves prisoners. The German soldier," I point out, "has not been beaten on his merits, but has simply been crushed by overwhelming masses of material. We have landed here because we did not

wish to stay in the Soviet zone. We should also prefer
not to discuss the matter any further, but would like
to have a wash and brush up and then have something to eat."

Some of the officers continue to scowl, but we are
able to perform our ablutions in the mess room so co-
piously that we make something of a puddle. We make
ourselves perfectly at home, why shouldn't we? We are
after all in Germany. We converse without embarrassment. Then we eat, and an interpreter comes and asks
us in the name of his commanding officer whether we
would like to have a talk with him and his officers
when we have finished our meal. This invitation interests us as airmen and we oblige, especially as all mention of "the whys and wherefores of the winning and
losing of the war" is taboo. From outside comes the
noise of shots and rowdiness; the coloured soldiers are
celebrating victory under the influence of liquor. I
should not care to go down into the ground floor hall;
jubilation bullets whistle through the air on every side.
It is very late before we get to sleep.

Almost everything except what we have on our
persons is stolen during the night. The most valuable
thing I miss is my flight log-book in which is recorded
in detail every operational flight, from the first to the
two thousand, five hundred and thirtieth. Also a replica
of the "diamonds," the citation for the diamond
pilot medal, the high Hungarian decoration and a lot else
are gone, not to mention watches and other things. Even
my bespoke peg-leg is discovered by Niermann under
some fellow's bed; presumably he had meant to cut
himself a souvenir out of it and sell it later as "a bit of a
high-ranking Jerry officer."

Early in the morning I receive a message that I am to
come to the H.Q. of the 9th American Air Army at
Erlangen. I refuse until all my pilfered belongings have
been returned to me. After much persuasion in which
I am told that the matter is very urgent and that I can
rely on getting my things back as soon as the thief has
been caught, I set off with Niermann. At Air Army

H.Q. we are first interrogated by three General Staff officers. They begin by showing us some photographs which they claim to have been taken of atrocities in concentration camps. As we have been fighting for such abominations, they argue, we also share the guilt. They refuse to believe me when I tell them that I have never even seen a concentration camp. I add that if excesses have been committed they are regrettable and reprehensible, and the real culprits should be punished. I point out that such cruelties have been perpetrated not only by our people, but by all peoples in every age. I remind them of the Boer War. Therefore these excesses must be judged by the same criterion. I cannot imagine that the mounds of corpses depicted on the photographs were taken in concentration camps. I tell them that we have seen such sights, not on paper, but in fact, after the air attacks on Dresden and Hamburg and other cities when Allied four-engined bombers deluged them indiscriminately with phosphorus and high explosive bombs and countless women and children were massacred. And I assure these gentlemen that if they are especially interested in atrocities they will find abundant material—and "living" material at that—among their Eastern Allies.

We see no more of these photographs. With a venomous glance at us, the officer making out his report of the interrogation comments when I have had my say: "Typical Nazi officer." Why one is a typical Nazi officer when one is merely telling the truth is not quite clear to me. Are these gentlemen aware that we have never fought for a political party, but only for Germany? In this belief also millions of our comrades have died. My assertion that they will one day be sorry that in destroying us they have demolished the bastion against Bolshevism they interpret as propaganda and refuse to believe it. They say that with us the wish to divide the allies against each other is father to the thought. Some hours later we are taken to the General commanding this Air Army, Wyland.

The general is said to be of German origin, from

Bremen. He makes a good impression on me; in the course of our interview I tell him of the theft of the articles already mentioned, so precious to me, at Kitzingen. I ask him if this is usual. He raises Cain, not at my outspokenness, but at this shameful robbery. He orders his adjutant to instruct the C.O. of the unit concerned at Kitzingen to produce my property and threatens a court martial. He begs me to be his guest at Erlangen until everything has been restored to me.

After the interview Niermann and I are driven in a jeep to a suburb of the town where an uninhabited villa is placed at our disposal. A sentry at the gate shows us that we are not entirely free. A car comes out to fetch us to the officers' mess for meals. The news of our arrival has soon got round among the people of Erlangen and the sentry has trouble in coping with our numerous visitors. When he is not afraid of being surprised by a superior he says to us: "Ich nix sehen."

So we spent five days at Erlanger. Our colleagues who have remained behind at Kitzingen we do not see again; there are no complications to detain them.

On the 14th May Captain Ross, the I.O. of the Air Army, appears at the villa. He speaks good German and brings us a message from General Wyland regretting that so far no progress has been made towards the recovery of my belongings, but that orders have just come through that we are to proceed immediately to England for interrogation. With a short stopoff at Wiesbaden, we are delivered to an interrogation camp near London. Quarters and food are austere, our treatment by English officers is correct. The old captain to whose care we are "entrusted" is in civilian life a patent lawyer in London. He pays us a daily visit of inspection and one day sees my Golden Oak Leaves on the table. He looks at it thoughtfully, wags his head and mutters, almost with awe: "How many lives can that have cost!"

When I explain to him that I earned it in Russia he leaves us, considerably relieved.

In the course of the day I am often visited by En-

glish and also by American intelligence officers who
are variously inquisitive. I soon perceive that we have
contrary ideas. This is not surprising seeing that I have
flown most of my operational flights with aircraft of
very inferior speed and my experience is therefore different from that of the allies who are inclined to exag-
gerate the importance of every extra m.p.h., if only as
a guarantee of safety. They can hardly believe my total
of over 2,500 sorties with such a slow aircraft, nor are
they at all interested to learn the lesson of my experience as they see no life insurance in it. They boast of
their rockets which I already know about and which
can be fired from the fastest aircraft; they do not like
to be told that their accuracy is small in comparison
with my cannon. I do not particularly mind these inter-
rogations; my successes have not been gained by any
technical secrets. So our talks are little more than a discussion of aviation and the war which has just ended.
These island Britishers do not conceal their respect
for the enemy's achievement, their attitude is one of
sportsmanlike fairness which we appreciate. We are out
in the open air for three quarters of an hour every day
and prowl up and down behind the barbed wire. For the
rest of the time we read and forge post-war plans.

After about a fortnight we are sent north and interned in a normal American P.O.W. camp. There are
many thousand prisoners in this camp. The food is a
bare minimum and some of our comrades who have
been here for some time are weak from emaciation.
My stump gives me trouble and has to be operated on;
the camp M.O. refuses to perform the operation on the
ground that I have flown with one leg and he is not
interested in what happens to my stump. It is swollen
and inflamed and I suffer acute pain. The camp au-
thorities could not make a better propaganda among
the thousands of German soldiers for their former officers. A good many of our guards know Germany; they
are emigrants who left after 1933 and speak German
like ourselves. The negroes are good-natured and ob-
liging except when they have been drinking.

Three weeks later I am entrained for Southampton with Niermann and the majority of the more seriously wounded cases. We are crowded onto the deck of a Kaiser freighter. When twenty four hours pass without our being given any food and we suspect that this will go on till we reach Cherbourg, because the American crew intend to sell our rations to the French black market, a party of Russian front veterans force an entry into the store-room and take the distribution into their own hands. The ship's crew pull very long faces when they discover the raid much later.

The drive through Cherbourg to our new camp near Carentan is anything but pleasant as the French civilian population greet even seriously wounded soldiers by pelting them with stones. We cannot help remembering the really comfortable life the French civilians often led in Germany. Many of them were sensible enough to appreciate that while they were living in comfort we were holding back the Soviets in the East. There will be an awakening, too, for those who today throw stones.

The conditions in the new camp are very much the same as in England. Here also an operation is at first refused me. I cannot look forward to being released, if only because of my rank. One day I am taken to the aerodrome at Cherbourg, and at first I believe I am to be handed over to Ivan. That would be something for the Soviets, to have Field Marshal Schoerner and myself as prizes from the war on the ground and in the air! The compass points to 300 degrees, so our course is set for England. Why? We land some twenty miles inland on the aerodrome at Tangmere, the R.A.F. formation leaders' school. Here I learn that Group Captain Bader* has effected my removal. Bader is the most popular airman in the R.A.F. He was shot down during the war and flew with two artificial legs. He had learnt that

---

*Read *Reach for the Sky*, the story of Douglas Bader's triumphant courage that overcame the peacetime loss of both his legs so thoroughly that when his country was attacked, he became an R.A.F. Wing Commander fighting the Battle of Britain. Another great book in the Bantam War Book Series.

I was interned in the camp at Carentan. He had himself been a prisoner of war in Germany and had made several attempts to escape. He can tell a different story from the inveterate agitators who seek by every means to brand us Germans as barbarians.

This time in England is a rest cure for me after the P.O.W. camps. Here I discover again for the first time that there is still a respect for the enemy's achievement, a chivalry which should come naturally to every officer in the service of every country in the world.

Bader sends to London for the man who made his artificial limbs with an order to make one for me. I decline this generous offer because I cannot pay for it. I lost all I had in the East and I do not yet know what may happen in the future. At any rate it will not be possible to pay him back in sterling. Group Captain Bader is almost offended when I refuse to accept his kindness and am worried about payment. He brings the man down with him, and he makes a plaster of Paris cast. The man returns a few days later and tells me the stump must be swollen internally as it is thicker at the bottom than at the top; therefore an operation is necessary before he can complete the artificial leg.

Some days after this an enquiry comes from the Americans, saying that I have "only been lent" and must now be returned. My rest cure is nearly over.

On one of my last days at Tangmere I have an illuminating discussion with the R.A.F. boys attending a course at the school. One of them—not an Englishman—hoping no doubt to anger or intimidate me, asks me what I suppose the Russians would do with me if I had now to return to my home in Silesia where I belong.

"I think the Russians are clever enough," I reply, "to make use of my experience. In the field of combating tanks alone, which must play a part in any future war, my instruction may prove disadvantageous for the enemy. I am credited with over five hundred tanks destroyed, and assuming that in the next few years I were to train five or six hundred pilots each of whom destroyed at least a hundred tanks, you can reckon out for yourself how many tanks the enemy's armament industry would have to replace on my account."

This answer provokes a general murmur of consternation and I am asked excitedly how I reconcile it with my former attitude towards Bolshevism. Hitherto I have not been allowed to say anything disparaging about Russia—their ally. But now I am told of the mass deportations to the East and tales of rape and atrocities, of the bloody terrorism with which the hordes from the steppes of Asia are martyring their subject peoples. . . This is something new to me, for previously they have been most careful to avoid these subjects; but now their views are an exact reflection of our own often enough proclaimed theses, and expressed in language which is frequently copied from us. Formation leaders of the R.A.F. who have flown Hurricanes on the Russian side

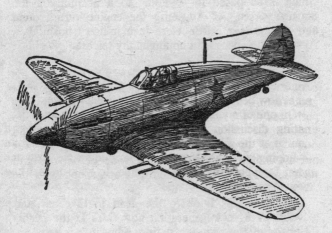

**Hawker Hurricane 2C**

at Murmansk tell their impressions; they are shattering. Of our crews which were shot down there hardly one was left alive.

"And then you want to work for the Russians?" they exclaim.

"I have been very interested to hear your opinion of your allies," I reply. "Of course I have not said a word about what I think, I have only answered the question you put to me."

The subject of Russia is never brought up in my presence.

I am flown back to the camp in France where I continue to be interned for a short time. The efforts of German doctors are finally successful in effecting a transfer to a hospital camp. Niermann has been released some days before in the British zone. He has several times wangled it so that he can stay with me, but he cannot put it over any longer. Within a week of leaving the French camp I am on an ambulance train which is supposed to be going to a hospital on the Starnbergersee. At Augsburg the engine turns round and steams into Fürth. Here in a military hospital in April 1946 I succeed in obtaining my release.

As one of the millions of soldiers who has done his duty and by the grace of providence has had the great good fortune to survive this war, I have written my experiences of the war against the U.S.S.R. in which the youth of Germany and many convinced Europeans laid down their lives. This book is no glorification of war nor a rehabilitation of a certain group of persons and their orders. Let my experiences alone speak with the voice of truth.

I dedicate this book to the dead in this war and to youth. This new generation now lives in the frightful chaos of the post-war period. May it, nevertheless, keep alive its faith in the fatherland and its hope in the future; for only he is lost who gives himself up for lost!

# BANTAM WAR BOOKS

Introducing a new series of carefully selected books that cover the full dramatic sweep of World War II heroism—viewed from all sides and in all branches of armed service, whether on land, sea or in the air. Most of the volumes are eye-witness accounts by men who fought in the conflict—true stories of brave men in action.

Each book in this series has a dramatic cover painting plus specially commissioned drawings, diagrams and maps to aid readers in a deeper understanding of the roles played by men and machines during the war.

## FLY FOR YOUR LIFE by Larry Forrester
The glorious story of Robert Stanford Tuck, Britain's greatest air ace, credited with downing 29 enemy aircraft. Tuck was himself shot down 4 times and finally captured. However, he organized a fantastic escape that led him through Russia and back to England to marry the woman he loved.

## THE FIRST AND THE LAST
by Adolf Galland
The top German air ace with over 70 kills, here is Galland's own story. He was commander of all fighter forces in the Luftwaffe, responsible only to Goëring and Hitler. A unique insight into the German side of the air war.

## SAMURAI by Saburo Sakai with
Martin Caidin & Fred Saito
The true account of the legendary Japanese combat pilot. In his elusive Zero, Sakai was responsible for downing 64 Allied planes during the war. *SAMURAI* is a powerful portrait of a warrior fighting for his own cause. (May)

## BRAZEN CHARIOTS by Robert Crisp

The vivid, stirring, day-by-day account of tank warfare in the African desert. Crisp was a British major, who in a lightweight Honey tank led the British forces into battle against the legendary Rommel on the sands of Egypt. (June)

## REACH FOR THE SKY by Paul Brickhill

The inspiring true story of Douglas Bader. The famous RAF fighter pilot who had lost both legs, Bader returned to the service in World War II as a combat pilot and downed 22 planes in the Battle of Britain. Shot down, Bader survived the war in a German prison camp. (July)

## COMPANY COMMANDER
## by Charles B. MacDonald

The infantry classic of World War II. Twenty-two-year-old MacDonald, a U.S. infantry captain, led his men in combat through some of the toughest fighting in the war both in France and Germany. This book tells what it is really like to lead men into battle. (September)

Bantam War Books are available now unless otherwise noted. They may be obtained wherever paperbacks are sold.